En reconocimiento a la confianza depositada por ustedes a lo largo
de estos seis años, hacemos entrega de esta obra, con nuestros
mejores deseos por que el próximo año
continúe lleno de prosperidad.

A Monetary History of Colombia

ANTONIO HERNÁNDEZ GAMARRA

A Monetary History of Colombia

Director, designer and editor
BENJAMÍN VILLEGAS

Prologue
JOSÉ ANTONIO OCAMPO

Foreword
ORLANDO GARCÍA

This book has been, produced
and published in Colombia by
VILLEGAS EDITORES
Avenida 82 No. 11-50, Interior 3
e-mail: villedi@cable.net.co
Telephone (57-1) 616 1788,
Fax (57-1) 616 0020
Bogotá, D.C., Colombia

© VILLEGAS EDITORES 2001

www.villegaseditores.com

Graphic research
JUAN DAVID GIRALDO

Art Department
DAVID RENDÓN

English translation
JIMMY WEISKOPF

Numismatic consultants
ANGELINA ARAUJO VÉLEZ
IGNACIO HENAO
YOLIMA ARIAS AZCUÉNAGA
JUAN MANUEL JAIME-BARRERA

Photography and reproduction of documents
ÓSCAR MONSALVE
ALBERTO SIERRA
JUAN CAMILO SEGURA
ERNESTO FRANCO
CRISTÓBAL VON ROTHKIRCH
PILAR GÓMEZ
ARCHIVO EL ESPECTADOR
HERNÁN DÍAZ, pages 175 and 179
LELIO PINZÓN, page 190

All rights reserved.
No part of this book may be reproduced, stored
in a retrieval system or transmitted, in any form
or by any means, electronic, mechanical,
photocopying, recording or otherwise, without
the prior written permission of Villegas Editores.

First edition
October, 2001

ISBN
958-8160-06-5

Prepress
ZETTA COMUNICADORES

Printing and binding
PANAMERICANA FORMAS E IMPRESOS

The editor wishes to thank
CREDIBANCO-VISA COLOMBIA
for providing the institutional sponsorship
for the first edition of this book.

The editor would also like to thank the permanent exhibition of the numismatic
collection of the Luis Ángel Arango Library, Banco de la República, for lending a
good part of the pictures reproduced in this book.

Front cover, *two pesos coin of 1907, obverse.*
Back cover, *one peso coin of 1907, reverse.*
Page 3, *Copper coin minted in Cartagena, 1812.*
Pages 4/5, *The Mesuno Treasure, found in the river Magdalena, opposite the town of Honda, in 1936.*
Page 6, *Mint mark of the "Casa de Moneda" (mint) of Santafé.*
Page 9, *1813 coin, known as the "india" or "china".*
Page 10, *coin of the republic of Gran Colombia, minted in 1824.*

CONTENTS

Foreword, *Orlando García*	13
Prologue, *José Antonio Ocampo*	15
Introduction	27
Metal Coinage	31
Free Banking and the Issuing of Paper Money	39
The Banco Nacional, Paper Money and the Monetary Controversy at the end of the Nineteenth Century	59
The Hidden Emissions and the Liquidation of the Banco Nacional	71
Monetary Crisis and Stability	81
Foundation of the Banco de la República and the Organization of the Banking System	99
The Gold Standard and Debt Prosperity	115
The World Economic Crisis and Monetary Orthodoxy	125
The Anti-cyclical Policy	133
Monetary Policy Between 1935 and 1950	143
The Reform of 1951 and the Vicissitudes of Coffe	153
Institutional Changes in the Nineteen-sixties. The Monetary Board and the Decree 444 of 1967	167
The Age of Inflation	171
The Reform of 1991	183
Appendix	195
Main Features of Metallic Money that has Circulated since 1821	197
Catalogue of Bills Issued since 1922	237
Index of Names	271
Bibliography	275

FOREWORD

Orlando García
President Credibanco-Visa Colombia

Opposite page, *Silver coin of eight reales, minted in 1847.*

Experts on monetary matters have always faced great difficulties in defining money. The consensus that has been worked out fundamentally addresses such questions as: what constitutes money or what does the monetary supply consist of ? But the controversy over the basic question – what is money? – continues.

One explanation is that used by Professor Lauchlin Currie in his book "The Supply and Control of Money in Colombia", when he cites the example given by the English economist Joan Robinson, who tells the story of a man who could not define an elephant, but was sure that he would recognize one when he saw it. The same happens with money.

Knowledge of the role of money in the economy is an important subject. It is indispensable for an understanding of the functioning of the economic system, essential for the management of economic policy and basic in the economic history of the country. The subject of money has a great influence on our daily life.

This book is a magnificent historical document about the money and monetary institutions of the nation. The author describes the events that make up this history in simple terms so that the subject becomes accessible to the non-specialist reader and, at the same time, offers a range of content and depth of understanding that give the book a high academic value and make it a useful tool for teaching monetary economics and the monetary history of Colombia.

Complementing the text is a beautifully-illustrated catalogue of the different kinds of money that have circulated in Colombia since the foundation of the Republic, together with important and sometimes curious details about their issuance. Also of great interest is the information about the development of the business of private banks towards the end of the nineteenth century and the transformation of the process of making primary emissions of money, a responsibility that initially lay in the hands of the commercial banks and then passed to the Banco Nacional, an institution that was invested with the exclusive right to issue bank notes payable to the bearer. Later, the monopoly over the issuing of bank notes representative of gold was given to the Central Bank, el Banco de la República.

After analyzing each of the reforms that took place in the monetary and financial fields during the twentieth century, the book devotes its final pages to the 1991 reform, which enshrined the Banco de la República's independence of the government by giving it the autonomous functions of a modern central bank The author's analysis of the inflationary tax that undoubtedly affected the distribution of income among different economic sectors and of the arbitrary apportioning of subsidies through the granting of development credits at lower interest rates than those of the market form the background to his magnificent description of the 1991 reforms.

The book finishes with a recent development, which, when it comes into effect (as seems likely), will open a new chapter in the monetary history of Colombia but will not, however, really effect the economy: an initiative, now under consideration by the Colombian Congress, to create a novel monetary unit in the year 2002, the new *peso*, equivalent to one thousand *pesos* in present currency.

For Credibanco and Visa Colombia the opportunity to provide the institutional sponsorship for the first edition of this book on the thirtieth anniversary of our foundation has been a motive of great satisfaction. Its meticulousness and depth are a tribute to the knowledge of Professor Antonio Hernández Gamarra, who has dedicated a good part of his professional career to the study and teaching of monetary subjects.

PROLOGUE

José Antonio Ocampo
Executive Secretary,
Comisión Económica para América Latina y el Caribe, CEPAL.
(Economic Commission for Latin America and the Caribbean)

Opposite page, Detail of a one peso bill, issued in Medellín by the Sociedad Minera del Zancudo, 1883.

I would like to thank my colleague and friend, Antonio Hernández, for honoring me with his invitation to write the prologue for his book "A Monetary History of Colombia".

It is a work that synthesizes nearly two centuries of Colombian monetary history, written with the precision of an economist who has dedicated several decades to a rigorous analysis of Colombian monetary matters, but at the same time easily understood by the non-specialist reader. The modesty which the author shows in its introduction is, therefore, unjustified. I would like to congratulate Credibanco-Visa for their wise decision to commission and publish this book.

The author begins by recognizing that, in modern societies, money is "a social convention based on trust". For this reason, he continues, its solidity depends on the existence of "institutions, that is to say, a set of social agreements, principles and rules that facilitate the acceptance, for the exchange of goods and service, of the different forms of money". The book sets out to trace the evolution of these institutions over nearly two centuries of monetary history, carefully analyzing the central features of each period's monetary institutions and the way that they responded or failed to respond to the demands of the country's economic development.

The two centuries under discussion were characterized by a profound transformation, not only of the Colombian economy, but the world economy as well and of the way that the functions of money and the institutions that maintain it are conceived. The difficulties that confronted our monetary system over many years as it helped to move our country towards a modern economy, and the problems it later faced while supporting our capitalist development, are analyzed with precision in this book. In this respect, an essential point was the way that the monetary regime responded to successive external shocks which the Colombian economy experienced - both the booms and the adverse situations associated with fluctuations in the price of coffee and the ups and downs of international credit.

The author also analyzes the internal factors that helped to shape this history, especially the War of the Thousand Days, which gave rise to the first outbreak of high inflation (or what might be roughly called hyper-inflation) in the economic history of Latin America. This traumatic experience led, as those who are familiar with the matter know, to a tradition of conservatism in monetary matters that lasted for several decades and explains why, when the Central Bank, el Banco de la República, was created in 1923, it had a joint private and public ownership and also the minority power given to the government on its Board of Directors up to 1963, when the Monetary Board began its work.

Changing ideas about the role of monetary institutions on an international level and their function in the evolution of the world economy were another decisive influence and serve as a background to the historical events that unfold in this book.

It is worth recalling that, in the nineteenth century, the gold standard was only imposed in a gradual and incomplete way, beginning in the eighteen-seventies, and created a tendency towards the unification of the monetary regimes that had existed until then in different parts of the world (the gold, silver and bimetallic standards).

That period was also characterized by the gradual emergence, under the leadership of the Bank of England, of notions about the central bank: its functions, powers and monopoly of issuance; its role as a banker for credit establishments and lender of last resort; and the use of rediscount as the central instrument of monetary policy.

Opposite page, *Detail of a bill of the Banco de Barranquilla, 1873.*

Equally typical of the period were situations marked by the inconvertibility of the national currencies of the countries that were on the periphery of the capitalist world, including those of Latin America. In Colombia, the monetary regime adopted during the eighteen-eighties and nineties by the reform movement that was known as the "Regeneration" was merely one of a number of experiments of this kind that took place in Latin America around that time, as was the slow breaking of the bonds of the silver standard, which the country, more as a matter of practice than norms, had inherited from the colonial regime.

The gold standard was abandoned by the European countries during the First World War and it became evident, during the nineteen-twenties, that it could not be reestablished in a stable way. During the Great Depression that began in 1929 it was buried forever: new visions of the role of monetary institutions which had come into being in the previous decades took its place. The most polished expression of this new thought was the emergence of the most characteristic philosophy of modern monetary institutions –monetary policy– , that is, the use of the instruments of monetary regulation to shape the performance of economies throughout the economic cycle.

This idea amounted to a fundamental break with the classical concepts of monetary regulation, which had evolved from the definition of its precious metal content towards the idea of conferring greater "elasticity" on metallic regimes through the complementary use of fiduciary money. The new vision found its maximum expression in the thought of Keynes, but there were precedents for it, even during the years when the gold standard ruled and, to a greater extent, in the years following the First World War, when the inconvertibility of European currencies was maintained. These experiences were what led Keynes to affirm in his now classic book, *A Tract on Monetary Reform*, published in 1923, that the gold standard was a relic of the era of the barbarians.

To this vision would be added, after the definitive collapse of the gold standard, the idea that the exchange rate of national currencies could also be subjected to modifications. That is, the idea of an exchange policy, which was definitively enshrined on an international level with the Bretton Woods agreements of 1944, which give rise to the International Monetary Fund.

This broadening of the functions of the state regulation of money was complemented by other innovations, the most outstanding of which is the direct regulation of transactions in foreign currency, that is, exchange control and the complementary regime of foreign trade licenses. Exchange control, with its different manifestations, was essentially a byproduct of inconvertibility, but its association with the authorization of specific operations of foreign trade first arose with the regulations imposed by the countries who fought in the First World War and, later, in the nineteen-thirties, was strengthened by the collapse of multilateral trade, which created the need to directly regulate transactions with each country in accordance with the corresponding bilateral accords.

This is the international background to our monetary history at the end of the nineteenth century and the beginning of the twentieth, and it is reflected in the successive stages that characterized it. Among them, we note: the effective maintenance of the silver standard, despite the legal adoption of the gold standard in 1871; the inconvertibility that took place during the Regeneration movement; the kind of functions and powers given to

Opposite page, *Detail of a one peso bill of the Banco de Bogotá, 1873.*

the Banco de la República at the time of its foundation, which made it an advanced central bank of the gold standard era; the radical changes in monetary and exchange management that resulted from the crisis of 1931; and their definitive consolidation in the financial reform of 1951.

The latter changes laid the foundations in our country for new ideas, voiced on an international level, about the role of money and foreign exchanges in economic policy. In this way, as the author indicates, the fundamental policy instrument of Colombia's Central Bank, as it was originally conceived –the rediscount rate– quickly lost its importance, giving place to a complex system of intervention that predominated for more than half a century: exchange and export controls, a modifiable exchange rate, variable reserve requirement ratios and forced investments in Banco de la República securities, including prior import deposits.

The most polemical aspect of the transition to the new model was, in the judgement of Antonio Hernández, the way in which the benefits deriving from the monopoly of issuance in inflationary conditions began to be apportioned, that is, the "inflation tax" which, as I pointed out several years ago, is, in great measure, a "devaluation tax" in countries like our own, since the Banco de la República largely appropriates the inflationary tax through the profits generated by the buying and selling of foreign exchange as the result of the nominal devaluation that accompanies inflation.

The manner in which the author describes the way that this tax is apportioned is categorical: "the ruling classes worked out an implicit social pact which, by means of credit financed with the primary emission of money at subsidized interest rates, apportioned the inflationary tax among certain sectors and in this way diminished the negative effects of inflation on these sectors". As a result, "the Banco de la República and monetary policy in general found themselves trapped by the need to administer a long list of credit lines destined for special purposes and at preferential interest rates".

There is no doubt that this situation implied a confusion between the regulatory functions of monetary and exchange policy and other kinds of functions that were being developed parallel to them: those of the development banks. The financial reform of 1951 gave both of these responsibilities to the Banco de la República. It is worth noting that the creation of development banks was another byproduct of ideas which had been developing on an international level since the 1930's about giving a more interventionist role to the State. They were a response to criticisms that the private sector does not always provide credit resources to the desired sectors –the rural sector and small and medium companies– nor does it grant adequate terms for loans, due to its tendency to maintain liquidity and concentrate on short-term financing.

This idea that there was a double justification for state intervention became a reality with the Bretton Woods agreements, which, in addition to the International Monetary Fund, created the World Bank as an instrument for reconstructing the countries ruined by the war and advancing the developing nations.

In the interests of precision, it is worth noting that the function of a development bank in Colombia was also carried out by other means, namely, through the creation of a multiplicity of new public agencies - the Caja Agraria (Agrarian Bank) and the Banco Central Hipotecario (Central Mortgage Bank) at the beginning of the nineteen-thirties; the Instituto

Opposite page, *Detail of a one peso bill of the Banco Popular de Bolívar, 1883.*

de Fomento Industrial (The Institute of Industrial Promotion) in 1940 and the Banco Popular (Popular Bank), Banco Cafetero (Coffee-Growers Bank) and Banco Ganadero (Cattle-Raisers Bank) in the nineteen-fifties.

In addition, new private institutions were created for the same purpose –the financial corporations in the nineteen-sixties and the savings and housing loans corporations in the following decade. Nevertheless the functions of a second-tier (rediscount) development bank were developed by the Banco de la República and it was only later that these responsibilities began to be given to other institutions like the National Electricity Fund (FEN) created in 1982; FINAGRO, an agricultural financial fund created in 1990; and the foreign trade bank, BANCOLDEX, created in 1990– and the transfer of the other special credit funds to the IFI. Added to this was the obligation placed on financial intermediaries, through norms that had a fundamentally governmental origin, to assign resources for certain development purposes.

This mixing of the functions of a central and a development bank doubtless caused problems and, in particular, distracted the Banco de la República from its main role as the governor of monetary and exchange policy. These problems explain one of the essential reforms of the Central Bank made by the new Constitution adopted in 1991, namely, the Constitution prohibits the Central Bank to create any credits for the private sector.

The virtues of the separation of these functions are now evident. What is more, the fact that Colombia has maintained one of the most complete systems of second-tier development banking indicates that the modern conception of the central bank is not incompatible with the creation of an active development bank. However, it was somehow natural, historically speaking, that the two functions would be confused, given that the inflationary tax created a number of resources that had to be assigned in a certain way and in our country they were largely allocated to the private sector through development credits.

Nevertheless, Antonio Hernandez's interpretation of this matter needs, I believe, some further clarification, particularly in four aspects. In the first place, the development of these mechanisms to assign the resources of emission clearly preceded the era of moderate but persistent inflation that began at the start of the 1970's. In addition, they played a passive role in the origin of this inflationary acceleration, since what happened in Colombia was part of a world inflationary process. Instead, we might say that the effect of these monetary mechanisms, as well as the regime of inflation-linked salary, exchange and financial adjustment, was to give Colombian inflation the persistence which has characterized it for the past quarter-century.

In the second place, it is worth remembering that the Special Credit Funds were also fed by foreign credit resources and by forced investments of different kinds, not only and maybe not even mainly by the apportioning of the inflationary tax.

In the third place, Colombia did not abuse these monetary mechanisms, at least when we compare our policies with those of other Latin American countries and recall our long history of moderate inflation and the rigorous way in which our monetary authorities always checked inflation when rises in price levels approached a certain limit (the 30% annual inflation barrier).

Finally, the public sector also appropriated part of the inflationary tax, through direct credits from the Banco de la República to the government at more highly subsidized rates

Opposite page, *Detail of a bond of the Tolima railway company, 1901.*

than those on credits to the private sector, and through the earnings on the buying and selling of foreign exchange (that is, the "devaluation tax") which formed part of the different manifestations of the Special Exchange Account.

It could be said that there was a relatively balanced distribution of the inflationary tax between the public and private sectors, although it was done through mechanisms that seem inappropriate today. This was especially true of the nineteen-eighties, when the assigning of resources from emission to the national government through the above-mentioned mechanisms helped to prevent an accelerated growth of internal public debt in the face of fiscal imbalances, high internal interest rates and the effects of devaluation on the *peso* value of the foreign debt.

The apportioning of the inflationary tax during the most recent stage of the history of the Central Bank has been just as problematical, although the debate on this subject has not been strictly put in these terms. There were essentially three basic mechanisms of monetary expansion after the strongly restrictive policy of 1991 and all of them benefited the private sector: the monetary accomodation of the strong accumulation of international reserves associated with private foreign debt, the gradual reduction of the non-monetary liabilities of the Central Bank and the sharp reduction in the reserve requirement ratios, which basically favored the commercial banks.

All of these contributed to the great boom in private spending and in the foreign and internal credit that financed it, later causing quite a number of problems, as the author points out. The traditional mechanisms of assigning the inflationary tax to the government, on the other hand, disappeared. One way of interpreting this set of circumstances is that the private sector wound up being the only beneficiary of the inflationary tax during a good part of the nineteen-nineties, although in ways that were very different to those of the past.

The government's participation in the benefits of this tax only came into effect at the end of that decade, when it began to receive income in the form of earnings by the Central Bank and the latter began to acquire national public debt securities in the secondary market.

For this reason, in contrast with the nineteen-eighties and despite the fact that the primary fiscal deficits (that is, before the payment of interests) were lower than the ones of that period, the government's non-participation in the distribution of the inflationary tax, joined to the strong rise in internal interest rates and the government's policy of contracting internal debt in order counteract the rapid increase of external private debt, led in the end to a strong rise in public internal debt. For this reason, by the end of the nineteen-nineties, interest payments became a much heavier burden on the fiscal situation than they had been at the end of the nineteen-eighties.

There is no doubt that the author's treatment of the recent crisis is a sensible one.

I completely agree with him when he says that the crisis would be incomprehensible without the strong expansion of public and private spending that had taken place before the crisis and the coincidental outbreak of problems in Asia in 1997 and in Russia in 1998. I also coincide with his view that, in terms of the growth of the monetary aggregates, Colombian policy was much more prudent from 1995 onwards than in the previous years, a fact that has been frequently ignored in recent discussions of the matter. But, without contradicting his assertion that "from a historical perspective perhaps it is too early to come up with a detailed and well-thought out analysis of the complex factors that led the Colombian economy to suffer the only decline in its Gross Domestic Product since the beginning of the nineteen-thirties", I would like to wind up my analysis of this important book with two commentaries.

Opposite page, *Detail of a ten* pesos *bill of the Banco Republicano de Medellín, 1889.*

The first has to do with the narrow link between monetary and exchange problems in Latin America. This is particularly true in the case of Colombia, since throughout its history our country has generally avoided the great macro-economic imbalances of a strictly internal origin that have affected other Latin American countries. For this reason, both the great booms and the great crises have usually been associated with external phenomena. This explains the decisive importance which devaluation has always had as a mechanism of adjustment in the face of the great crises that have confronted our economy since the nineteen-thirties.

In fact, not only on that occasion but also in the mid-1950's, the 1980's and, once more, in the recent crisis, devaluation played a fundamental role in such adjustment.

In each case devaluation only came after a certain delay, which created problems of different kinds. Thus, the defense of the exchange band during the recent crisis forms part of the series of episodes involving a delayed adjustment of the exchange rate that characterized the main crises of the country during the twentieth century.

The second commentary refers to the fact that the deterioration of the net wealth of the private sector was much greater in the recent crisis than in those of the 1950's and 1980's and much more similar, in this sense, to what went on during the crisis of the 1930's. What is more, on both occasions, this deterioration was the result of a phase of accelerated indebtedness on the part of the private sector, followed by period in which this indebtedness became much more expensive, even though two entirely different mechanisms were at work: deflation in the 1930's and the rise in nominal interest rates in the 1990's.

The losses represented by the deterioration of net worth in the 1930's were largely nationalized through the relief given to mortgage debts and the absorption of mortgage banks by the Banco Central Hipotecario. Nevertheless, this solution, as well as the high rates of foreign indebtedness of the public sector, were not onerous in the end, thanks to the moratorium on foreign debt, which was facilitated by the international context of the period, which included a more or less explicit acceptance of the Latin American moratoriums by the administration of Roosevelt in the United States.

Although a part of the mortgage debts has also been nationalized in recent years, neither the aggressive use of this mechanism nor moratoriums have been available in recent years. Apart from other differences of an economic kind (the existence of wide margins for an easy substitution of imports in the nineteen-thirties, for example) and, of course, political ones as well, the above contrasts help to explain our present circumstances. And, finally, it is worth recording that the international financial markets that play a role in the so-called "emerging" markets never fully recovered from the Asian and Russian crises.

The above reflections have been a way of expressing my thanks once more to Antonio Hernández and Credibanco Visa for making this book available to readers who are interested in the monetary history of Colombia and for inviting me to write its prologue.

Rieles de Oro entregados pr. el Fundidor al Fiel desde hoy 23 de Julio hta 16 de Ag.to 1822	Moneda de Oro entregado p.r el Fiel al tesorero desde 30 de Julio hasta hoy 21 de Ag.to de 1822
	075
51-0-3-0	50-0-4-0
62-1-1-0	50-0-4-0
62-0-2-0	50-0-4-0
62-0-0-0	50-0-4-0
58-4-4-0	50-0-4-0
64-0-0-0	50-0-4-0
58-0-0-0	50-0-4-0
58-2-4-0	50-0-4-0
61-2-0-0	50-0-4-0
537-2-6-0	50-0-4-0
62-4-0-0	50-0-4-0
56-7-0-0	50-0-4-0
51-0-0-0	50-0-4-0
68-0-0-0	Ag.to 19 50-0-4-0
66-0-0-0	50-0-4-0
845-5-6-0	50-0-2-0
64-4-4-"	50-0-2-0
72-2-0-0	50-0-2-0
65-2-0-0	1051-1-6-0
1.043-6-2-0	

Se cerró en 16. de Agosto 1822.

Se cerró en 21 de Ag.to de 1822

Aquí cesó la moneda Española

INTRODUCTION

Opposite page, *Document in which the authority over gold coinage was given to the Colombian treasury on August 21, 1822.*

The everyday meaning of the word money is very different from that of the word used by specialists. It is a semantic vagueness that is the source of paradox and not a little confusion.

In daily life money and wealth are often considered to be synonyms, as we see by the way that people mean the same thing when they say that someone is very rich or that he has a lot of money. In specialist language the wealth of an individual refers to the total of the material goods that he owns, whether they be real estate, capital goods, stocks or any other form of property. Money is only that part of such wealth which is made up of metal coins, bank notes or bank deposits.

Money in the latter sense has little or no intrinsic value. The fact that it is accepted in exchange for other goods which do have such a value is due to the confidence of the different individuals or institutions that play a role in the economy, who will, in turn, exchange it for other goods and services. People accept money because they know that others will.

In modern societies, money is, then, a social convention based on trust and its invention follows very elemental economic principles. For one thing, its use reduces the cost of transactions, when compared to the option of exchanging goods for goods.

It permits buying and selling to take place without the need for barter. If a person wants to sell something and get something else in return, it is not necessary to make a direct swap of items. For another, it turns out to be cheaper to print bank notes or make account entries than produce other goods —for example, gold or silver— that may serve as money.

But these, the main virtues of money, are often the reason for its greatest weakness. If the low cost of producing currency leads it to be issued in excess, confidence in it is undermined and the monetary system established around it will collapse.

For this reason, the solidity of a monetary system is based on the existence of institutions —that is to say, a set of social agreements, principles and rules— that facilitate the acceptance, for the exchange of goods and services, of the different forms of money placed into circulation by the authorities invested with this power. Institutions and authorities which must constantly create the confidence that is necessary for money to effect and contribute to the good functioning and, in particular, the stability of the economic system.

With this in mind, the main aim of this work is to examine the evolution of the institutions and authorities which, in the course of Colombia's history as an independent republic, have been in charge of authorizing, regulating and controlling the supply of money. This book likewise attempts to set forth the fundamental principles which have guided the taking of decisions about this matter in different periods of our history. It also endeavors to offer the reader a clear picture of the evolution of monetary policy. In a complementary way, it frequently deals with the different kinds of money which are physically represented by Colombian coins and bank notes, whose main characteristics are described in both of the catalogues found at the end of the text.

For a number of reasons this book can only offer a panoramic view of the subject matter it deals with. It covers a broad historical period marked by an abundance of specific and closely-interrelated changes in monetary, exchange and credit policies.

Furthermore, these events are related to the multiplicity of factors that have affected the course of our monetary institutions, including the specific kinds of conflicts of interest that have influenced decisions about such policies.

Therefore, the scope of this book does not allow for a detailed analysis of many aspects that are relevant to its main themes, such as an in-depth analysis of the economic theories that prevailed, on an international level, in different periods. Nor does it set out to explore the different alternative explanations for or interpretative controversies surrounding many of the episodes it relates. Also, by its very nature, it has few pretensions about being markedly original. On the contrary, the specialist reader will understand that it owes a lot to the works of Guillermo Torres García, José Antonio Ocampo, Mauricio Avella Gómez, Fabio Sánchez Torres, Adolfo Meisel Roca, Alejandro López M. and Jorge Enrique Ibáñez, among others. The last three were responsible for a major part of the book, "*Banco de la República. Antecedentes, Evolución y Estructura*" ("The Banco de la República: Its Background, Evolution and Structure".)

This is not to say that the author fully shares the traditional interpretations about the development or reforms of our monetary institutions. In some cases, on the contrary, the book openly disagrees with these interpretations. To mention only a few examples, it challenges traditional views about the causes of the liquidation of the Banco Nacional at the end of the nineteenth century and the origins of the Banking Reform of 1951, and questions the usual explanation of the date on which the minister of Finance (*Ministro de Hacienda*) was designated a full member, with voting rights, of the Board of Directors of the Banco de la República.

Before finishing this introduction, one technical matter has to be clarified. The figures on inflation included in the statistical appendix at the end, used as an analytical tool throughout the book, are measured with the Consumers Price Index (CPI). As is well known, over short periods this index may not be a good indicator of the inflation of demand, because of the multitude of circumstantial factors that determine it. Nevertheless, for a long period, like the one covered in this study, this precariousness is not important, apart from the fact that there are no alternative indicators for the most recent periods.

I would like to express my thanks to the following persons: Gerardo Hernández, executive manager of the Banco de la República, for his help in finding and clarifying many of the data found in the book; Angelina Araujo Vélez, head of the numismatics section of the Library and Arts department of the Banco de la República, who had a big part in creating the catalogue which describes the bank notes which have circulated in the country since 1922; and Martha Jeanet Sierra, head of the Rare Books and Manuscripts room of the Luis Ángel Arango library, for providing documentation that was invaluable for the writing of this book. I also owe thanks to Camilo José Hernández López, for his efficient work as a research assistant, both for the main text of the book and, especially, the catalogues found at the end.

Finally, I am grateful to Dr. Orlando García, president of Credibanco-Visa, who came up with the idea of doing this book, which would not have been possible without his intellectual stimulus and the financial support of the important institution he presides.

Opposite page, *Document from the historical archives of the "Casa de la Moneda" which declares the initiation of Republican money: "From here on the new money began..." 1822.*

Rieles de Oro entregados p.r el Fundidor al Fiel desde 4 de Sep.re hasta hoy 30 del mismo.

Moneda entregada p.r el Fiel al Tesorero desde 10 de Sep.re hasta 8 de 8bre de 1822 — Nuebo Tipo

```
 56 - 1 - 0 - 0        50 - 0 - 4 - 0 ..... ##
 62 - 4 - 0 - 0        50 - 0 - 4 - 0 ..... ##
 61 - 4 - 1 - 0        50 - 0 - 4 - 0 ..... ##
 56 - 3 - 0 - 0        50 - 0 - 4 - 0
 55 - 4 - 0 - 0        50 - 0 - 4 - 0
 57 - 7 - 0 - 0        50 - 0 - 4 - 0
 58 - 1 - 5 - 0        50 - 0 - 4 - 0
 53 - 3 - 4 - 0        50 - 0 - 4 - 0
─────────────          29 - 0 - 2 - 0
462 - 4 - 2 - 0        25 - 0 - 2 - 0
 62 - 2 - 0 - 0        50 - 0 - 4 - 0
 62 - 0 - 2 - 0        50 - 0 - 4 - 0
 55 - 2 - 1 - 0        50 - 0 - 4 - 0
 63 - 2 - 5 - 0        50 - 0 - 4 - 0
 62 - 4 - 5 - 0        50 - 0 - 4 - 0
 64 - 3 - 0 - 0        50 - 0 - 4 - 0
 62 - 1 - 0 - 0        50 - 0 - 4 - 0
 66 - 0 - 0 - 0        50 - 0 - 4 - 0
 63 - 0 - 0 - 0        50 - 0 - 4 - 0
 64 - 7 - 0 - 0        50 - 0 - 4 - 0
─────────────         ─────────────
1088 - 2 - 7 - 0      1101 - 3 - 0 - 0
```

Se uzzó en 30 rs.

Estos rieles han servido p.a la moneda de la Republica

Desde aqui empezo la moneda nueva con el Busto y armas de la Republica

METAL COINAGE

Opposite page, *Series of Colombian coins, from the colonial* macuquinas *to the coins of the Republic. The* macuquina *continued in use up to the mid-1840's, some time after the country became independent.*

Up to 1871, the money that circulated in the territory that is now known as Colombia was made up, for all practical purposes, of metal coins with different kinds of legal standards, weights and mint materials.

During the Spanish colonial period, the monetary system was based on *el peso de plata* (the silver *peso*) of a $0.902^{2/3}$ standard: the figure expresses the percentage of precious metal in every unit of weight.

The silver *peso* was divided into eight *reales*. Pesetas (two *reales*), *reales*, *medios* (half) *reales* and *cuartillos* (quarters) were also minted. A regulation issued in 1771 reduced the standard of gold and silver coins to 0.901 and a later measure, in 1786, set the standard for gold coins at 0.875. As a result of these colonial norms, the republic of Colombia inherited coins of different specifications, among others what was known as the *macuquina*, which, in addition to not having a homogenous standard, was uneven in weight and design.

This diversity was complicated by the effects of the struggle for independence, during which the warring armies minted different kinds of coins to cover their military expenses.

Among them was the one known as the india, with a standard of $0.583^{1/3}$, put into circulation to support the army of don Antonio Nariño, one of the leaders of the independence movement; the copper coins minted in Cartagena that were known as chinas; and the *caraqueña* (the "Caracas"), so-called because it was minted in Venezuela by Pablo Morillo, leader of the royalist forces: it also circulated in Nueva Granada, the colony roughly corresponding to modern Colombia.

Faced with the economic and commercial obstacles caused by the existence of a variety of currencies of uneven value, the Constituent Congress, the constitutional congress for the newly-founded republic held in Cucutá in 1821, passed a number of measures with the aim of unifying them. In the first place, it ordered the minting of a quarter-ounce coin of refined platinum, equivalent to the *peso fuerte* ("strong" *peso*), as well as coins of two and four *pesos* fuertes. It also arranged for the circulation of *cuartillos* and *medios cuartillos* that would be minted in copper and would have a weight equivalent to a half and a quarter ounce, respectively. In the second place, it ordained that the gold and silver coins that

Above, *Antonio Nariño. Lithograph by Lemercier after an engraving by José María Espinosa, printed in Paris by Lisveille. To finance his army, in 1813 Nariño ordered the minting of a coin known as the* india.

REPUBLIC OF COLOMBIA.

No.

ONE HUNDRED POUNDS STERLING.

£100.

I, FRANCISCO ANTONIO ZEA, Envoy Extraordinary, and Minister Plenipotentiary of the Republic of Colombia, for the purpose of establishing political and commercial relations with the different Powers of Europe, do, by this present General Bond, make known, that the Government of the said Republic having determined, under the Authority of the Supreme National Congress, to raise a Foreign Loan of Two Millions of Pounds Sterling, for the purpose of

1stly. Paying off the existing engagements of the Republic in Great Britain.

2dly. Giving a powerful impulse to its Agriculture,—to the working of its Mines of Gold, Silver, and other Metals, and to the general development of its immense natural Resources.

And having authorized me to enter into a Contract for the said Loan, and having granted me full special Powers for that purpose, signed by the President of the State, SIMON BOLIVAR, and countersigned by the Minister for Foreign Affairs, J. R. REVENGA, I have, in the Name, and as the Representative of the said Republic of Colombia, contracted a Loan of Two Millions of Pounds Sterling, by virtue of the aforementioned special Powers, the Original of which is deposited with Messieurs *Charles Herring, William Graham,* and *John Diston Powles,* Agents for the Colombian Government for this Loan; which Sum of Two Millions of Pounds Sterling, I acknowledge to have received from the said *Charles Herring, William Graham,* and *John Diston Powles,* and in return for which, I have, in the Name of the Government of Colombia, which I represent, issued an equal value in Special Bonds, classed A, B and C, in manner following: viz.

Class A.—2,000 of £500 each £1,000,000
— B.— 2,000 of £250 each   500,000
— C.— 5,000 of £100 each   500,000
                                          £2,000,000

With Fifty-five half-yearly Dividend Warrants annexed thereto.

And I do hereby declare that the Conditions on which the said Loan has been raised, are as follows:

1st. That there shall be paid an Annual Interest of Six *per Cent.* to the Bearers of the said Bonds, in half-yearly Payments, namely, on the 1st of May, and on the 1st of November in each Year, commencing on the 1st of November of the present Year 1822.

2dly. That the payment of the said Interest shall be made in London, (free of all Expense) at the Banking-house of Messieurs *Barclay, Tritton, Bevan* and Co. on presentation of the half-yearly Dividend Warrants.

3dly. That a twentieth part of the Bonds for the said Loan shall be annually paid off at Par, commencing in the year 1830, and ending in the year 1849.

4thly. That Notice shall previously be given of the Numbers and Amounts of the Bonds which are to be paid off in each year.

5thly. The Government of Colombia reserves to itself the liberty of paying off at Par a larger proportion of Bonds than the aforesaid Annual Twentieth Part, or the whole of them, giving in such case, Six Months public notice of its intention so to do.

And as Security for the Payment of the Interest, as also for the Liquidation of the Principal of the said Loan, I do hereby, acting in the Name and on the Behalf of the Government of Colombia, solemnly pledge to all the Holders of the aforesaid Special Bonds the following Revenues of the State, the produce of which very far exceeds the purposes to which it is now destined, namely,

1st. The Duties of Importation and Exportation as established by the Tariff of the Supreme National Congress, dated the 21st September 1821.

2dly. The Revenues arising from the Mines of Gold, and of Silver.

3dly. The Revenues arising from the Mines of Salt.

4thly. The Revenue arising from the Grant of the exclusive Privilege to trade in Tobacco, so long as the same shall exist, or from such other Imposts as may be levied on this Branch of Revenue in the event of the exclusive Privilege being abolished.

And, in virtue of the full Powers with which I am invested, I declare, that the Government of the Republic of Colombia, does, by these Presents, constitute itself responsible, and legally and solemnly bound, to all the Persons collectively interested in this Loan of Two Millions of Pounds Sterling, and individually to each of them, for the amount of the Special Bonds of which for the time being they may be the Holders.

In Faith whereof,—I, in the Name, and as the Representative of the Government of the Republic of Colombia, do give the present General Bond, signed by me, and sealed with the provisional Seal of the State.

Dated in Paris, the 13th March, 1822.

We, hereby certify, that the before-mentioned Special Power signed by SIMON BOLIVAR, and J. R. REVENGA, authorising the Contract for this Loan, is deposited with us; and that we hold the same for the Account of all Parties interested in this Loan.—London, March 13, 1822.

I do hereby certify, that the Bearer of this Special Bond, is a Creditor of the Government of Colombia for the Sum of ONE HUNDRED POUNDS Sterling, which I acknowledge to have received; and which forms a part of the Loan of Two Millions of Pounds Sterling secured by the foregoing General Bond.

Signed by me in the Name of the Republic of Colombia, at Paris, the 13th March, 1822.

Secretary.

Opposite page,
A "Zea" foreign debt bond of 100 pounds sterling, Paris, March 13, 1822. The new republic commissioned Francisco Antonio Zea to obtain foreign loans in order to reactivate the economy, which was in ruins after the War of Independence.

Right below,
A "Zea" foreign debt bond for 100 pounds sterling (reverse).

would circulate in Colombia should have the same weight and standard as those laid down in the colonial laws since 1786.

Because of the scarcity of fiscal resources, the shortage of platinum and the technical difficulties involved in their minting, there was little circulation of platinum coins. For this reason, gold and silver were restored as metal coinage in 1826.

For the former, it was decided to issue coins of a 0.875 standard, in accordance with Spanish laws, and mint el *peso colombiano de oro* (the Colombian gold peso, equivalent to sixteenth of an ounce), *el escudo* (equivalent to two *pesos*), *el doblón* (the doubloon, that is, the double, equivalent to four *pesos*), la *media onza* (the half ounce) and la *onza* (the ounce). For the latter, there would circulate el *peso colombiano de plata* (the silver Colombian peso, equivalent to eight *reales*), el *medio peso*, la *peseta* (equivalent to two *reales*), el *real*, el *medio real*, and el *cuartillo de real*. For the *pesetas* and higher units the standard would be 0.900 and for the real and lower units, $0.666^{2/3}$. In addition, to avoid difficulties caused by the *macuquina* to the new coinage in circulation, it was ordered out of circulation and reminted in accordance with the standard for low-denomination silver coins.

In 1836, shortly after the disintegration of Gran Colombia, the short-lived (1819-1830) republic made up of present-day Venezuela, Colombia, Panama and Ecuador, a regulation was passed with the aim of unifying the standard, weight, value, type and denomination of the coins of Nueva Granada, the colonial name used once more to describe the new republic in the period 1831-58. By virtue of this norm, el *peso colombiano de plata*, with the same characteristics as those established in 1826, came to be known as the *granadino de plata*, and el *peso colombiano de oro* with a standard of 0.875 and weight of 1.691 grams was now called the *granadino de oro*.

In 1838 all of the silver coins which did not bear the seal of Colombia or Nueva Granada were ordered out of circulation, to be reminted into *cuartillos*, *medios reales* and *reales* with a standard of $0.666^{2/3}$. In effect, this was a new attempt to take the *macuquina* coin out of circulation, which was easily forged and trimmed, causing a great deal of insecurity when the time came to pay for goods and services or comply with sales contracts between economic agents. This measure only came to be effectively enforced in 1848, during the first presidency of Tomás Cipriano de Mosquera.

Above,
Coins of "Gran Colombia", the short-lived (1819-1830) republic made up of present-day Venezuela, Colombia, Panama and Ecuador: 1 real de plata, Bogotá; eight gold escudos, Popayán, 1830. Such coins, stamped with another seal, continued to be used in Venezuela and Ecuador after the break-up of that republic.

Opposite page, *Document stating the debt owed to Guillermo Robinson by the republic of Gran Colombia, signed by José María del Castillo, 1824. Later, as an independent country, Colombia borrowed money to reconstruct its economy, exhausted by the effort of the war for the independence of Venezuela, Ecuador and Peru.*

Consolidated Debt of the republic of "Nueva Granada", the colonial name for Colombia used once more in the period 1831-58. Subscription at 5%, December 31, 1838.

Above, *Original drawing of the Coat of Arms and Flag of Nueva Granada in an official letter by Lino de Pombo to the Secretary of the War and Navy Office, Law 9 of May, 1834. De Pombo, as Secretary of Foreign Relations of Nueva Granada, signed a treaty with Venezuela and Ecuador for the payment of the foreign debt.*

Below, *Coins minted between 1830 -1837, the period when Gran Colombia was succeeded by the republic of Nueva Granada.*

Twenty five years after the measures passed by the Constituent Congress of Cucutá, the Colombian Congress approved new legislation on the national currency. In June, 1846, it adopted as the monetary unit el *real de plata*, with a weight of 2.5 grams and a 0.900 standard. The coins of 8 and 2 *reales* were adopted as multiples of this monetary unit, the latter with a weight of five grams and thus the equivalent of the French franc of this period: the subdivision of the unit was el *medio real*.

For low-value currency the minting of copper coins equivalent to un *décimo* (a tenth or dime) and a *medio décimo de real* was ordered. Even though this same measure ordered the minting of gold coins of different denominations (*el escudo, el doblón, el cóndor* and *la onza*), no legal relation was established between the value of gold and that of silver and therefore the first acted more as a merchandise than as a means of payment.

Despite their advantages – the unification of the standard for all coins, the laying down of a strict proportion between their weight and exchange value, the establishment of a logical order of multiples and subdivisions – the 1846 norms were modified several times in the following years. In 1847 the issuing of el *granadino de plata* with a weight of 25 grams and a standard of 0.900 was authorized. In 1853, the monetary unit was changed again, becoming el *peso*, equivalent to the *granadino de plata*. In 1857, the multiples and subdivisions of the monetary unit were rearranged. There were further reforms when, in 1867 and in 1873, authorization was given again for the minting of silver coins with standards of 0.900, 0.835 and 0.666.

In addition to allowing, again, for a lack of uniformity in the precious metal content of the different silver coins, these legal measures established that each kilogram of silver would produce 40 *pesos*, independently

Above, *Florentino González (1805-1874). Lithograph by the Thierry brothers, Paris, 1851. Politician, journalist, jurisconsult, public figure and professor, he was a staunch supporter of radical policies. He served as Finance Minister, Interior Minister and Foreign Relations Minister under different administrations.*

Above, *José María Plata (1811-1891). He was a minister on several occasions representing the radical movement.*

Above, *A cuartillo de plata coin, Popayán, 1834. In 1836 the Congress unified the money of Nueva Granada, establishing the standards, patterns, values and denominations of gold and silver coins.*

tion in our country up to the beginning of the 1870's were the predominance of silver as a means of payment and the withdrawal from circulation of coins of a higher intrinsic value, following, as was to be expected, the dictates of Gresham's law.

To relieve the shortage of silver, some financial experts like Florentino González in 1848 and José María Plata in 1854, tried to take advantage of Colombia's position as a producer of gold but not silver and impose a bimetallic monetary system, based on the predominance of gold, but it was not a success. The failure of these proposals was due to ancestral customs, in that the pattern of currency had been dominated by the circulation of silver coins since colonial times and also because, as we shall shortly see, Colombian legislation created incentives to banish gold as a means of payment. Apart from being exported like any other kind of merchandise, gold was mostly used to settle the deficit arising from foreign trade, since it was the money that was usually employed as a means of international payment.

In the sixteenth century Thomas Gresham had set the principle that governs a situation when people are faced with a choice between two currencies of the same nominal value, one of which is preferable to the other because of metal content. They will spend the bad money, and hoard the good money or export it or sell it at a premium. In a colloquial way, bad money drives good money out of circulation.

In accordance with this principle it was predictable that gold coins would stop circulating, a phenomenon that became accentuated when silver stopped being used as a currency in the world and its price fell compared to the price of gold. Darío Bustamente points out that "the fiscal law of 1873 had established the legal exchange rate between gold and silver as 1 to 15.5, the proportion which had applied in world markets for many years. But while this rate fell in the international market due to the

of the standard at which the coins were minted. This was illogical, since while a kilogram of metal with a standard of 0.900 would, in fact, produce 40 *pesos* of 25 grams, with the same amount of metal at that standard you could produce 43.10 *pesos* in coins with a 0.835 standard and 54 *pesos* if the standard of the coins were 0.666.

The measures of 1867 and 1873, as well as one of 1853, fixed the price of the gold unit at 15.244 units of silver, when in the international market was 15.5, a decision which helped to intensify the existing chaos in monetary circulation, given that a persistent legal instability was added to an inconsistency in the exchange value of coins with respect to the intrinsic content of metal and the varying price of gold in terms of silver.

In addition to these contradictions, the characteristic features of currency circula-

Right,
Proposal for the Coat of the Arms of the Republic of Nueva Granada. Original drawing by Lino de Pombo, Secretary of the Office of Foreign Relations, Law 9 of May, 1834. De Pombo signed frontier-delimitation treaties with Venezuela and Ecuador.

Below,
Gold Mine, watercolor by José María Gutiérrez de Alba, 1874. In the 1870's, Colombia was the setting for a lucrative international exchange of gold for silver coins.

demonetizing of silver, it was not modified in Colombia, thus putting a premium on the export of gold. Bringing 15.5 units of silver to the country and changing them for one unit of gold was thus a very good deal, since the same unit of gold would obtain more than 15.5 units of silver when it returned to the international market… It was thus that most of the gold in circulation was exported in a matter of a few years, so that our currency became one that mostly revolved around silver and continued to depreciate".(Bustamente, 1974, p. 563-564).

Some analysts maintain that the export, in line with Gresham's law, of gold and of silver coins with a higher standard did not necessarily lead to a reduction of the money supply, insofar as this supply could be made up of coins of a lower quality. However, it must be said that it reduced the amount of metallic money in circulation and the monetary supply suffered because metal coin was exported both to pay for the excess value of imports over exports and to take financial advantage of the disparity between the national and international markets.

FREE BANK AND THE ISSUING OF PAPER MONEY

Opposite page, *Tomás Cipriano de Mosquera*, who was president of Colombia four times, led important social and economic changes. In 1846, during his first term, the Congress adopted the silver real as the monetary unit.

Right above, *Germán Gutiérrez de Piñeres, oil painting.* Patriot from Cartagena, he was responsible for the first issue of paper money in Cartagena, around the year 1813.

Right below, *Facsimile of a* real, signed by Germán Gutiérrez de Piñeres. These bills had a low circulation because of the small size of the issue and the fact that they were printed on ordinary paper, without any security features.

The mid-nineteenth century economy of Colombia was subject to international trade cycles that resulted in monetary fluctuations and notorious variations in government revenue (because of the importance of customs duties in its total income): all of this had an impact on economic activity.

These export cycles did not take place in a political or social void. After the war of independence the merchant class called for the abolition of the colonial rules that had acted as an obstacle to the growth of production and had imposed all sorts of limitations upon the free flow of goods to and from the country.

As part of the effort to dismantle the colonial structures and establish freer trade, a set of political and economic reforms were carried out from the middle of the nineteenth century onwards. Among these it is worth mentioning the following: the abolition or reduction of a number of taxes; the liberation of the land market, especially through demortization, that is, the conversion of ecclesiastical property into private property; the abolition of slavery; and the improvements in the infrastructure of roads, river transport and ports.

These reforms culminated with the drafting of the 1863 Constitution, which enshrined a complete political decentralization and reduced state intervention to a minimum. From an economic point of view, this laissez faire attitude led to a greater mobility in productive factors by freeing manpower and the use of capital. It was in this context of economic freedom that the private bank arose, whose first expression was the creation of the Banco de Bogotá.

This bank and others that followed it were born under the shelter of law 35 of

Right,
2 pesos bank note, issued in the early days of the republic of Gran Colombia, with the shield of the Republic in the center.

Below,
Portrait of José Hilario López (1849-1853) detail from a bill of the Banco de Bogotá. During his government liberal-type reforms were carried out, such as the abolition of slavery and the abolition of ecclesiastical privileges. In the monetary field, the free export of gold was authorized.

Manuel Murillo Toro. President of Colombia (1864-1866; 1872-1874). As Treasury Minister and later as President he carried out the great reforms of the mid-19th century, which adapted a backward economy to the new ideas of free trade. Law 35 of 1865 allowed for the foundation of many private banks.

1865, which gave the banks founded in the Republic the freedom to issue bank notes, which were admissible as money for the payment of national taxes and fees or, in general, for any other kind of transaction managed by the national government. It also gave them the right to grant credits, receive sight deposits from the National Treasury and pay the nation's creditors, charging the government a commission that could not exceed 1% of the value of such payments.

In exchange for the right to issue bank notes for twenty years, the banking institutions were obliged to maintain in circulation an amount of payable-to-bearer bank notes no higher than twice the value of the metallic money that they kept in their vaults. They were also obliged to accept government supervision over these transactions and to exchange their paper money for metal coin on the demand of the bearers.

Thus, we can say that law 35 of 1865 initiated free banking in our country, that is, a monetary system in which private banks issue bank notes which can be redeemed for metal coins whose characteristics are defined by the State. This was a profound change in our monetary institutions and also in our credit system, since it placed in the hands of private enterprise a handling of credit that was formerly a monopoly of the Church.

In this way circulating money came to take the form of bank notes issued by

Opposite page,
Bond for the debt of the "Estados Unidos de Colombia", the federation of Colombian states that replaced the Republic of Nueva Granada. Signed by Aquileo Parra as Treasury Minister. In 1845, the Mosquera administration committed itself to resume payments of its part of the foreign debt of the extinct republic of Gran Colombia.

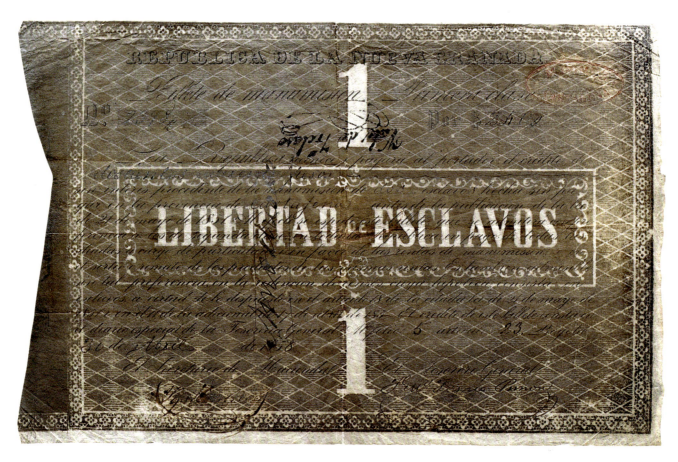

Opposite page,
Two bills paid to slave-owners for the manumission of slaves. The Law of May 21, 1851, which freed the slaves on January 1, 1852, authorized these bonds as an indemnification.

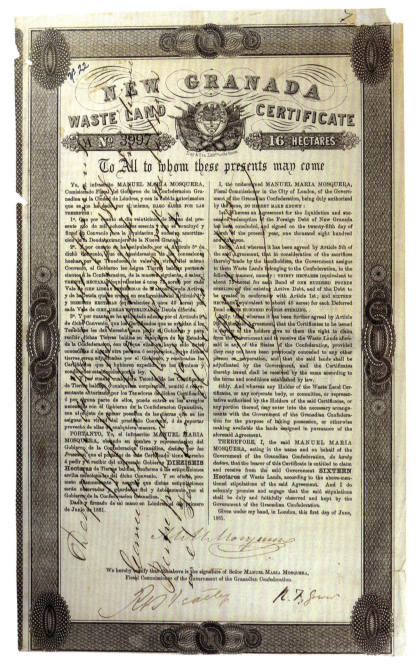

Left,
Land grant certificate for 16 hectares of waste land, issued to Manuel María Mosquera, 1863.

Right,
Map of the region of Mompós in 1844, General Archive of the Nation. In the following year, a regular steamship service was established on the river Magdalena.

the private banks and complemented by metallic money, thus giving rise to the existence in our country of fiduciary money - a paper money representing metallic coinage. This statement does not ignore previous attempts to put paper money into circulation, a point we will deal with in a moment, but it stands because such initiatives had a very restricted character.

In 1813 in Cartagena Germán Gutiérrez de Piñeres, one of the leaders of the independence movement, ordered the issuing of 300,000 *pesos* with a denomination of un *real*, a currency of minimum security since it was printed on ordinary paper. In 1821 a decree was passed ordering the salary of public employees to be paid in the form of libranzas of 6, 12, 18 and 24 *pesos*, bills, issued under the authority of the Vice President of Cundinamarca (a province in central Colombia), that could be exchanged for salt that was produced in the mines of Zipaquirá, Nemocón and Tausa.

In 1838, during the presidency of José Ignacio de Márquez (1837-41), the General Treasury of the Republic was authorized to issue and place into circulation *billetes de Tesorería* (Treasury bills) of 5, 10, 20, 25, 50, 75, 80 and 100 *pesos*. They were to be paid, on a voluntary basis, to employees and creditors of the Republic and were also admissible as payments in the tax offices of the State: they could also be converted into their equivalent in metallic money at the request of the bearers.

In 1847 Florentino Gonzaléz, Treasury Minister under Mosquera, got the Congress to approve a law which authorized the creation of a private bank called the Banco de la Nueva Granada, which did not operate because the businessmen who were expected to be its stockholders were, for a number of reasons, unable to capitalize it. Despite this failure, in 1848 President Tomás Cipriano de Mosquera gave the Treasuries of the center and south of the country the authority to issue two types of Treasury bills: those representing silver, with values of 40, 80, 160, 200, 400, 600 and 800 *pesos*, redeemable for their equivalent in coins minted in the same metal, and those representing gold, which were also redeemable in coin, at denominations of 5, 10, 25 and 50 *pesos*. All of these notes were to be admissible as payment for taxes and would be given, on a voluntary basis, to those who wished to receive them in payment for government debts.

Through laws passed in 1851 and 1852, President José Hilario López (1849-53) decreed the issuing and amortization of a number of bills aimed at the payment of the debt owed to slave-owners for the manumission of slaves, which had not been paid up to that time.

In 1861, under decree 2591, Tomás Cipriano de Mosquera, pressed to pay the expenses of the war of 1860, authorized the General Treasury of the Estados Unidos de la Nueva Granada (the federation of Colombian states or provinces that replaced the Republic of Nueva Granada in 1858) to issue Treasury bills for a value of up to 500,000 *pesos*, in denominations of 1, 2, 3, 10, 20, 50 and 100 *pesos*. These bills were to be admissible, at their nominal value, as payments for 50% of import duties, 60% of the price of salt sold in the mines owned by the State and 100% of export duties.

Initially, the acceptance of these bills, at their nominal value, was only obligatory in the case of government creditors, except foreigners, and the creditors of government employees. For the creditors of private debts they had a voluntary character. Since they had little acceptance, the government decreed their obligatory receipt for private and public debts, a short-lived measure that represented the first attempt to establish something like the modern system of government legal tender in the country.

In order to guarantee compliance with the measure and prevent the bill's depreciation, the government ordered that anyone who exchanged these bank notes at a discount of more than 2% of their nominal value would be subject to such penalties as the annulment of civil rights, fines of between 10 to 1,000 *pesos* and the loss of employment in the case of public employees. Despite Mosquera's attempts to get the courts to enforce the measure, the government was unable to maintain the value of the bills and as a result, the government abolished their status of legal tender in 1863: the bills were amortized as a national debt and retired from circulation.

Below, *Tomás Cipriano de Mosquera, photograph taken during the Rionegro Convention, 1863. In 1861 he made the bills issued by the government into legal tender, for the first time in Colombian history, but the reform only lasted a short time.*

Opposite page,
5 and 50 pesos *bank notes of the Banco de Bogotá. 100* pesos *bank note (obverse and reverse) of the Banco de Bogotá. The 1865 law on free emission allowed for the creation of this private bank in 1870 and gave solidity to the circulation of private bank bills.*

In 1866, under the presidency of Mosquera, the government again obtained authorization to issue Treasury bills and in the same year to establish el Banco Nacional de los Estados Unidos de Colombia (the National Bank of the United States of Colombia), which would be an institution in charge of issuing money and bank drafts and handling deposits and discounts and, as such, authorized to issue bank notes acceptable as payment for taxes except for the part corresponding to the amortization of the foreign debt. But this institution never flourished either.

Ordered, in one way or another, to cover government expenses, not to regulate money in circulation, none of these bill issues had any success, either because they were too small in size to fulfill the purpose for which they were intended or because there was a general fear that they would be devalued, as happened with those issued in 1861.

For the above reasons, we can safely say that it was only with the creation of el Banco de Bogotá and by virtue of the freedom of issuing granted under law 35 of 1865 that an effective circulation of bank notes first came into being.

The Banco de Bogotá, established by public deed 1923 of the Second Public Notary of Bogotá, November 15, 1870, began operations at the beginning of 1871 with a capital of 235,000 *pesos*, divided into nominal stocks of 2,500 *pesos* and bearer stocks of 100 *pesos* each. The main stock-holders were Bendix and Salomon

Above,
Miguel Samper, calling card; Mariano Tanco, daguerreotype; Salomón Koppel, oil painting. The three were founding stockholders of the Banco de Bogotá, together with Bendix Koppel, Carlos Schloss, Manuel Murillo Toro, Carlos O'Leary y Eusebio Bernal, among others.

Below,
First headquarters of the Banco de Bogotá, engraving by R. Moros Urbina, for the publication Papel Periódico Ilustrado, 1884. Founded in 1870, its initial success was partly due to the support of the radical governments. By 1888 it had 84.3% of the metallic money deposited in the banking establishments of Bogotá and 53.2 % of the total for the country.

Right,
Bills of the private banks: Banco de Boyacá and Banco Americano. Despite the notorious expansion of their operations, the private banks suffered from crises of confidence, some of them caused by political instability and others by the effects of export cycles.

Below,
50 pesos bill of the Banco de Colombia. This bank was founded in 1875, with a capital of 181,400 pesos.

Right,
Bank notes of private banks: Banco de Pamplona, 1883, and Banco Tequendama in the town of La Mesa, Cundinamarca, 1881.

Below,
1 peso bill issued by the Sociedad Minera del Zancudo, founded in Medellín in 1883. It bears the portrait and signature of Carlos Coriolano Amador, a businessman from Antioquia who became the richest man in the country. He was involved in almost all of the economic activities of his period: banking, mining, construction, cattle-raising and agriculture.

Koppel, Carlos Schloss, Miguel Samper, Manuel Murillo Toro, Carlos O'leary, Eusebio Bernal and Mariano Tanco. By the second half of 1875 this bank had deposits in current accounts of a bit more than 10 million *pesos* and circulated bank notes worth 776, 935 *pesos*, in denominations of 5, 20, 50 and 100 *pesos*.

The creation of the Banco de Bogotá was followed by the founding of the Banco de Antioquia and the Banco Santander in 1872, the Banco de Barranquilla and the Banco del Cauca in 1873, the Banco de Bolívar and the Banco Mercantil in 1874 and the Banco de Colombia in 1875. Between the latter date and 1886, the year in which the private bank began to decline for reasons we shall examine later, a total of 30 banks were founded, as can be seen in Table 1.

Despite this large number of banks, it is worth noting that from the beginning there was a marked concentration of capital and deposits in a very few of them. By way of illustration, in 1888 the Banco de Bogotá had 84.3% of the metallic money deposited in the banking establishments of Bogotá and 53.2 % of the total for the country.

There is a consensus among analysts that, as in the case of the Banco de

Left and below, *Bank notes of private banks: the Bancos Antioquia, Riohacha, Bolívar and Prendario de Soto. The Banco de Antioquia, founded by law 149 of 1872, was the second private bank established in Colombia.*

Opposite page, *Bank notes of the Banco de Barranquilla and the Banco de Cundinamarca founded in 1873 and 1881, and del Progreso. The great boom in private banking lasted from 1870 to 1886, when they fell into decline because of the centralist policies of the reform movement known as the "Regeneration".*

Table 1

PRIVATE BANKS FOUNDED BETWEEN 1870 AND 1886			
		Date of Foundation	Initial Capital (pesos)
BOGOTÁ			
Banco de Bogotá		1870	235.000
Banco de Colombia		1875	181.400
Banco popular		1877	150.000
Banco de Cundinamarca		1881	22.000
Banco de la Unión		1881	55.700
Banco de Crédito Hipotecario		1883	202.350
Banco Internacional		1885	n.d.a
ANTIOQUIA	**CITY**		
Banco de Antioquia	Medellín	1872	694.000
Banco Mercantil	Medellín	1874	40.000
Banco Restrepo & Cia.	Medellín	1875	n.d.a
Banco de Medellín	Medellín	1881	1.539.000
Banco Popular	Medellín	1882	100.000
Banco Industrial de Manizales	Manizales	1882	240.000
Banco de Sopetrán	Sopetrán	1882	100.000
Banco de Oriente	Rionegro	1883	125.820
Banco de Vicente B. Villa e Hijos	Medellín	1883	20.000
Banco de Progreso	Medellín	1883	60.000
Banco de Botero Arango e Hijos	Medellín	1883	n.d.a
Banco del Zancudo	Medellín	1883	n.d.a
ATLANTIC COAST	**CITY**		
Banco de Barranquilla	Barranquilla	1873	312.500
Banco de Bolivar	Cartagena	1874	145.000
Banco de Cartagena	Cartagena	1881	100.000
Banco Popular de Bolivar	Cartagena	1883	54.000
Banco Unión	Cartagena	1883	160.000
Banco Márquez	Barranquilla	1883	125.000
Banco Americano	Barranquilla	1883	565.000
Banco del Estado	Cartagena	1884	n.d.a
Banco de Riohacha	Riohacha	1885	150.000
OTHER REGIONS	**CITY**		
Banco de Santander	Bucaramanga	1872	300.000
Banco del Cauca	Cali	1873	300.000
Banco del Norte	El Socorro	1881	101.600
Banco del Tolima	Neiva	1881	200.000
Banco de Pamplona	Pamplona	1882	86.225
Banco Prendario de Soto	Bucaramanga	1883	10.000
Banco de Santander	Bucaramanga	1883	200.000
Banco del Estado	Popayán	1884	102.400

n.d.a: no data available

Source: Compiled on the basis of information in Meisel Roca, Adolfo; *"Los bancos comerciales en la era de la banca libre, 1871-1923"*, ("The commercial banks in the era of free banking,1871-1923".) In *EL BANCO DE LA REPÚBLICA: Antecedentes, Evolución y Estructura*, ("THE BANCO DE LA REPÚBLICA: Its Background, Evolution and Structure").1990, Pages. 145,150,153 and 157.

Bogotá, the main stockholders of the private banks were businessmen linked to foreign trade and that these institutions helped to enlarge the supply of money, despite the fact that in most cases their bank notes had a restricted and local circulation.

On the quantitative importance of the circulation of the bank notes of the private banks, the historian Guillermo Torres García writes in his study: "Señor Aquileo Parra, in his 1874 *Treasury Report*, speaks of the wide circulation of the bank notes of the Banco de Bogotá; señor Nicolás Esguerra, in his 1875 *Treasury Report*, points to the fact that the banks, through their bank notes, offered very important services to industry and profitably made up for the scarcity of money that was felt as a result of the exportation of metal coinage to the European markets; señor José María Villamizar Gallardo, in his 1876 *Treasury Report*, argues that if the bank notes of that time had not made up for the shortage of coin, commercial transactions would have been 'completely paralyzed'; more or less the same kind of opinion was held by señor José María

Page 52,
Bank notes of the private banks: Banco Popular de Bogotá, 5 pesos, bearing the words "moneda de talla mayor" (large-size money), 1877; Banco de Medellín and Banco de Cartagena, 1882.

Page 53,
Bank notes of private banks. Banco de Santander, 1873; Banco de Sopetrán and Banco de Pamplona, both founded in 1882. The Banco de Santander was born in 1872, around the time that the Colombian Society of Farmers was founded.

Left and below, *Emigdio Palau, José Villamizar Gallardo, José María Quijano Wallis and Nicolás Esguerra, defendors of the right of the private banks to issue paper money.*

Quijano Wallis in his 1878 *Treasury Report*; señor Emigdio Palau and señor Simón Herrera, Treasury Secretaries in 1879 and 1881, respectively, spoke in highly favorable terms of the bank notes". (Torres García, 1980, p.88-89).

Despite these remarks on the healthy effects of the establishment of the private bank, it should be noted that these institutions went through a number of crises as a result of a lack of public confidence in the private banks as a whole: this happened in 1876-77, 1879 and the beginning of the 1880's. The first and last of these problems coincided with foreign crises and the one in 1879 had to do with the political instability provoked by rumors about a new civil war. As a result of these problems, the Banco de Bogotá faced difficulties in converting bank notes

into metal coins at the end of 1876 and the beginnings of 1877. Likewise, there was a run on the banks in Medellín in 1876 and in 1878 the Banco Mercantil of that city had to close its doors.

To begin with, the creation of the private banks led to a lowering of the nominal interest rate, which then stabilized between 1871 and 1875. In 1876, on the occasion of the overseas crisis, these rates underwent a sharp rise which was quickly reversed by the end of the decade. During the eighteen-eighties and up to the time when the government tokk the decision to control it, the nominal interest rate showed moderate rises. These fluctuations were not very significant, however, when compared with the variations observed in prices and for this reason it is accurate to say that the real interest rate was governed by the fluctuations of inflation.

Even though the figures on the latter variable are meager, analysts tend to think that inflation fell between 1871 and 1880 and that the real interest rate thus rose in that period. Inflation was naturally linked to the export cycle, which influenced monetary supply, and to an inelastic agricultural production and the political consequences of civil wars, when food normally became scarce.

Right,
Aquileo Parra (1876-1878). During his administration there was a sharp fall in exports and signs of a liquidity crisis in the private banks.

Below,
Mining scene. Vignette taken from a 5 pesos bill of the Sovereign State of Bolívar.

Right,
Bank notes of private banks: Banco de Márquez, which had its headquarters in Barranquilla from 1883; Banco del Norte founded in el Socorro in 1881; and Banco del Cauca. The 1870's was a time of prosperity for the merchant class who became the main stockholders in the private banks.

Right,
Bank notes of private banks: Banco Unión de Bogotá, 1883; Banco Popular de Soto, with headquarters in Bucaramanga; Banco Internacional, 1884; and Banco de Bolívar.

THE BANCO NACIONAL, PAPER MONEY AND THE MONETARY CONTROVERSY AT THE END OF THE NINETEENTH CENTURY

Opposite page, *Rafael Núñez (1880-1882; 1884-1888). Vignette from a 20 centavos bill of the Banco Nacional, 1887.* Head of the Regeneration movement he led a broad program of economic reforms, which include the creation, in 1880, of the Banco Nacional as a bank of emission, discounts, loans, bank drafts and deposits.

Right, *50* centavos *and 50* pesos *bank notes of the Banco Nacional,* signed by Juan María Pardo, Felipe Paul and Juan de Brigard, among others.

Following pages, *Bills of the banks of the Sovereign States of Cauca, 1886, and of Bolívar, 1877 and 1883, with signature or portrait of Rafael Núñez. Bills from the last years of the Estados Unidos de Colombia: Banco Nacional; Treasury of the State of Santander; Banco Republicano of Medellín.*

The election to the presidency of Rafael Núñez in 1880 took place in the context of doubts about the government's handling of the export cycle and dissatisfaction with the political regime established by the Rionegro Constitution of 1863.

After 1850 there were recurrent foreign trade cycles. A phase of expansion in the period 1849-1857 was followed by relative stagnation between 1858-1869: there was a decline in the exports of hats and quina bark (for quinine) but the fall in the price of quina bark was compensated for by an increase in tobacco exports. The period between 1870-1882 was generally one of rapid expansion, despite the fall of 1876-1877, since the fall in tobacco exports was more than compensated for by the rise of coffee exports and a notable increase in the export of quina bark, which became the principal export product in this period. Beginning in 1882-83, quina bark virtually disappeared as an export, causing a recession in the whole sector which lasted almost until the end of the eighteen-eighties, when the export boom in coffee began.

As was to be expected, given the rigidity of imports, these exporting cycles affected monetary circulation, even when the fall beginning in 1883 was restrained both by the emergence of the private bank and the great amount of silver that was imported, which was used to finance the exports of gold.

On the political front, as Jorge Orlando Melo points out, "the Conservatives' dissatisfaction with the Liberal-party governments was heightened by the conviction that the institutions established in 1863 did not offer adequate guarantees for the progress of the country; the excessive autonomy of the provinces had led to a permanent political crisis among the state

governments, which were subject to frequent changes and revolutions. Logically, this climate of unrest was considered to be harmful for economic development and a substantial sector of the Liberals began to think it was necessary to substantially improve the central government's capacity to maintain peace". (Melo, 1987, p. 154).

These two problems –instability in exports and political dissatisfaction– were the background for the reforms undertaken by Rafael Núñez, who, in contrast with the radical Liberals, defended state intervention in economic affairs, especially in matters of customs, money and credit.

As a development of these interventionist ideas, in his inaugural address of 1880 President Núñez outlined a government program to reform customs tariffs with the aim of protecting and increasing national production, strengthen government revenues in order to solidify its intervention in the course of the economy and stimulate credit activity through the creation of an agency that would serve as an instrument of development.

The above ideas constituted an ideological challenge to the defenders of free trade based on the principles of the Manchester School. In this way political controversies about such subjects as civil liberties, the right to political opposition and the need for cleaner elections merged with economic ones about the role and dimensions of the State, the policy of public spending and its finance and, of course, the management of money and credit.

As was to be expected, the ideas of Núñez were opposed by the radicals and provoked a deep split in the heart of the independent Liberals, among whom were numbered such notable figures as don Miguel Samper, partner of the Banco de Bogotá, and Salvador Camacho Roldán, founder of the Banco de Colombia and author of the 1871 law which imposed the gold standard. Thus it was natural that such figures opposed Núñez and the principles he inspired, which were known as the policy of Regeneration.

Despite this opposition, the reforms proposed by Núñez were carried out, among them law 39 of 1880, by which the government was authorized to establish the Banco Nacional, which, apart from promoting the development of credit, was founded as an auxiliary agent for carrying out fiscal operations.

Even though the law stipulated that 20% of the initial 2,500,000 *pesos* capital of the Banco Nacional would be freely offered to the public, this stock subscription did not result: some writers say that it was boycotted, others that private capital was not favorably inclined towards an entity in which the government was going to be both the main stockholder and a major debtor. For this reason the Banco Nacional became a strictly public establishment, since this was foreseen in the law in a case where the stocks were not taken up by the private sector.

One million of the two million *pesos* that the government needed to capitalize the Banco Nacional were financed with part of a foreign loan of 2.5 million *pesos* granted to the government by the Morton, Bliss and Co. firm of New York. The loan was guaranteed by the stocks which Colombia owned in the Panama Railway Company. The remaining million was paid, almost half and half, through the government's own funds and through the surrender of some Treasury promissory notes. From that time to the present day the latter financial mechanism has been the customary practice for capitalizing the public bank.

Law 39 of 1880 established the constitution for the

Left above,
Two bank notes of the Banco Nacional, 1884.

Below,
Scene of a coffee plantation in the decorative vignette of a 1 peso bill of the Banco de Tequendama, La Mesa, Cundinamarca, 1881.

Right,
Law 39 of June 1, 1880, which authorized the executive branch to found a National Bank in the capital of the nation.

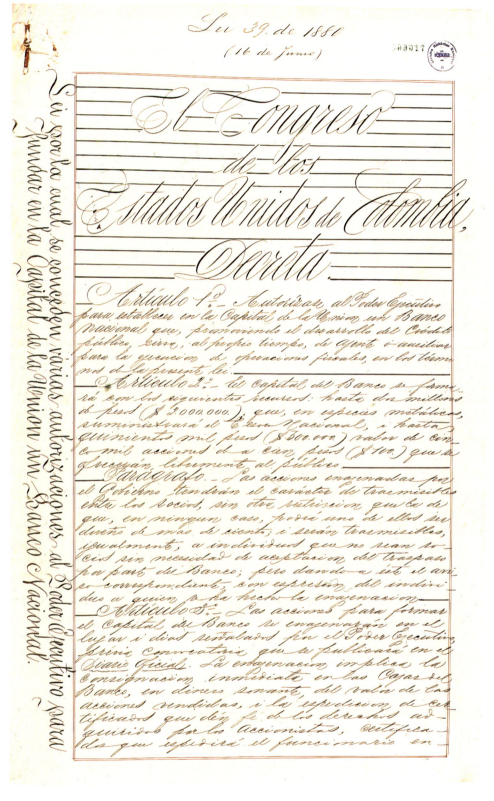

bank, which gave the executive branch the right to draft its statutes by decree and give it the status of a corporation (*compañía anónima*): from then on, the statutes could only be reformed by the stockholders assembly through a 2/3 majority vote of the stocks represented at the assembly, which meant that the government had a veto power with regard to any modification. By virtue of these statutory norms, the Bank was authorized to carry out ordinary operations of discounts, loans, emissions, bills of exchange and deposits.

Right,
Original matrix of the 50 centavos coin, known as the "cocobola", with the effigy.

Credit operations would require a guarantee from two signatories, previously assessed by the Administrative Council of the Banco Nacional; collateral that could be easily liquidated was also admissible, so long as it covered 130% of the value of the loan, as were mortgages on rural properties or urban ones located in Bogotá, so long as the value of the credit was not higher than 25% of the mortgaged goods. When the guarantees were in the form of mortgages, the maximum term for credits would be one year and when they were backed by signatories or collateral they could not exceed 180 days.

The Banco Nacional was given the right to receive deposits of money from the public, acknowledging its obligation to pay interest according to the stipulations of the Administrative Council.

In addition, the institution was invested with the exclusive right to issue bank notes payable to the bearer, but the executive branch of the government might also extend this right to existing private banks or those that might be established in the future, so long as they expressly agreed to accept the bank notes of the Banco Nacional as cash in their offices.

Despite this authorization the national government reserved to itself the right to mint, on its own account, the silver coins of *cuarto de décimo*, *medio décimo*, *décimo*, *dos décimos* and *cincuenta centavos* at a standard of 0.666 or 0.835, in accordance with the Fiscal Code of 1873 and also nickel coins of one *centavo* and a half *centavo*. One of the *cincuenta* (fifty) *centavos* coins most widely circulated was known as the *cocobola* and bore the effigy of doña Soledad Román, wife of president Rafael Núñez.

This peculiarity, whereby metal coins were issued by the government and not the central bank, lasted until the passing of the 1991 Colombia Constitution and law 31 of 1992.

Right, *Carlos Holguín and Rafael Núñez, in a political cartoon done by Greñas, published in* El Zancudo, *1890*.

The amount of issued bank notes was restricted to twice the capital of the Banco Nacional and the government was made permanently responsible for the solvency of the institution. In order to guarantee the convertibility of these bills into metal money, in line with the stipulation that they be payable at sight at the request of the bearers, it was established that the Banco Nacional would maintain in its vaults an amount of metal money equal to at least 25% of the value of the bank notes in circulation and that the remaining 75% would be represented by credits or other assets with a term of no longer than 180 days.

To begin with, the bank notes would be issued in denominations of 50 *centavos* to 100 *pesos*, but in March, 1885, due to the shortage of low-denomination currency, the Banco Nacional was allowed to issue bank notes of 10 and 20 *centavos*. These bills were first printed in Bogotá by the Paredes and Villaveces firm and later by the American Bank Note Company of New York, which towards the end of the eighteen-eighties printed the bill of the Banco Nacional that had the widest circulation. This was the *un peso* bill, printed in yellow and a bluish black, colors similar to those of the *toche,* a Colombian bird, and this became the popular name for the note.

In accordance with law 39 of 1880, the Banco Nacional had an Administrative Council of nine members, six of them named by the executive branch of the government and three by private stockholders: there was a five-member Board of Directors, three of whom were named by the government, one being the Secretary of the Treasury, who was its President.

Since private stockholders did not participate, all of the members of both the Board of Directors and the Administrative Council were named by the government. The first Board of Directors, presided by Simón Herrera as Secretary of the Treasury, was made up of Luis María Pardo, Alejandro Arango, José Vicente Uribe, José Borda and Francisco García as principal members, and Jorge Holguín, Miguel Quintero, Silvestre Samper, Bernardino Medina and Leopoldo Arias, as deputies. Felipe Fermín Paúl was its first managing director and this post was held between 1882 and 1896 by such outstanding public figures as Antonio Roldán, Jorge Holguín, Nicolas Osorio, Arturo Malo O'leary, Juan de Brigard and the abovementioned Simón Herrera.

The fiscal difficulties of the Banco Nacional and the reluctance of potential private stockholders and depositors in general to accept it meant that other stipulations of law 39 of 1880 were not carried out either. In fact, the Banco Nacional granted little credit to the private sector and with the passing of time came to be a financing institution almost exclusively of the government, to the point that some analysts have not hesitated to call it a branch office of the Treasury.

Furthermore, with the coming into effect of decree 260 of 1885 the convertibility of the bank notes into metallic money was suspended, a measure which was consolidated with the passing of decree 104 in 1886, by which the one *peso* bill of the Banco Nacional would be, for all legal effects, the monetary unit and accounting money of Colombia. Law 87 of 1886 refuse them in government or private transactions and the payment of taxes. It also prohibited stipulating any other kinds of currency in contracts that involved the payment of money in cash or cash installments.

In this way, as Mauricio Avella points out, "the paper money of the Banco

Above,
One peso bill of the Banco Nacional. Because of its importance within the mass of money in circulation it was the most representative of the bank notes issued by the Banco Nacional. It was known as the "toche", after a bird which the same yellow and black colors.

Below,
Alejandro Arango, José Vicente Uribe and Simón Herrera, members of the first board of directors of the Banco Nacional, of which Juan María Pardo, José Borda and Francisco García were also members.

Nacional acted, in the first stage, as a classic bank note, convertible into metallic money.

In the second, by government intervention it was exempted from the requirement of convertibility and obliged to stave off problems when the executive branch's financial requirements became extreme. Finally the bills of the Banco Nacional reached their final stage of development by turning into the nation's currency". (Avella Gómez, 1987, p. 13).

The measure giving these bank notes the status of legal tender was followed by new regulations which restricted the liberties which the private banks had enjoyed till then in matters of issuance and credit. Under law 57 of 1887, which adopted the new measures and unified the relevant legislation, a Commercial Law was passed and it was stipulated that:

• The right to issue bank notes payable to bearer which the private banks had enjoyed would be suspended, while the Banco Nacional would have this right as an exclusive privilege;

• The bank notes in circulation issued by the private banks were to be withdrawn from circulation and changed for legal tender;

• The maximum interest rate for mortgage credit would be 8% and for other cases, 10%;

• The legal minimum reserve requirement would be 33%, under the stipulation that the banks would have to keep in their vaults assets equivalent to a third

Below,
The closure of numerous private banking institutions after 1887 led to a situation in which the bills originally printed by them were stamped with the overlaid seal of the Banco Nacional and placed into circulation as Banco Nacional bills. One of these overscaled bills, originally printed by the Banco de Bogotá.

of the value of the bank notes in circulation and of the deposits in current account;

• The sum of these two liabilities could not exceed the minimum reserve and the 90-day term debt portfolio;

• The government would employ its right to inspect and exercise vigilance over the private banks, as laid down in number 17 of the 1886 Constitution;

• Contravention of these regulations would give rise to the closing down of operations of the offending entities.

There was no room for doubt: with the status of legal tender given to the paper money of the Banco Nacional and the banking reform of 1887 a hard blow was struck at the private banks. The number of such institutions fell from 30 in 1881 to 14 in 1892. This closure of private institutions gave rise to a curious situation in the circulation of bills. Possibly for reasons of economy, the Banco Nacional wound up having to overprint its own seals on and put into circulation bank notes bearing the name of private banks.

According to some historians, the measure making the bank's paper money legal tender was a temporary fiscal resource, mainly arising from the government's need to pay for the expenses of the war of 1885. They base their argument on the fact that successive government measures undertaken in the period of the Banco Nacional's existence, among them laws 116 of 1887 and 93 of 1892, ordered the withdrawal from circulation of paper money. Others say that, in addition to the government's financial problems, the causes for establishing these banks notes as legal tender were to found in the vicissitudes of foreign commerce, the export of metallic money and the government's inability to obtain foreign loans with which to finance its recurrent fiscal deficits and from the monetary point of view, reduce the effects of the exports of coinage.

Independently of this controversy, and despite the fact that opponents of the Regeneration continued to fight against the monetary, banking and financial policies of the government after 1887, there is no doubt that the decisions on legal tender and banking reform that were adopted in the years 1886 and 1887 meant that the State now had the right to exercise a monopoly over the emission of currency. In this way, the de facto exercise of economic policy put an end to theoretical discussions about the nature of paper money, convertibility, obligation and free stipulation.

Left, *1976 stamp honoring the "Great Citizen", Miguel Samper Agudelo (1825 - 1899). Lawyer, politician and statesman, he was sharpest and most persistent critic of the monetary policy of the "Regeneration" movement.*

These debates saw a confrontation between two diametrically opposed positions: that which believed in the authority and the right of the State to establish a national currency and that which saw in the exercise of that authority a violation of individual liberties, to the extent that the circulation of state money was imposed in a coercive way. The defenders of the state monopoly over the issuance of currency were the men in power, especially Miguel Antonio Caro and Jorge Holguín, and their principal opponents were the independent Liberals, especially Salvador Camacho, Miguel Samper, Modesto Garcés, José Borda and José Camacho Carrizosa.

The opponents of paper money believed that it lacked the fundamental characteristic of intrinsic value and therefore defended the obligation of converting paper money into precious metal, since only in this way would there be a guarantee on the forced loan which they considered the issuance of paper money to be. In this respect, Miguel Samper stated that "metal money does not worry anyone, while paper money introduces an element of uncertainty into business which is unsettling to everyone. This paper is a forced loan which the governments impose on the economy when they lack legitimate and ordinary resources in times of crisis… the advantage of this form of loan lies in the fact that it affects all social classes and no one feels that he is being personally singled out for vexation; but this advantage is accompanied by an injustice and a danger. The injustice consists in the fact that the great bulk of people who live off wages, salaries or fixed property rents suffer from the overall rise in prices… thus these classes wind up paying a veritable tax, which does not enter into the official list of government taxes. The danger we have referred to has to do with paper money tempting people to spend more, supported by the facility with which the government can meet this expense by printing more paper money, which leads to catastrophe when it becomes a habitual recourse". (Samper, 1977, p. 110-111).

The defenders of paper money, for their part, upheld its symbolic value. They argued that as soon as it was accepted and kept its purchasing power in terms of the total amount of goods produced and consumed in the economy, the problem of convertibility became irrelevant, as did its status as legal tender, because in these circumstances it would conserve its power to settle debts.

Another important issue in these polemics revolved around whether you could or could not stipulate credit obligations in monetary units other than the bank notes of the Banco Nacional. For the partisans of paper money it was clear that free stipulation could not be permitted, since this would place the bills of the Banco Nacional on the same level as those other monetary mechanisms and lead to its eventual repudiation, which would injure the establishing of a national

Above,
Detail of bill with an overprinted seal of the Banco Nacional. When these bills, originally issued by the private banks, were withdrawn from circulation, the Banco Nacional utilized them again under its own seal.

Below,
Jorge Holguín Mallarino (1848 - 1928). Statesman and military leader from the Valle del Cauca, he was the President of Colombia on two occasions, an office previously held by his brother Carlos. Defendor of Conservative policies and a leading figure of the "Regeneration" movement and of the long Conservative rule that came be known as the "Conservative Hegemony".

currency. For their part, the defenders of free choice regarded this prohibition as yet another government trick to restrain personal liberty and ignore the natural laws of the economy.

There is no doubt that these arguments were based both on matters of principle and political affiliations. To a certain extent, those who were opposed to paper money did so because they were afraid that the ruling party would use it to finance unorthodox fiscal operations destined to strengthen its power. According to Indalecio Liévano Aguirre, on the other hand, what really made the opponents of paper money and the Banco Nacional indignant was "the fact that the government should have a bank where it could deposit its revenue, a responsibility entrusted to the Banco Nacional at that time, a bank that, when carrying out fiscal operations, would earn the commissions which the private banks had enjoyed in the past. The supposed scientific arguments... were no more than a disguise to hide the private interests of the opposition". (Liévano Aguirre, 1985, p.209).

Despite the political and economic controversies which have been referred to, there is an overall consensus amongst the writers who have analyzed the functioning of the Banco Nacional, including the most severe critics of the Regeneration governments, namely, that the issues of paper money placed in circulation in most of the years between 1880 and 1898 were not excessive.

This, despite the fact that, starting in 1886, successive government regulations – among them decree 229 of 1886 and the laws 20 and 71 of the same year – increased the amount of the issue, and that by quite different means, which we shall be examining closely in the next section, the bank violated the so-called "dogma of 12 million". This principle, laid down in law 124 of 1887, was strongly defended by President Núñez in the following words, "we shall set a 12 million (*pesos*) maximum on national paper money; as honorable and prudent men we promise the great economic interests that we shall not surpass this limit for any reason".

As has been pointed out, from 1887 onwards the nominal interest rates were fixed by legal decree, which meant that the real interest rate would depend on inflation. As the latter increased between 1885 and 1890, in this period the real interest rate was very low or negative, a situation which was reversed between 1891 and 1898, when inflation fell.

A. Greñas

XXXVI

THE HIDDEN EMISSIONS AND THE LIQUIDATION OF THE BANCO NACIONAL

Opposite page, *Shield of the Regeneration, according to Greñas,* cartoon published in "El Zancudo" *in 1890. A clear sign of the opposition towards the Regeneration governments by certain sectors of the country.*

Right, *Miguel Antonio Caro, acting President between 1892-1898, in the absence of the titular President Rafael Núñez. He was the staunchest defendor of the monetary and financial policies of the Regeneration.*

Despite a relatively stable economic situation, law 70 of 1894 ordered the liquidation of the Banco Nacional. For the reasons we have explained above it cannot be said that this decision arose from an excessive monetary expansion, galloping inflation, a crisis in foreign markets or an economic depression. None of these occurred around the middle of the eighteen-nineties. Rather the decision was due to ethical and political considerations, as became evident in April and May, 1894, on the occasion of a newspaper controversy between *El Correo Nacional* ("The National Post"), the paper opposed to President Caro, and *El Telegrama*, defender and spokesman for the government in power, a dispute that had begun at the time of the presidential elections of 1892.

In this election a Conservative Party faction, headed by Carlos Martínez Silva, Treasury Secretary during the administration of Carlos Holguín (acting President 1888-1892), proposed the candidacy of Rafael Núñez for President and Marceliano Veléz for Vice President, in opposition to the national faction, which backed Núñez but wanted Miguel Antonio Caro as the candidate for Vice President.

The selection of the Vice President was a critical matter, since, as in fact happened, it was expected that Núñez would not be the acting President. To begin with, Núñez chose not to intervene in the selection of one or the other candidate for the vice presidency but he wound up asking Vélez to withdraw. This ensured the election of Núñez and Caro for the 1892-1898 term. In the words of Liévano Aguirre, Núñez chose Caro because "it meant the maintenance and integrity of the 1886 Constitution, whereas Veléz represented a revisionist tendency. Caro was chosen as the candidate because he was the best symbol of a policy that was founded on the integrity of the 1886 Constitution and con-

sequently of the policy of the "nationalist" Conservatives. Vélez represented a completely contrary policy, as demonstrated by his writings and those of his followers, which showed a tendency towards greater political and administrative decentralization and called for a weakening of state power and a revision of the economic and financial reforms of the Regeneration government". (Liévano Aguirre, 1985, p. 486). This point of view is shared by Charles Bergquist, who sees Vélez as a critic of the regime of paper money: when Vélez published his criticism of the fiscal policies of the Regeneration Núñez turned against him.

Right,
Bank notes of the Banco Nacional, of the years 1885 and 1881.

Right and below, *Portraits of Rafael Núñez on two 20 centavos bank notes of the Banco Nacional, 1887.*

Thus, the presidential elections of 1892 marked a point of no return for the unity of the ruling party. The division that year between Caro and the supporters of Vélez, who were headed by Carlos Martínez in the name of the "historical" Conservatives, widened in the following years when the opponents of the government intensified their attacks on the fiscal policy and the regime of paper money. According to Bergquist, the inflexible, authoritarian style of Caro contributed to the polarization of the Conservative factions, but the division also reflected economic factors and especially, the position of the different groups with regard to the fiscal and monetary policy of the government.

In his address to the Congress of 1892 Caro replied to his opponents, one month after his being named acting President by virtue of the absence of Rafael Núñez, who was still the nominal President. He gave a stubborn defense of the paper money regime and its beneficial effects by saying that "in the six years during which this exchange instrument has been used industrial activity has taken off with a surprising strength". (Caro, 1956, p. 60). The acting President's message also stressed the need to make the norms on monetary issuance more flexible.

Above, *Nicolás Osorio, Arturo Malo O'Leary and Carlos Martínez Silva. The first two, as managers of the Banco Nacional, and the last, as Treasury Minister under Carlos Holguín, were involved in the investigations into the clandestine emissions of the Banco Nacional. Malo O'Leary was fined and sent to prison for his role in these emissions.*

Disagreeing with Núñez on the dogma of the 12 million *pesos*, he stated, "this amount, as opposed, say, to 6 or 24 or 30 millions, was not determined in a capricious or arbitrary way, but by calculating a correct balance between 12 million and the economic activity of the country as represented by the sum of public revenues. The natural proportion is an equivalence between the bulk of paper money and the total value of public taxes. The base that was adopted in this case, which was below the above-mentioned limit, was pretty moderate. But if that figure was sufficient so long as the conditions which determined it still stood, it does not continue to be so if there is a considerable variation in the factors that enter into the calculation of the currency needed for internal changes. From this we correctly infer that the promise not to surpass this limit –which was made in 1887 and backed by a law, which by its very nature may be reformed– stays in effect only so long as the reasons for it remain the same, but it does not have an absolute character or a perpetual consecration for all times and circumstances". (Cited by Torres García, 1980, p. 186-187).

Caro also censured the proposals on free stipulation since "with a simultaneous, legally-authorized acceptance of different kinds of currency that would tend to be mutually antagonistic, the legal equivalence between bank notes and a given metallic

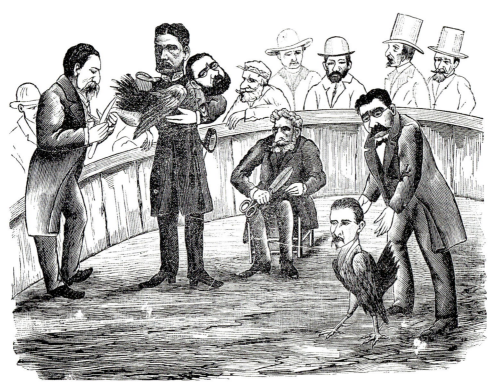

Below, *Political cartoon by Greñas in* El Zancudo *on the choosing of the Vice President during the 1892 campaign. Carlos Martínez Silva launches the candidacy of Marceliano Vélez and Carlos Holguín "sharpens the spurs of the cock", Miguel Antonio Caro. With scissors in hand, Rafael Núñez watches the scene.*

Above, *100 pesos government bond to finance the construction of the bridge at Girardot, signed by Carlos Martínez as Treasury Minister of the administration of Carlos Holguín.*

money would be implicitly mocked, a legal tender of fiduciary money would no longer rule, the nation would go back on the word pledged by its laws and from that moment onwards anything that tended to strengthen confidence in national paper money would be considered a false promise". (Caro, 1956, p. 62).

One of the main opponents of the government was the director of the *Correo Nacional*, Carlos Martínez Silva, who had founded that newspaper on September 1, 1890. On April 4, 1894 he published an editorial proposing a change in the orientation of the government with regard to state education, governmental finances, the issuing of paper money, the organization of the Banco Nacional and the management of foreign credit: he concluded by calling on the government to stop excommunicating its opponents.

These criticisms and proposals led *El Telegrama* into a harsh reply which appeared on April 12, 1894, and was thought by many to have been written by Caro (acting President 1892-98), because the article said that the depreciation of paper money was the main cause of the worst misfortunes of the country and insinuated that the abuse of issuing had taken place during the time that Carlos Martínez Silva had been Treasury Minister in the government of Carlos Holguín.

Martínez Silva picked up the hints and demanded that a formal denouncement of the crime attributed to him should be made. This led to another round, in which El Telegrama stated that since there were 26 million *pesos* in bank notes in circulation and the law had only authorized the emission of 17 million *pesos*, the former Treasury ministers that might have been responsible for the excessive issues had to explain their conduct in a categorical way. Thus the debate on the hidden emissions of the Banco Nacional was launched.

As a result of this controversy and the scandal it provoked, new revelations were published, the most detailed of which was a "Report of the Accountant of the Banco Nacional about the transactions of purchase and sale of some public credit documents,

Above, *Reverse of a bank note of the Banco Nacional, with the signature of Juan de Brigard as Cashier.*

Below, *Bank note of the Banco Nacional, with an allegorical portrayal of the Isthmus of Panama.*

carried out between the Banco Nacional and the Banco de Bogotá, and the general emission of bills". Published on May 19, 1894 in the *Treasury Report* of that year, this document contained a lengthy account of all the issues made since April, 1889, naming the persons who had a role in authorizing them and giving the dates and reasons for the issues.

These publications and debates led the Prosecutor of the High Court of the (State of) Cundinamarca (fiscal del Tribunal Superior de Cundinamarca) to begin an investigation of the matter on May 10, 1894, whose example was followed by the House of Representatives in August of the same year: the House named a committee to inquire into the illegal issues of the Banco Nacional.

The committee designated by the House of Representatives on August 3, 1894 and charged with the investigation of possible criminal actions behind the illegal issuing of Banco Nacional bank notes submitted its report on November 14 of that year. It examined eleven cases of presumed irregularities, among which the most important, by virtue of their amount and political implications, were the issues for the clearance of old debt in 1889 when Carlos Martínez Silva was the Treasury minister and those for the change of the silver coins with a standard of 0.500 in 1891.

The report concluded by placing before the Senate charges against the former Treasury ministers Carlos Martínez Silva, Vicente Restrepo, Marcelino Arango and acting minister Miguel Abadía Méndez. The charges ranged from the authorization of excess issues, violation of the statutes of the Banco Nacional and failure to comply with legal obligations to the illegal issuance of paper money.

On another front, the prosecutor of the High Court of Cundinamarca asked that proceedings be taken against those who might have been responsible for the improper activities of the Banco Nacional and Banco de Bogotá that had been reported in the press.

At the end of these proceedings, the Supreme Court ordered the dropping of the case against Simón Herrera for the fabrication and introduction of the bank notes ordered by the government in 1886 and for

Right,
Two promissory notes of 10 and 100 pesos to repay expropriations from private citizens during the 1895 war.

the issues made during his term of office. The Supreme Court also dropped the charges against Nicolás Osorio, manager of the Banco Nacional, and its auditor, Carlos Eduardo Coronado, for their participation in the illegal issues of Banco Nacional bank notes prior to 1891. The same was done with the charges of dishonesty laid against Nicolás Osorio. However, it decided to continue the prosecution of the latter for loss, usurpation, misappropriation or poor administration of the funds of the Treasury Ministry. Similarly, it upheld the prosecution of Arturo Malo O'leary for his participation in the illegal issues made under his management, his part in transactions with the stocks of the Ferrocarril de la Sabana railway company and the uttering of false public and private documents. Criminal proceedings were further undertaken against Carlos Eduardo Coronado for having signed a false balance sheet. The case against the former manager of the Banco de Bogotá, Juan de Brigard, was dropped.

In his well-known book on the monetary history of Colombia, Professor Guillermo Torres García states that none of the accused was sent to prison as a result of these events, but as we have just seen, the prosecution of two of the managers and the financial auditor of the Banco Nacional was upheld. Nevertheless, in the interests of accuracy, it must be pointed out that, following an appeal, the Supreme Court of Justice, in the end, revoked the measures against the auditor of the Banco Nacional,

Above, Parque de Santander (Santander Park) at the end of the 19th century, oil painting by Juan Cárdenas, 1976. On the southern side of the park the headquarters of the Banco de la República would be built sixty years later.

Carlos Eduardo Coronado; absolved the former manager Nicolás Osorio of the charge of misappropriation or usurpation of public funds; and annulled the penalties against him for the other charges leveled in the proceedings. The only one who was not let off was Arturo Malo O'leary, who was sentenced to a 15 months prison term and the payment of a fine of 398, 292.5 *pesos*.

Even though it is clear that the debate over hidden emissions had a political background, the above proceedings show that several of the episodes investigated by the committee of the House of Representatives in the second half of 1894 and examined during the appeal process by the Supreme Court of Justice in 1894-1895 were unequivocally criminal acts. And it was precisely these events which were responsible for the passing of law 70 of 1894, which ordered the closure of the Banco Nacional and the amortization of the paper money which had been issued by it.

To achieve the latter end, the government was to make use of revenues from the following sources: two fifths of the 25% of the import duties that had been ceded to the departments (states) of Colombia in 1886; the recoverable value of the portfolio of the Banco Nacional; the stocks in the railway companies and Panama Canal that belonged to the nation; and earnings which the gov-

ernment would obtain from granting the private banks the right to issue bank notes.

The liquidation of the Banco Nacional was to have concluded in January, 1895, but in view of a norm stipulating that the process might be suspended in the case of civil unrest and the political strife that led to the war of 1895, the government prorogued the existence of the Bank until January, 1896, when it finally disappeared, to be replaced by the so-called Liquidating Office of the Ministry of Treasury. Despite these rules and regulations, a number of laws passed in 1898, created an odd situation: *they authorized the Banco Nacional to issue bank notes when the bank no longer had a legal existence.* For this reason catalogues of Colombian money list currency issued by this institution after its official liquidation in 1896.

The Banco Nacional had never been a central bank in the strict sense of the term used for modern institutions. It was never a lender of last resort for other credit institutions, nor did it regulate the monetary reserves such institutions had to maintain. But there is no doubt about its importance in the monetary history of Colombia. It was through this institution that the State first exercised its right to monetary emission, not as an arbitrary assumption of power but as an inalienable and legitimate function of government.

MONETARY CRISIS AND STABILITY

Opposite page, *José Manuel Marroquín (1900-1904). During his government the War of the Thousand Days took place and as a result of the excessive emission of money there occurred what might be called the first hyper-inflation in the history of Latin America.*

The presidential campaign for the 1898-1904 term, which wound up with the election of Miguel Antonio Sanclemente as President and José Manuel Marroquín as Vice President, was marked by a sharp divergence of opinion between the "nationalist" Conservatives, on the one hand, and the "historical" Conservatives and Liberals on the other.

In the political field, the "historical" Conservatives and the Liberals called for greater civil liberties, a reduction of presidential power, increased administrative decentralization and a reform of public education. On the economic front, they proposed ending export taxes and reducing those on salt, meat and essential imports. They wanted to prohibit an increase in the amount of paper money in circulation and authorize a gradual amortization of it leading to the restoration of metallic money. They further demanded free choice in the currency used in contracts and the free issuing of bank notes by the private banks. To defend this program, the Liberals chose Miguel Samper as the presidential candidate and Foción Soto as the vice presidential one: they were the obvious leaders of the movements that were in favor of a greater degree of political and economic freedom.

Following a campaign marked by strong ideological debate and accusations

Left, *Manuel Antonio Sanclemente, elected as titular President for the 1898-1904 term, was overthrown by Marroquín.*

Below, *Promissory note for indemnification of foreigners, June 15, 1888. At the end of the 19th century Colombia was threatened by foreign powers on several occasions. In 1898 Cartagena was besieged by five Italian warships. The motive was Colombia's failure to comply with a ruling by the President of the United States, who had arbitrated a dispute in favor of an Italian citizen, Ernesto Cerruti, who had claimed compensation from the Colombian government for expropriations he had suffered in the war of 1885.*

Right,
50 pesos bill, February 15, 1900, signed by Salomón Koppel, among others, and with a portrait of Manuel Antonio Sanclemente.

Below,
General Benito Ulloa and officers of the Liberal army of Cundinamarca.

of electoral fraud, Marroquín assumed power on August 7, 1898 in the absence of President Sanclemente and faced an acute fiscal crisis that had led to the suspension of payments of government salaries and the service of the public debt. The situation was aggravated by an ultimatum presented to Colombia by the Italian government and backed by a military threat to Cartagena. The motive was Colombia's failure to comply with a ruling by the President of the United States, who had arbitrated a dispute in favor of an Italian citizen, Ernesto Cerruti, who had claimed compensation from the Colombian government for expropriations he had suffered in the war of 1885.

The precarious financial situation was also affected by a decrease in customs revenues, resulting from a fall in the international price of coffee and the disincentive

Right,
100 pesos bill, September 30, 1900, with a portrait of José Manuel Marroquín. This bill bears the name of the Banco Nacional but its issue date is subsequent to the bank's liquidation.

Below,
Conservative army at a banquet held around 1900.

to exports caused by an export tax that been in effect since the government of Caro.

To begin with, this crisis forced Marroquín to seek a private loan, which did not result. The government then asked the Congress for authorization to issue paper money for a value of eight million *pesos*, a sum that was raised to ten million *pesos* by the Senate.

Despite opposition in the House of Representatives, which was dominated by the "historical" Conservatives and had as its only Liberal congressman Rafael Uribe Uribe, the measure was passed, but on the condition that the government initiate a series of political reforms.

As a result the stock of issued bank notes, which had remained stable at a sum of 30,862,359 *pesos* between 1895-1897, rose to 38,302,000 *pesos* in 1898. This monetary growth became exorbitant after October, 1899, when in order to cover the

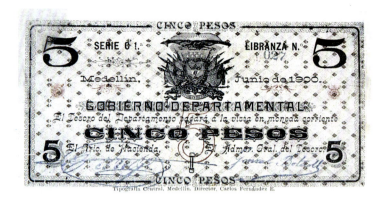

expenses of the war that began in that month, the President of the Republic issued decree 520, which authorized the government to issue and put at the disposition of the General Treasury of the Republic whatever amount of paper money the executive might need to restore public order. Since none of the bills printed in the United States were available in Colombia, the measure also authorized the immediate placing into circulation of used bills in a poor physical state that were going to be incinerated.

This was the start of a multitude of decrees through which the government, pressed by the financial needs arising from the war, ordered its printing house, the Litografía Nacional, to produce paper money without cease.

The following figures tell the story of what happened. In the thirteen years between 1886, when government paper money was made into legal tender, and 1899, when the war began, the amount of bank notes in circulation had multiplied by a factor of at least 10 and maybe as much as 13, depending on the analyst. That is, it had grown from 4 million *pesos* to something between 40 and 53 million *pesos*. In the three and a half years between October, 1899 and the middle of 1903 the means of payment rose by around 800 million *pesos* and by 1905 the money in circulation rose to 847, 216, 313.10 *pesos*. The Litografía Nacional paper money was responsible for about 78% of this total. The most widely circulated bank notes were those of 10, 20, 50 and 100 *pesos*, in contrast with the importance which the one *peso* of the Banco Nacional had 15 years before.

The result of this very rapid monetary expansion was a dizzying rise in the level of prices which brought the annual average rate of inflation up to a level of more than 100% between 1900 and 1903, with a record figure of 389% in 1901. This process led to complete anarchy in determining relative prices and was also reflected in the depreciation of the *peso* with regard to the pound sterling, with an average annual devaluation of around 150% in the years 1900-1902.

This chaotic monetary and exchange situation, which wrecked the system of

Left and below, *Four government bills issued during the War of the Thousand Days. The financing of this conflict through exorbitant issues of money gave rise to the biggest inflation in the economic history of Colombia.*

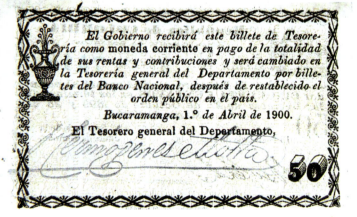

Above, Obverse and reverse of bills of 1 and 5 pesos, issued by the "provisional" Liberal government during the War of the Thousand Days. Ocaña, 1900.

payments, was worsened by the heavy damage which the violence caused to the coffee sector, both in production and costs. Manpower became scarce and dear and the same happened with transport and this coincided with a fall in international coffee prices.

For the rest, the fall in coffee exports had negative repercussions on public finances, because of the big role played by customs duties within overall government revenues.

In the analysis of Jesús Antonio Bejarano, "at the end of the war... the country was in ruins, with a coffee economy overwhelmed by both the external crisis and the internal conflict; an inherently precarious transport system dismembered; public finances, foreign exchange and monetary circulation undone; and prices completely out of control". (Bejarano, 1987, p. 174).

Reconstruction of the economic infrastructure began when the war was over. Towards this end decree 217 was issued in February, 1903. It prohibited issues of paper money as a fiscal resource and ordered the Litografía Nacional to return to its proper work, which was to produce stamps and sealed legal paper and do printing jobs for private customers. The lithographic plates with which the bank notes had been printed would be placed in the hands of a new institution called the Junta Depositaria (Depository Board), which would act as a custodian for these lithography plants and ensure that they would only be used to print the bank notes needed to replace deteriorated ones. This was the way of guaranteeing that the amount of bank notes in circulation would remain stable. The same decree ordered that the Emission Board and the Depository Board would be jointly responsible for the work of incinerating old bills in order to ensure a strict compliance with the measure. It further stated that the lithographic matrixes were to be destroyed as soon as the foreign-made bank notes needed to effect the change-over reached Colombia.

Above,
Banco Nacional bank notes with overprinted seals that allowed for their provisional circulation, in accordance with the decree of October 30, 1899.

Right,
Obverse and reverse of a 50 pesos bill issued by the Reyes administration. The allegorical drawing shows the intentions of the government's economic policy: to promote agriculture and industry.

To strengthen the policy laid down in decree 217 of February, 1903, the Congress of the Republic passed law 33 of the same year, which regulated the monetary system and envisaged the amortization of paper money. The new monetary unit would be the gold *peso* of a 0.900 standard and a free stipulation of the legal currency for contracts was allowed, which might be either this monetary unit or paper money.

A *Junta de Amortización* or Amortization Board was created to administer the circulation of paper money. It was made up of five members: two chosen by the House of Representatives, two by the Senate and one by the executive. The main functions of this Board were to sell gold in exchange for paper money, incinerate the latter and set the foreign exchange rate on the basis of an analysis of the market. The gold needed for the amortization of paper money would be obtained from the resources allocated to the Amortization Board by the same law: these were yields from a number of mines, revenues from pearl fisheries along the country's coasts, port fees and customs duties on the export of goods in general.

It is now evident that law 33 of 1903, whose author and staunchest defender was José Camacho Carrizosa, was not very effective, since it depended for its success on the creation of a fiscal surplus to amortize the paper money, which was difficult to achieve because of the precariousness of public revenues and the costs of reconstructing the country after the war. A surplus in the country's trade balance was also an important condition, for there was no other way to mint the metallic money needed to replace paper money.

We should also point out that the law suffered from a technical defect, in that it set out to restore to the bank notes the purchasing power which they had lost during the period of inflation. For the rest, despite these regulations, the amount of paper money in circulation increased between 1903 and 1905, because it was only after the latter year that the amount of money in circulation stabilized. The reforms did manage, however, to stabilize the exchange rate from 1903 onwards.

In 1905, during the presidency of Rafael Reyes (1905-09), the Banco Central was founded and new legislation on the monetary regime was passed. The former measure was part of a broad program to guarantee macro-economic stabilization and stimulate economic growth, which also included regulations on the handling of the

Opposite page,
Rafael Reyes (1904-1909). Under a broad program to encourage macro-economic stabilization and economic growth, his administration was responsible for the creation of the Banco Central in 1905.

Right, *José María Sierra and Nemesio Camacho, who, with Pedro Jaramillo and others, organized the Banco Central, under an authorization given by legislative decree 47, 1905, during the administration of General Reyes.*

exchange rate, a fiscal reform, changes in tariff and customs rules and different incentives for industrial growth.

The creation of a new emission bank, under legislative decree 47 of 1905, authorized José María Sierra, Nemesio Camacho, Pedro Jaramillo and other individuals to organize in Bogotá a bank that would bear the name of the Banco Central. Among the factors behind the founding of this bank were the need to convert paper money into metallic money, the high interest rates existing in the money market due to the scanty supply of credit, fluctuations in the exchange rate, the disappearance of metal money as a circulating medium and the existence in the country of private capitals that might help to solve these problems.

The Banco Central would have a capital of 8,000,000 gold *pesos*: the above-mentioned licensees were to subscribe 60% of this capital and the general public the remaining 40%.

The stocks not taken up by the latter category of investors might be subscribed by the government, under the same conditions that applied to private investors. To obtain the stocks, investors had to commit themselves to a cash payment of 50% payable within six months from the time of subscription, with the remaining 50% to be laid out according to the terms found in the statutes.

The Banco Central was granted the privilege of issuing bank notes equivalent to and freely convertible into gold for a period of 30 years. The amount of bank notes issued could not exceed twice its paid-in capital and it had to keep on deposit in its vaults an amount of gold equivalent to 30% of the value of the bank notes in circulation. It was also given the free use of the government telegraph and postal services for its operations, as well as an exemption from customs duties on the import of its bank notes. It was further ordered that, in Bogotá or other cities where it had branches, all Treasury revenues would be deposited in this bank.

In addition, the Banco Central was given the administration of the government revenues reorganized by legislative decree no. 41 of 1905, which included taxes on liquors, hides, tobacco, cigarettes and matches. These revenues had been administered by a company whose owners were the same capitalists behind the founding of the Banco Central, who consented to cede this contract to that bank under the same conditions as the one they had originally signed with the government.

Through the Amortization Board, the government handed over to the bank all

Below, *1 peso bill of 1904, signed by Carlos Arturo Torres, Treasury Minister under the government of Rafael Reyes.*

of the bank notes which the Board had ordered to be printed in England to replace those from previous editions. To effect the change-over, only deteriorated bills would be withdrawn from circulation initially, to be followed by a progressive withdrawal of others. The legal deadline for the withdrawal from circulation of the bills of old denominations was April 1, 1907, after which they would have no exchange value. This date was later postponed until July, 1914, under decree 1429 bis of 1908.

But the measure went even further, by stating that the new bank notes put into circulation to replace the old ones could be converted into metal money, a job that decree 47 of 1905 gave to the Banco Central. The conversion of paper money into metallic money would be achieved by allocating for this purpose, in 1906, 25% of the revenues established by legislative decree number 41 of 1905, which would be increased to 50% from 1907 onwards.

For the effects of the conversion of paper money into metal money, legislative decree 47 of 1905 ordered that 100 *pesos* of paper money were equal to one gold *peso*. This change of the monetary unit was ratified by law 59 of 1905, which stated that the monetary unit and account money of the nation would be the gold *peso*, divided into 100 *centavos*, with a weight of 1.672 grams and a standard of 0.900.

The multiples of this unit were to be: the *doble cóndor*, whose value was 20 *pesos*; the *cóndor*, equivalent to 10 *pesos*; and the *medio cóndor*, equivalent to 5 *pesos*. The fractions of the unit, to be minted in silver, were the *medio peso*, equivalent to 50 gold *centavos*; the *peseta*, equivalent to 20 gold *centavos*; and the real, equivalent to 10 gold *centavos*. Silver coins would be minted at a standard of 0.900 and 33 grams of silver would be the equivalent of a gram of gold. By virtue of this norm, it was established that only 10 silver *pesos* could be emitted for every 100 gold *pesos* in circulation. The government was further authorized to issue coins of 1, 2 and 5 *centavos* in copper, nickel or bronze, whose value in circulation might not surpass 2% of the amount of gold in circulation.

Law 59 of 1905 established free stipulation in contracts, authorized the government to contract a private company to mint the new coins and ordered that budgets at all levels of public administration should be accounted in terms of the gold *peso*. The measure confirmed the channeling of special revenues towards the conversion of paper money into metal money, at a proportion of 100 *pesos* of paper money for one gold *peso*.

As we have said, this process would be undertaken by the Banco Central, now that the Amortization Board *(Junta de Amortización)*, downgraded to an office of the Ministry of the Treasury, was only to carry out the minor tasks of receiving the new bills printed abroad and burning the old ones.

In practice, the measures found in law 59 were a triumph for those who had al-

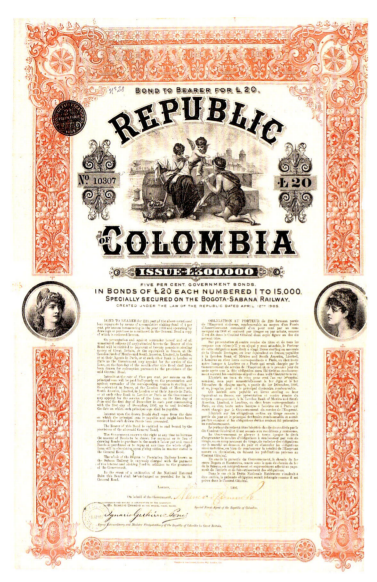

Left,
English bond for the Ferrocarriles de la Sabana railway company, 1906. Each bond was for 20 pounds sterling and the total emission was 300,000 pounds.

ceived them at their effective value, not the value that was printed on them. For the rest, the Colombian people were pleased with this official depreciation of their money, which was immediate and effective, for several reasons: the country, ruined by three years of bloody civil war, longed to erect a new economic life on the foundation of safety and certainty; the population, worn down by the nightmare of paper money and the universal fever of speculation which this had led to, was anxious for peace and yearned for norms to guide future calculations that would not be so changeable and uncertain; the popular instinct clearly understood from the very beginning that giving a value of one billion pesos to paper money and returning to the gold standard by the normal avenues were things that would be beyond the reach of the possible resources of the State for many years". (quoted by Torres García, 1980, p. 236).

Despite this change in the monetary unit, the Banco Central was not successful in placing its bills into circulation, which, as Guillermo Torres García explains, were dubbed "day boarders" by the wits of Bogotá, because they went into circulation in the morning and returned to the vaults of the bank in the afternoon. Nor was the Banco Central successful in converting paper money into metallic currency. Once the foreign exchange rate had stabilized and fluctuations in the purchasing power of paper money disappeared, a new measure passed in 1907, law 35, ordered that resources destined to the conversion of paper money into metallic money would be used by the government for the ordinary expenses of the Treasury. In this way was blocked the withdrawal from circulation of the bank notes issued by the Banco Nacional before the outbreak of the civil war, which retrospectively became known as "the War of the Thousand Days" (*la Guerra de los Mil Días*), and by the Litografía Nacional during the course of it.

This same law 35 of 1907 brought a new change in the monetary unit, one without much technical sense, since once

ways opposed the monetary policy of the Regeneration, especially the obligation to receive legal tender for contracts rather than having a free choice of currency: a conclusion that has led Charles Berg quist to say that while the Liberals lost the war, they won the peace.

As was to be expected, the change in the monetary unit would not have much of an economic effect on relative prices and compliance with contracts. What was being changed, in the end, was the way of measuring the money in circulation, not the amount of it. As Esteban Jaramillo commented at that time: "In accordance with very respectable analysts, we must conclude that this extreme measure was not unjust, since the members of the public who were bearers of the bank notes had, at the time of this conversion, re-

Below, *5 and 10 pesos bills issued during the government of General Reyes, before the creation of the Banco Central.*

again coins of the same nominal value could be minted with different standards, thus forcing the high quality ones out of circulation.

The confusion brought by the monetary system established under law 35 of 1907 and the fiscal provisions contained in it were not an obstacle to a new attempt to withdraw paper money from circulation and replace it with coins of variable standards. In fact, partly as a criticism of the monetary policies of the government of Rafael Reyes and the poor results of the Banco Central's efforts to withdraw paper money from circulation, law 58 of 1909 approved the signing of a contact between the government and the Banco Central which ended all of the contracts between the executive branch and that institution. In this way, despite the strong opposition of don José María Sierra, the Banco Central lost its privileges: it continued to function as a private bank until 1928, when it fused with the Banco de Bogotá.

A complementary measure, law 69 of 1909, created the Junta de Conversión or Conversion Board, with the aim of making monetary and exchange policy independent of government influence: it was made up of three members designated by the Congress and had the double responsibility of stabilizing the exchange rate and withdrawing paper money from circulation.

To achieve these two aims, a gold fund was established that would be able to use half of its resources to intervene in the exchange market to buy and sell foreign currency so that fluctuations in the exchange rate would not exceed the limits set by the same Board. The other half of the funds were destined for the withdrawal from circulation of paper money, for which, in contrast to the 1903 measure –which

Right, *100 pesos bond of the Ferrocarril del Norte railway company, for the line between Zipaquirá and Chinquinquirá, signed by Tobías Valenzuela, Treasury Minister.*

hoped that bank notes would progressively increase in value– a sole exchange rate was set which made 100 *pesos* of paper money the equivalent of 1 *peso* of gold.

As we shall see below, the Junta de Conversión was completely successful in stabilizing the exchange rate but the opposite was true of its attempts to withdraw paper money from circulation, which were impeded by recurrent fiscal problems.

With the income from different sources of revenue allocated to it under law 69 of 1909, the Conversion Board managed to accumulate reserves of around 1.5 million *pesos* in gold by 1913 and foresaw that by the end of the year this would amount to 20% of the bank notes in circulation, that is, 2 million gold *pesos*. Among other sources, the revenue came from the yields of the emerald mines of Muzo and Coscuez; rents from the mines of Santa Ana, La Manta, Supía and Marmato; 2% of import taxes; and the profit from the difference between the real and nominal value of the silver coin in circulation. Nevertheless, fiscal difficulties prevented the Fund from accumulating more resources.

What happened next was a clear violation of the principle of law 69, which had established that "in no case, nor for any motive, nor on the order of any authority may the Conversion Fund be used for investments other than those set forth in this law, on penalty of the deed being considered a fraud against public revenues for which the members of the Board and the employees that order and agree to the surrender of funds will be held criminally responsible". But in 1914, faced by a fall in imports and customs tariffs due to the outbreak of the First World War, the legislature passed law 126, which authorized the government to make use of the resources of the Conversion Fund when its monthly revenues fell below 1,250,000 *pesos*. The change found in law 126 of 1914 was reaffirmed by other measures –such as law 65 of 1916, law 15 of 1918 and law 61 of 1921 – and the result was that the replacement of old denomination bills by metal currency was once more postponed.

Unable to achieve what it had been created to do in the monetary field, the Junta de Conversión, beginning in March, 1916, decided to replace the old bills with new ones representing gold in denominations of 1, 2, 5 and 10 *pesos*. The American Bank Note Company received the order to print the bills, whose edition date was July 20,

1915. These bills representative of gold were issued by the Republic of Colombia and were known as *billetes nacionales* (national bank notes) until their retirement from circulation.

For the effects of carrying out the replacement of the old bills and maintaining in a good state those that were put into circulation, a printing of 20 million *pesos* in bank notes representing gold was authorized. Of these, 10 million would be of one *peso*, 2 million of two *pesos*, five million of five *pesos* and 3 million of ten *pesos* denomination. The money put into circulation between 1916 and 1924 is found Table 2.

The deadline for replacing the old bills was to be June 30, 1918 but this was later extended to June, 1919. But this was not completely enforced either, since a small number of these old bills continued to circulate until 1923.

At the time that the attempts to convert paper into metal money were being made, the Fiscal Code adopted under Law 110 of 1912 decreed that the monetary unit of the

nation was the gold peso, divided into one hundred *centavos*, that weighed 1.957 grams and would be minted at a standard of $0.916^{2/3}$. The multiples of the *peso* were the *doble cóndor* (20 *pesos*), the *cóndor* (10 *pesos*), the *medio cóndor* (5 *pesos*) and the *cuarto de cóndor* (2.50 *pesos*). The latter two coins were the equivalents, in terms of weight and standard, of the pound sterling and half pound sterling, coins that freely circulated in the country. The fractions of the gold *peso* were made up of silver coins, with a 0.900 standard, of 10, 20 and 50 *centavos* and a weight of 0.25 grams per *centavo*.

In order to give solidity to the gold monetary unit and reduce the circulation of silver coins, you were not allowed to

Above, *The allegorical figure of "the Miner" by Francisco Antonio Cano was used both on coins minted in 1915 and a series of stamps in 1932.*

Table 2

CONVERSION BOARD **AMOUNT OF BANK NOTES REPRESENTATIVE** **OF GOLD ISSUED BETWEEN 1916 -1924**						
Figures in *pesos*						
Emission Act No.	**Date**	**Denomination**				
		$1	$2	$5	$10	TOTAL
1	March 1, 1916	5.400.000	1.760.000	1.200.000	1.440.000	9.800.000
2	December 19, 1917	30.000	20.000	20.000	30.000	100.000
3	January 24, 1911	10.000				10.000
4	May 10, 1918	40.000	20.000	5.000		65.000
5	June 20, 1918	40.000				40.000
6	July 1, 1918	40.000				40.000
7	*	40.000				40.000
8	July 20, 1918	50.000				50.000
9	October 31, 1918	10.000		10.000	5.000	25.000
10	October 31, 1918	10.000				10.000
11	March 5, 1920	100.000				100.000
12	December 9, 1920	10.000				10.000
13	April 12, 1921	10.000				10.000
14	July 4, 1921	20.000				20.000
15	April 20, 1922	10.000				10.000
16	September 23, 1922	20.000				20.000
17	April 14, 1923	20.000				20.000
18	August 30, 1923	20.000				20.000
19	November 24, 1923	10.000		15.000		25.000
20	December 20, 1923		20.000		5.000	25.000
21	January 5, 1924	40.000	20.000		20.000	80.000
	TOTAL	5.880.000	1.840.000	1.300.000	1.500.000	10.520.000

* No date given in the source used to compile the table.
Source: Table compiled in the basis information in Avella Gómez, Mauricio, *Pensamiento y Política Monetaria en Colombia 1846 - 1945*. ("Monetary Though and Policy in Colombia, 1846-1945".)

Left, *Rafael Uribe Uribe, Liberal-party leader who was assassinated in 1914. After the disappearance of the Banco Central as an emission bank, he led the movement to create a new institution of this kind.*

Below, *Mortgage certificate, issued by the private banks on bills with an overlaid seal that had originally belonged to the Banco Central.*

settle a debt of more than ten *pesos* with silver coins. The lowest-denomination coins were cupro-nickel ones, of 1, 2 and 5 *centavos* and a weight of 2, 3 and 4 grams, respectively, which, for similar reasons, could not be used to settle a debt of more than 2 *pesos*.

With the prohibition on issuing paper money and monetary regimes that supported the circulation of metal money based on gold, the amount of money in circulation during the first two decades of the twentieth century was largely governed by the surpluses or deficits in foreign trade, except for the period of First World War, which had a strongly disruptive effect. Thus, between 1910 and 1913, there was an import of gold coins equivalent to 4 million gold *pesos*. During the war, however, gold was exported despite the trade surplus. With this export the amount of money in circulation tended to fall, a trend which was only reversed in 1919, with the import of 9 million *pe-*

sos worth of gold coins from the United States, the minting of gold coins and the placing into circulation of *Certificados sobre Consignación de Oro, las Cédulas de Tesorería* and *Cédulas Hipotecarias*, which will be explained below.

The minting of money after 1919 is explained by the fact that, once the United States allowed the renewal of payments in gold, the foreign surpluses accumulated during the war by Colombian exporters were cashed in gold and later minted. The *Certificados sobre Consignación de Oro* (Gold Certificates) originated as a response to the limited minting capacity of the *Casa de Moneda* (government mint) of Medellín. In this mint gold that was to be minted was exchanged for gold certificates of 2.5, 5, 10, 20, 50 and 100 *pesos*. Since the government received these certificates as payment for taxes and later exchanged them for minted gold, it might be said that they carried out a monetary function.

Exhausted by an acute fiscal deficit inherited from the administration of José Vicente Concha (1914-1918), the administration of President Marco Fidel Suárez (1918-1921) resorted to two expedients to solve its financial difficulties: increase monetary circulation and stabilize the exchange rates. The first of these was the issuing of *Cédulas de Tesorería* (Treasury Bills), which had the dual function of dealing with the fiscal deficit and increasing circulating currency, since they were accepted as money.

4 million *pesos* of these Treasury Bills were issued, to be paid by the government to those who would voluntarily accept them as payment for government debts, such as salaries of public officials and

Right above,
Two and a half pesos *coin, 1919.*

Below,
Treasury Bond issued as money the Conversion Board, under law 6 and decree 169, 1922. The original bill corresponds to one of the kind that the Conversion Board ordered to be printed in 1915.

money owed to contractors. The bills, in denominations of 1, 2, 5, 10, 15 and 50 *pesos,* were payable to the bearer and the government received them at their nominal value for tax payments. The proceeds of the tax on stamps and sealed legal paper were used to amortize them. The *Cédulas de Tesorería* made use of bank notes of the former Banco Central, with an overprinted government seal, and they were withdrawn from circulation by the Banco de la República from 1923 onwards, as shall be explained below.

The second expedient employed by Esteban Jaramillo, Treasury Minister of President Suárez, to increase the amount of money in circulation, was the acceptance, by government tax offices, of the bank notes issued by the Bank of England on an equal basis with national currency. This measure sought to increase circulating money and stabilize the exchange rate, which had tended to appreciate during the First World War due to the positive trade balance and the blockade of gold exports by the United States and the European countries. The Supreme Court of Justice ruled that the measure was unconstitutional, a decision that led to polemics between minister Jaramillo and the Court and put an end to the circulation of English bank notes.

These two initiatives were complemented by the emission of *Cédulas Hipotecarias* (mortgage certificates) by the private banks, to pay part of their loans. These papers, used for purchases of real estate, entered the market and circulated as a means of payment. In addition, law 6 of 1922 authorized the emission of 6 million *pesos* in low denominations, through what were called *Bonos del Tesoro* (Treasury Bonds).

To conclude, it might be said that since 1903 successive Colombian governments

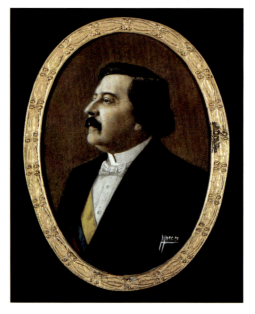

Above,
José Vicente Concha (1914–1918) and Marco Fidel Suárez (1918-1921). Concha faced very severe monetary difficulties on the occasion of the First World War. Suárez ordered Treasury Bills to be placed into circulation as money and allowed English bank notes to circulate on an equal basis with Colombian ones.

had proposed the withdrawal from circulation of legal tender bank notes and the establishment of a system of money based on gold. Despite the fact that, due to their fiscal problems, the achievement of these aims was not successful, the period between the end of the "War of the Thousand Days" and the beginning of the nineteen-twenties was characterized by economic growth and a climate of stability in prices and the exchange rate.

After the creation of the Conversion Board in 1909, the exchange rate kept the *peso* nearly on a par with the dollar until 1922, except in 1920 and 1921, when, due to a shortage of foreign earnings, it rose to 1.12 and 1.17 *pesos* per dollar, respectively.

In relation to the behavior of prices, inflation was moderate throughout this period; in fact, there were slight falls in prices between 1905-1907, 1912-1914 and 1921-1922. The only period when there was a relatively high inflation was in 1919-1920, when prices rose by nearly 20%.

The economic expansion of the period deserves a wider comment. Because of the civil war and internal developments in this sector, coffee-growing shifted from the departments of Cundinamarca, Santander and North Santander towards Antioquia, Caldas and el Valle del Cauca. This regional change in the coffee sector was of great economic importance, since it meant the end of the large hacienda plan-

Below,
Modesto Garcés and Lucas Caballero, who, with Rafael Uribe Uribe, José Camacho Carrizosa and Carlos Calderón, were responsible for several proposals for the establishment of a central bank of emission between 1914 and 1922.

tations, which were replaced by small coffee farms.

This, in turn, led to a separation of the activities of production and commercialization of the bean and, to a certain extent, to smaller variations in internal prices as a result of fluctuations of the international price, all of which contributed to a marked expansion of the national economy, not only because of the demand created by coffee revenues but also due to the improvement of the country's transportation network and increased investment in the coffee sector.

In addition, the tariff reforms of 1903, 1905 and 1913 protected the production of a number of agricultural goods, which, added to the process of urbanization, encouraged the growth of some agricultural sectors, like cotton, barley, wheat and tobacco, between 1903 and 1920. This process of expansion also reached to the industrial sector, where it was seen in the initiation of petroleum exploration, the foundation and modernization of sugar mills, a growth in the production of cement and sulfuric acid, the emergence of a consumer goods industry (for example, such products as drinking chocolate, beer, soft drinks, candles and matches) and, one of the most important, the appearance of a modern textile industry, mainly in the departments of Antioquia and Cundinamarca.

Thus, a process of export-driven development took place, thanks to the overseas sales of coffee, which was complemented by a notable increase of the internal market. However, this material development ran into a serious obstacle, which was the absence of a financial system that would provide the credit needed for further economic expansion and of a medium of circulating currency suitable for the efficient development of productive activities, since, as we have seen, the creation of the money supply faced many difficulties and the financial system functioned in a precarious way.

A number of political leaders who were aware of these problems, among them Rafael Uribe Uribe, Lucas Caballero, José Camacho Carrizosa and Carlos Calderón, made repeated proposals for the establishment of a bank of emission. Beginning in 1914, there was a growing controversy over the institutional framework that would be needed to issue circulating currency and the debate about the plurality or unity of emission was joined to arguments about the legal status of such an institution and whether it would or would not be convenient to allow foreign capital to participate in it.

Despite the fact that the partisans of a unity of emission were gaining ground, there was little consensus about other aspects of the proposed reforms. This was evidenced by events in the Congress, where no fewer than eight proposals to organize a central bank were discussed between 1917 and 1922. None of these initiatives prospered and it was only in 1923, with the passing of law 25, that a real reform took place. This law authorized the government to promote and undertake the foundation of the Banco de la República, a measure which was complemented by one dealing with the organization of the credit system, law 45 of 1923 on banking establishments.

Right,
Political cartoon in Fantoches, *1929: Miguel Abadía and Esteban Jaramillo, accused of encouraging debt prosperity, are expelled from the paradise of squandering by Uncle Sam. Peñuela and Renjifo, ministers of the Abadía government, watch from a tree.*

FOUNDATION OF THE BANCO DE LA REPÚBLICA AND THE ORGANIZATION OF THE BANKING SYSTEM

Opposite page,
The Pedro A. López building, designed by Robert M. Farrington, which was the headquarters of the López bank until 1923, when it was bought by the government to serve as the first headquarters of the Banco de la República.

Right,
Eugenio Andrade, Treasury Minister under Jorge Holguín, presented in 1921 the proposal for the law that led to the foundation of the Banco de la República.

By 1922 the currency in circulation had expanded through the use of the ad-hoc measures described in the previous chapter, but the Colombian economy still faced serious difficulties in achieving a well-functioning system of monetary circulation and credit supply.

Meeting the former requirement was hampered by legal limitations on the government's power to expand or contract the amount of money in circulation with the flexibility required to meet a changing business climate, as became evident through the shortage of money supply before 1918 and its very rapid expansion after 1919. In addition, the existence, as a means of exchange, of so many different and unequal kinds of currencies made monetary circulation even more difficult and created anomalies in the strict enforcement of contracts. They included silver and nickel coins, gold coins, current bank notes representative of gold and older ones that survived the epoch of the big emissions), Treasury Bills, Treasury Bonds and the certificates issued by the private banks.

With the aim of solving the problem of circulating money, a meeting of private bankers took place in Bogotá in the months of August and September, 1921. These discussions resulted in the drafting of a bill that was put before the ordinary sessions of the Congress later that year, which set out to create a private-sector emission bank Two other proposals along the same lines were submitted to the legislature around the same time.

The first, presented to the Senate by the congressman from Santander, Eugenio Gómez, sought authorization for a foreign loan and the foundation of an emission bank that would be called the Banco Colombiano. The second, on the same sub-

ject, was presented to the House of Representatives by Eugenio Andrade, Minister of the Treasury during the administration of Jorge Holguín (1921-1922), who had taken charge of the government after the resignation of the titular President Marco Fidel Suárez.

In proposing that the new bank of emission be called the Banco de la República, the latter initiative resurrected a name that had been used in a contract, authorized by the government of Carlos E. Restrepo (President between 1910-14) in 1913, granting a concession for such a bank to the French company Dreyfus et cie. The name had been chosen as gesture in honor of the "Republican" coalition of Liberals and Conservatives that governed Colombia between 1910-1914. But the contract was rejected by the Congress and the bank was never created.

The extraordinary sessions held in the Congress of the Republic in 1922 wound up combining the projects of Senator Gómez and Minister Andrade into a single measure, which resulted in law 30 for the foundation of the Banco de la República, which authorized the government to undertake the creation of bank for emissions, bank drafts, bills of exchange, deposits and discounts, in accordance with the stipulations of the law and those which would be incorporated into its statutes.

The main features of this legal measure had to do with the contractual character of its foundation, which sought to prevent government abuse of its purpose, functions and structures; the special juridical status awarded to it, through an autonomous legal regime that would not be subject to interference by the government; the minority power given to the government in the Bank's Board of Directors; and the requirement that the Governor of the Bank be elected by a practically unanimous vote, which would weaken the executive branch's influence over his selection.

Among its functions, the Bank was given a unique right to issue the legal currency of Colombia on behalf of the State; it would be the government's banker, by virtue of its power to receive funds from and grant credits to the government within the limitations set forth in the law; it would be the lender of last resort, through its power to make loans to private banks; it would exercise monetary control by means of setting, within certain limits, the interest rate on the loans it granted, and it would control the interest rates that private-sector banks might charge for their loan operations.

When Pedro Nel Ospina assumed his four-year term as President in August, 1922, he found that the private banks, smarting from the Congress's disparagement of their own proposal, were not interested in becoming partners of the Banco de la República under the terms of law 30 of 1922. This brought the initiative to a halt but, determined to overcome the difficulties, the Ospina government convoked another round of meetings with the bankers. This resulted in a new legislative proposal that became law 117 of 1922, which enlarged and reformed law 30 but did not substantially effect its definition of the functions and structure of the Banco de la República. The revisions essentially concerned the liquidity of the Bank's assets, the purposes for which it would issue bank notes and the forms of credit that it might grant to the public sector.

Around the same time that law 117 of 1922 was passed, the government obtained authorization from the Congress to contract a mission of international experts to advise it on the reorganization of government services, revenues and taxes. Although some sectors of public opinion in Colombia wanted European experts to be

Left, *Pedro Nel Ospina (1922-1926), championed the establishment of the Banco de la República as the first central bank of Colombia and promoted the general banking law which guided the Colombian financial system during nearly the whole of the twentieth century.*

Right,
News item about the foundation of the Banco de la República, which mentions the exclusion of Liberals from its first Board of Directors. El Tiempo newspaper, July 21, 1903.

hired, the government wound up choosing American ones and on the recommendation of the U.S. State Department, the then Colombian ambassador to the United States, Enrique Olaya Herrera, chose Professor Edwin Kemmerer to head the mission. Kemmerer was an expert on monetary and banking matters from Princeton University who had been a financial advisor to the Philippines (1903-1906), Egypt (1906), Mexico (1917), Guatemala (1919) and, after his work in Colombia in 1923, did the same job in Chile, Poland, Ecuador, Bolivia, China, Peru and Turkey until 1934.

Given Kemmerer's wide experience and in view of the fact that he had been contracted at the beginning of 1923, when laws 30 and 117 of 1922 had still not been developed, it was natural for the government to postpone the creation of the Banco de la República until it received his opinion about the two measures.

Professor Kemmerer took over the organization of the Mission and chose as his collaborators Howard Jefferson, expert in banks and their organization, who had worked in the Federal Reserve Bank of New York; Frederick Rogers Fairchild, professor of the University of Yale and expert in tax matters, who had held the post of Secretary of the National Tax Association in the United States; Thomas Russell Lill, expert on accounting and financial organization, a subject on which he had advised the government of Mexico; and Frederick Luquiens, Professor of Spanish at the University of Yale, who would act as secretary and translator of the Mission. Their Colombian counterparts were Esteban Jaramillo, who, as has been said, had occupied the post of Treasury Minister in the Suárez government and Vicente Villa, a Colombian businessmen who lived in New York, was a close friend of President Ospina and had been in close contact with Enrique Olaya Herrera during the initial stage of organizing the Mission.

The American experts reached Bogotá in March, 1923 and, as part of their working methodology, which had the aim of becoming closely acquainted with existing Colombian legislation and gauging the

Above,
Bank bond issued by the Banco López in 1921.

Below,
Political cartoon of Uncle Sam and Colombia. The foundation of the Banco de la República became feasible thanks to the payment in 1922 of the first installment of an indemnification granted to Colombia by the United States for the loss of Panama.

receptivity or otherwise of their proposals, held meetings and interviews with bankers, industrialists, businessmen and public officials. To strengthen their links with the political and financial elite of Colombia the members of the Mission also participated in a wide range of social activities: they played tennis and golf and went to all sorts of gatherings.

Although there was discord within the group about working methods –Luquiens and Fairchild complained about the intensity of the 8 hour, Monday to Saturday timetable and began to take time off, which led Kemmerer to distance himself from them– by the end of May they had already prepared five legislative bills, backed by technical arguments. These included:

- the establishment of the Banco de la República as a central bank of emission and discount;
- norms about the tax on stamps and sealed legal paper;
- the general banking law;
- the national budget law;
- the law on the Controller's office.

With the aim of getting the legislature to analyze these initiatives, the executive branch convoked the Congress to hold extraordinary sessions beginning on 28 May, upon which Kemmerer and his colleagues prepared another five legislative measures:

- a project for a law on taxes on passenger transport;
- a project for a law that introduced changes in the number and nomenclature of the Ministries and included, among other suggestions, changing the name of the Treasury Ministry to the Ministry of Finance and Public Credit;
- a project for a law that would make changes in the organization for collecting and administering State revenues;
- a project for a law on negotiable financial instruments;
- a project for a law on income tax.

Between May 28 and July 19, the period of the extraordinary sessions, the Congress adopted almost all of these measures. The only projects it did not approve were those for taxes on passenger transport and the income tax.

Even though these laws were important for the consolidation and modernization of the administration of the state and ensured a better equilibrium between the government's revenues and expenses, thus making the proposed monetary and credit schemes more viable, the most important

Above, *Edwin Walter Kemmerer y Esteban Jaramillo. The first, as the head of the mission of foreign experts, and the second, as his Colombian counterpart, played a decisive role in the creation of the financial and fiscal reforms of 1923, especially law 25, which authorized the government to found the Banco de la República.*

laws for the achievement of these aims were the one that defined the basic structure of the Banco de la República and the law on banking institutions.

The first of these measures closely followed the stipulations laid down in laws 30 and 117 of 1922, as can be seen when one reads the arguments put forth in favor of law 25 of 1923, by which the Congress authorized the government to promote and undertake the foundation of bank for emissions, bank drafts, deposits and discounts, which would be called the Banco de la República and have a life of 20 years that could be extended, at the request of the Bank, by a government resolution.

The capital of the Banco de la República was set at ten million gold *pesos*, represented by nominative stocks of one hundred gold *pesos* each that were not transferable to foreign governments. The stocks were divided into four classes: A stocks, which the government would subscribe; B stocks, which Colombian banks which carried out commercial banking operations would subscribe; C stocks, which foreign banks which carried out business in Colombia would subscribe; and D stocks, to be subscribed by the general public. All of the stocks would be paid for in gold and have equal rights with regard to dividends.

The government would supply 50% of the capital and have a right to three seats on the ten-member Board of Directors of the Banco de la República. Of the seven remaining members, four would be chosen by the Colombian banks, two by the foreign banks and the other by the private shareholders who owned class D stocks. Half of the members elected by the Colombian and foreign banks had to be professional bankers, while the other half had to be businessmen, farmers or professionals, that is, the three members of the Board of Directors of the Bank from the latter category did not necessarily have to represent stockholders.

There were no professional restrictions on the member chosen by the private stockholders, but they could only exercise their right to elect this member after having paid

Right,
Members of the first U.S. advisory commission: Howard Jefferson, Frederick Rogers Fairchild and Frederick Luquiens (translator).

Below,
The mission headed by E.W. Kemmerer arrives at the Sabana railway station in Bogotá in 1923, where they are welcomed by Aristóbulo Archila, Treasury Minister of Pedro Nel Ospina.

a million *pesos* of capital. There was be a three-year term of office for the members designated by the government, but to begin with, it would choose one member who would serve for one year, a second for two years and a third for three years, so that from then on one of these directors would be replaced each year. The term of office for the members not chosen by the government would be two years and a similar mechanism to ensure a periodical changeover of board members was applied to the Colombian and foreign banks, who, in the initial election, would choose half of their representatives to serve for one year and the other half for a period of two years. The directors would have deputies who were to be elected in the same way, at the same time and for the same period of their respective principals.

The law ordered that the Governor of the Banco de la República would be designated by the Board of Directors, by a vote of at least seven members and could not be a government official nor the manager, director or employee of another bank.

The Board of Directors was given the power to decide on the class of credits which the Banco de la República could award, subject to the restrictions laid down in the law, which included a prohibition on making loans, discounts or investments against credit instruments, bonds or bills of exchange with a term of more than 90 days, except in exceptional cases when the term might be extended to 180 days. In addition, the Bank was not allowed to accept collaterals which did not have, as signatories, at least two responsible firms, including that of the bank that made the discount; nor could it accept those credit instruments whose discount implied the destining of funds for speculative purposes or permanent investments like the purchase of lands, buildings, etc.

The credit that might be given to the public sector was restricted to 30% of the paid-in capital and the reserves of the Banco de la República, but it would be permitted to exceed this limit up to June, 1929, during which period it would lend to the government 10% of its capital (1 million *pesos*) plus 3,216,000 *pesos*: the government committed itself to use the 4,216,000 *pesos* loan to redeem the Cédulas de Tesorería which had been circulating since 1919. The loan would be guaranteed with 10% *Cédulas de Tesorería* payable at five years. To make government access to the Bank's resources even more restrictive the law stated that, with

Right,
Before the creation of the Banco de la República, many kinds of money circulated in the country, among them Treasury Bonds and Treasury Bills. Both of these were identified by seals printed on top of the bank notes whose fabrication was ordered by the Conversion Board in 1915.

the exception of the above-mentioned credit for the withdrawal from circulation of the *Cédulas*, any credit to the public sector would require the favorable vote of seven members of the Board of Directors.

In addition to being able to carry out credit operations, the Banco de la República was given the authority to receive deposits from the private banks, negotiate with them the purchase or sale of gold in coin or bars and to serve as a clearing house for checks. However, these operations could only be carried out with the stockholder banks.

On interest rates, the Board of Directors was given an unrestricted power to fix the rate which the Banco de la República would charge in the moment of lending resources to banks and private individuals and an indirect right to influence the interest rates on credit in general, because the statutes stated that no stockholder bank could discount credit instruments through the Banco de la República if it charged its clients interest rates higher than 3% of the Bank's rate for instruments of the same class and term.

For the general public, the Bank was authorized to buy and sell bank drafts, gold in coins or bars, bills of exchange deriving from foreign trade if their term was no longer than 90 days, bank acceptances, bills of exchange or promissory notes issued or to be paid in Colombia with the same 90 day limit, and bonds and other securities emitted by public agencies, the latter faculty being subject to the restrictions imposed by law. In addition, the Banco de la República could receive sight-deposits from the general public. Nevertheless, despite the norms authorizing the discount of financial instruments for private individuals, the Banco de la República refused to carry out such operations until the end of 1931.

The Banco de la Repúblic was given the exclusive privilege of issuing bank notes representative of gold, within the terms fixed by the Fiscal Code of 1912, which defined the nation's monetary unit. Without being legal tender, such bank notes would be considered as currency for all legal effects and would be received in payment for taxes or debts owing to the government. The bank notes would be issued in exchange for gold coins or bars and for the purchase or discount of foreign bills of exchange and bank drafts, with the restrictions on terms that have already mentioned. They could be also be issued against credits granted to the government, the stockholder banks and private individuals.

The bank notes would be convertible into gold in the main office of the Bank in

Bogotá or exchanged for checks to be cashed for gold when there was not sufficient gold in its branch offices. In exceptional cases, with the affirmative vote of six members of the Board of Directors and the approval of the Finance Minister, they could be exchanged for sight bills payable in gold in New York.

To facilitate the convertibility of these bills, the government committed itself to allow the Bank to exercise a free commerce in gold, with the right to import or export it, without taxes or obstacles and to turn into coin, as a matter of priority, the gold

Above,
During the economic crisis of the 1930's, the Banco de la República issued these Silver Certificates to replace the coinage minted in that metal.

that it might receive for that end. To guarantee this convertibility, it was established that the Bank would maintain in its vaults an amount of gold equivalent to 60% of the sum of its monetary liabilities (that is, its bank notes in circulation and deposits in these bills held in banks or by the public) and the *Cédulas de Tesorería* that had been circulating as money since 1919.

To enforce compliance with the gold reserve requirement, any shortfall in the reserves of the Bank would be penalized by fines payable to the National Treasury and proportional to the amount of the reserve shortfalls at a growing percentage. In addition, to make these precautions more rigorous, when the Bank failed to maintain the required reserve, the interest rates that it charged on its loans could not be lower than 8% and to this rate would be added half of the percentage paid to the Treasury as a fine. Thus, for example, if the Bank had to pay a fine of 6% of this shortfall, the rediscount rate could not be less than 11%.

The Banco de la República was authorized to receive government funds and act as its fiscal agent and by virtue of this power take charge of the functions which the Conversion Board had carried out since 1909. In accordance with this mandate it was decided that the Bank would act as the government's agent for the withdrawal from circulation of the different kinds of money that had served as mediums of exchange, especially the Treasury Bonds and Bills. As we have mentioned, to redeem the latter, the Banco de la República granted the government a credit of 3,216,000 *pesos*, a loan which the Treasury deposited in the Bank so that these resources could be used to redeem the *Cédulas* by exchanging them for gold or its own bank notes.

Once they were received in payment for taxes or deposited in the offices of other banks, the *Cédulas* could not return to circulation and they would also be exchanged for gold or bank notes of the Banco de la República. In the same way, the government promised to surrender to the Bank the resources which the Conversion Board had for redeeming the Treasury Bonds in circulation: these resources were complemented by funds from the national budget that were granted as from the 1924 financial year. Earnings and other resources which the government would receive from the Bank's operations, including the fines on reserve shortfalls, would be used to redeem the national bank notes representative of gold that had been issued in 1915. With the aim of avoiding tricks with the latter measure, the law ordered that it would be covered by a special contract between the Banco de la República and the government.

In addition, the banks that had issued mortgage certificates that circulated as money were prohibited from becoming partners of the Banco de la República, unless they committed themselves, through a contract with the Bank Superintendency, to withdraw them from circulation within a maximum term of fours years counted from the foundation of the Banco de la República.

All of the above measures were taken with the aim of unifying the monetary unit and complemented by a norm which obliged the government to obey the orders of the Bank's Board of Directors with

Below, *Mortgage Certificate and provisional bank note issued when the Banco de la República began operations: Gold Certificates held in the* Casa de Moneda *of Medellín were overprinted with its seal and put into circulation.*

regard to future emissions of silver, nickel, copper and other metal coins.

Finally, law 25 determined that the Banco de la República would be obliged to supply the Bank Superintendency with any reports it might require and inform the public about the development of its operations, particularly the amount of bills in circulation, deposits, loans and discounts, and stocks of gold.

Through a system of penalties and incentives, the law encouraged the private banks to become stockholders in the Banco de la República. Among the former, we have already mentioned that non-stockholder banks could not accede to rediscounts. Among the latter, the reserve requirement for the stockholder banks was to be half that of the non-stockholder ones.

For the purpose of adopting all of the preliminary measures needed to organize the bank, such as those relative to the issuing of stocks and the election of the first directors, the law created an organizing committee made up of the Treasury Minister and four other members chosen by the President of the Republic as representatives of the Colombian banks (2), the foreign banks (1), and the businessmen or professionals (1).

.It is easy to deduce from an examination of the text of law 25 of 1923 that both this norm and law 30 of 1922 were carefully prepared in order to avoid the problems that had made the founding of an emission bank fail in the past. All of the interested parties had a share in its paid-in capital, that is, Colombian and foreign bankers, private individuals and the government, which was able to come up with its contribution in gold because it had received, in the second half of 1922, a first installment of the indemnification paid to Colombia by the government of the United States for Colombia's loss of Panama, which had been a state of Colombia up to 1903.

The organization of the Board of Directors was also well conceived, since it gave representation to the stockholders and spokesmen for the productive sectors and established a balance among the different interests that participated in the founding and operation of the Banco de la República.

 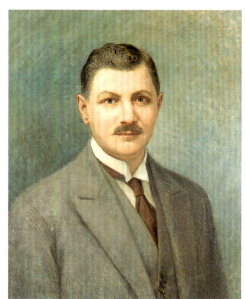

Right,
José Joaquín Pérez, Governor of the Banco de la República, July, 1923 - April, 1924. Oil painting by Carlos Valenzuela, 1942.
Félix Salazar Jaramillo, Governor of the Banco de la República, January, 1924 - April, 1927. Oil painting by Georges Brasseur, 1948.
Julio Caro, Governor of the Banco de la República, April, 1927 - October, 1947. Oil painting by Georges Brasseur, 1948.
Mariano Ospina Vázquez. Co-founder and Secretary of the Banco de la República. Oil painting by León Cano, 1943.

This was reinforced by the requirement of a seven-tenths majority to make fundamental decisions, like the naming of the Governor and the awarding of credit to the government.

The above measures would stop the government from making an unwarranted interference in the management of the Banco de la República. The head of the Mission, Kemmerer, had reached the following conclusion after meeting with different representatives of the political and financial elite: "the most general and emphatic doubt about the success of the Bank was that it might remain subject to an improper influence by the government and wind up failing because of politics, a fear which seems fully justified by the banking history of Colombia" (Kemmerer, 1923, p. 28). In addition, the presence on the Board of representatives of the productive sectors had the specific objective of easing their fears about the management of interest rates in favor of the bankers and to the detriment of the interests of the agricultural, industrial and commercial sectors.

As regards the credit policy of the Bank, the maximum 90-day term that applied to its operations sought to ensure liquidity for the institution's assets, because this was the only guarantee that its functions as a discount and rediscount bank would develop in harmony with monetary and banking stability, the free

Below, *Carlos Adolfo Urueta and Manuel Casabianca, who, together with Sam B. Koppel, Félix Salazar and Treasury Minister Gabriel Posada, were named as members of the Organizing Committee of the Banco de la República on July 16, 1923 and given four months to complete the job.*

convertibility of bills, and stable exchange rates. The same considerations were responsible for the restrictions on its credit operations with the government, although it was understood that an exception had to be made to the legal provision that set a general limit to its indebtedness, with the aim of unifying the currency in circulation through the amortization of the Cédulas de Tesorería.

It is worth nothing that the Bank's unlimited power to modify the discount rates was considered to be its most powerful weapon, since the exercise of this right enabled it to "protect the monetary market of the country, prevent big outflows of gold, check dangerous speculations and conserve an amount of metallic reserves sufficient to inspire confidence in its capacity to deal with any possible crisis". (Kemmerer,1923, p.33).

To fully understand the effectiveness which Kemmerer attributed to this instrument of monetary control, it is worth remembering that when expounding his arguments in favor of law 25 of 1923 he had written: "The Banco de la República bears a great weight in being wholly responsible for conserving the monetary market in Colombia, defending the country's gold reserves and enabling the stockholder banks to maintain their payments in metallic money at times of emergency. In great part, it will carry out these functions by raising the rediscount rates when it judges that the banks are too widely extended, or that the monetary market is subject to doubtful speculations, or that gold is leaving the country in dangerous amounts or in any other circumstances when the stability of the monetary market in Colombia is found to be threatened. If, at such times, the banks, finding themselves in possession of considerable funds, do not depend on the Banco de la República for rediscounts and refuse to follow its lead, as has often happened in England and other countries, and at the same time continue to increase their loans, the Banco de la República must have the capacity to comply with its obligation to protect the national monetary market. It makes effective its interest rates, which will oblige the banks to follow its lead so as to conserve their strength and have the capacity to prevent or deal with future crises". (Kemmerer, 1923, p. 36).

Approved by the Congress on July 4, 1923, law 25 was signed by President Ospina and Treasury Minister Gabriel Posada a week later. As was foreseen in article 10 of the law, the Organizing Committee would have four months in which to take the measures needed to organize the Bank, for which end it was given a budget of 20,000 gold *pesos*. The members of the Committee were appointed on July 16, 1923, held their first meeting that day and finished their work on July 22. In ad-

Right, *Illustrated explanation of the items of national government income and spending, on a picture of the 1925 Colombian* peso. *In the book* Colombia Cafetera *by Diego Monsalve.*

dition to the Treasury Minister, the members were Manuel Casabianca, Sam B. Koppel, Félix Salazar J. and Carlos Adolfo Urueta.

The short life and rapid deliberations of the Committee were due to a financial panic that began on Sunday July 15, when there arose rumors about the financial difficulties facing the company of Pedro A. López. These rumors led to a run on the Banco López, which was closely linked to that commercial trading company: as depositors, especially those with saving accounts, proceeded to retire massive amounts of savings, the bank faced a liquidity crisis, in spite of its reputation for solvency.

Faced by this grave crisis, which threatened to extend itself to the Banco de Bogotá and other banking houses located in the capital, on July 16 President Ospina and the Organizing Committee decided to consider one of the Kemmerer Mission's recommendations: that the Banco de la República initiate activities on Thursday the 18th.

The idea did not receive a wholehearted support, since some of the members of the Committee were in favor of declaring a moratorium on payments.

Below, *Four scenes from the financial panic unleashed by the crash of the Banco López, July, 1923. Orderly line at the doors of the bank; Arrival of trucks full of bank notes to pay clients; Uproar in front of the bank; Intervention of the police.* Cromos magazine, July, 1923.

In view of the different kinds of operational difficulties this initiative would bring and considerable doubts about its legality, on Wednesday July 18 it was decided that the first idea, which was Kemmerer's, was not feasible and that it would be wiser to open the Banco de la República on Monday July 23rd. Towards this end and taking advantage of the fact that Friday the 20th was a holiday, the government declared Thursday the 19th and Saturday the 21st to be holidays as well, which provided a four-day period in which to overcome the most pressing difficulties. Kemmerer's sense of humor is evident in the words of an essay recalling these events, when he wrote that it was a bit ironic for the government to declare these public holidays on the pretext of paying homage to the Congress of the Republic for its arduous task of issuing the laws which the Mission had proposed.

In those four days everyone got down to work. The deeds of the Banco de la República were drawn up; its statutes were drafted; the government subscribed all of the class A stocks; 5, 473 class B stocks were subscribed by the Banco de Bogotá, Banco de Colombia and Banco Central; the Board of Directors that would be in office until December 31, 1923 was designated; José Joaquín Pérez Salazar was named Governor and Gustavo Michelsen Secretary; and it was decided to organize emergency transport to deliver to the Bank the Gold Certificates held in the Casa de Moneda of Medellín, so that they could be immediately overprinted with the Bank's seal and put to circulate as provisional bank notes of the Banco de la República.

As might have been foreseen, during the week between Monday July 16th and Sunday July 22nd of 1923, there were intense debates within the Organizing Committee, because in addition to the complex operational problems they had to solve, some members were doubtful about the legality of some of the proposed solutions. One example will serve: on July 15th the government, with the intention of settling the liquidity crisis of the Banco López, decided to buy its headquarters for 750,000 *pesos* and use it as the seat of the Banco de la República. Years after, Kemmerer wrote of this initiative: "considering that the Organizing Committee was authorized by law to spend money for such purposes up to a limit of 20,000 *pesos*, an expenditure of 750,000 *pesos* on a building before creating a Board of Directors or giving a legal foundation to the Bank turned out to be a little ultra vires (beyond the legal powers) ... even when it might be necessary to interpret the law to the extreme of abusing it. This, at least, was the attitude of the government officials in charge of resolving the matter, who argued that a sum of

Above, *Stamp commemorating the 50th anniversay of the founding of the Banco de la República.*

750,000 *pesos* for the building of the Bank did not form part of the 20,000 *pesos* limit, which only was meant for the minor expenses of organization and not a capital investment of such a magnitude", (retranslated from the Spanish version of the original English text, Banco de la República, 1994, p. 124).

They also expressed doubts about the legality of using the Gold Certificates as bank notes of the Banco de la República and some members of the Organizing Committee warned about the legal penalties involved in placing into circulation a currency not authorized by the law.

But in the end the plan for opening on July 23, 1923 was accepted. That was the day on which the Banco de la República opened its doors, approving rediscounts for approximately 1,500,000 *pesos* for the Banco de Bogotá, the Banco Central and the Banco de Colombia, and disposed to change the *Cédulas de Tesorería,* the *Bonos del Tesoro* and the national bank notes representative of gold for the Bank's provisional bank notes, which tranquilized the markets, putting an end to the financial panic and stabilizing the exchange rate.

The rapid creation of the Banco de la República was welcomed, because it came into existence at the precise moment when it was needed and warded off a crisis that threatened to have devastating effects on the Colombian economy. Nevertheless, *El Tiempo* newspaper complained about the absence of representatives of the Liberal party on the first Board of Directors of the Bank and claimed that some of the businessmen who served on it were not representative of their economic sectors.

This last concern would give rise to the first reform in the norms for the Banco de la República, through law 17 of 1925, which established stricter requirements for the election of the representatives of the productive sectors and gave the government the right to veto the choice made by the banks when they did not observe the spirit of the law.

While the foundation and structuring of the Banco de la República was fundamental to stabilizing the money in circulation, as became evident in the financial crisis that coincided with its initiation, it was not sufficient to deal with all of the problems that beset that Colombian financial apparatus in 1922. These flaws manifested themselves in the existence of an inefficient banking system, since the banks' portfolio was not liquid enough to ensure a good functioning of financial intermediation, especially insofar as there was a frequent refinancing of credits. The system lacked precise regulations about the kinds of loans or investments that the banks could make, particularly those relating to the acquisition of stocks or risk investments in industrial or agricultural enterprises. In addition, the regulations on the capital needed to found a bank and its relation to the deposits gathered from the public were not appropriate and there was no adequate supervision of the banks by the authorities.

These flaws also required a profound legal reform and new kinds of institutions. This, precisely, was what came into being with the promulgation of law 45 of 1923 on banking institutions, which were defined as "any individual, corporation, society or establishment which habitually carries on the business of receiving funds for general deposit or makes advances in the form of loans, or effects discounts, or does any of these operations".

In addition to this definition, law 45 of 1923 includes other provisions having to do with the different kinds of banks and the divisions that might constitute them; the deposits they might receive; and their capital, earnings and minimum reserve requirements. It also established the characteristics, salaries, powers and duties of the *Superintendente Bancario* or Bank Superintendent, a post created by the law to oversee the Banco de la República and the private banks, and regulated such matters relating to commercial banks as the requirements for the founding partners, the number of directors, the minimum capital in relation to deposits, restrictions and limitations on their operations, and accounting norms. It further established the requirements banks had to meet in order to open fiduciary and savings branches; and finally, issued rules for mortgage banks and the mortgage branches of commercial banks.

With the establishment of these definitions and norms through law 45 of 1923, the banking system was now able to act as a financial intermediary and manage its system of payments much more efficiently than in the past.

For the first purpose, the banks would receive deposits in current account, savings deposits and term deposits that, in conjunction with their capital and excluding their reserve requirement, would permit them to make loans on the condition that such loans had a term of less than one year or exceptionally of two years. For the second, the transference of deposits in current account by means of checks in the customary way and the creation of a system of compensation gave greater security to transactions and reduced costs for the payment of goods and services and the honoring of contracts.

In this way the creation of the Banco de la República and the organization of the banking sector consolidated a new financial system that began its work by seeking the unification of the currency and laid the foundations for a rapid expansion of banking credit, as we shall see in the following section.

An interesting question from the historical point of view is: what were the reasons that allowed these institutional transformations to be carried out in 1923 and not, say, before that time? Some analysts think that, although some of the ideas behind the reforms had been mooted as far back as 1905, a period of time was needed for the appropriate conditions to develop in Colombia. For others, the change had to do with the special economic circumstances of the post-war period, especially the new desire of U.S. capital to penetrate the Latin American economy in general and that of Colombia in particular, which required a stable financial system that would guarantee such investors an orderly expansion of their interests.

Except for some fine points of academic reasoning, the two theses are not mutually exclusive, since it is evident that by the year 1923 the widening of mercantile activities in the Colombian economy and the increased interest in Colombia on the part of foreign capital merged in such a way that it finally became possible to establish a new financial structure that would respond to the growing demand for financial services.

The above-mentioned institutional change took place in a climate of relative political harmony. No political parties defended ultra-nationalistic economic ideas and the reforms received wide support from the Colombian capitalists who were interested in enlarging urban markets and understood that the emergence and consolidation of the financial system was indispensable for their aims.

Below, *Political cartoon. The Colombian people ask Pedro Nel Ospina (seated on the Banco de la República) to share, not accumulate, wealth.*

THE GOLD STANDARD AND DEBT PROSPERITY

Opposite page,
Pedro Nel Ospina. As well as promoting the foundation of the Banco de la República, his government realized such reforms as the creation of the Bank Superintendency and the Controller-General's office.

Below,
1 peso bank note. First edition of the Banco de la República, July 20, 1923, signed by José Joaquín Pérez, Governor, and Gustavo Michelsen, Secretary. The bills of this denomination circulated between 1923 and 1974.

In accordance with law 25 of 1923, the first years of the Banco de la República's operations took place within the framework of the theoretical principles of the gold standard, which gave central banks the responsibility for regulating money, credit and foreign exchange.

The regulation of money was supposed to ensure that the Banco de la República exercised, in fact as well as name, the monopoly over the issue of bank notes representative of gold that it had been granted by law. To regulate credit it was necessary that the Banco de la República carry out, in an effective way, its functions as the lender of last resort to the private banks, both with regard to the amount of money in circulation and the defense of its gold reserves. Its intervention in exchange rates was intended to keep the exchange rate stable and ensure the convertibility into gold of its bills.

To carry out these principles, the Banco de la República initially dedicated itself to unifying and strengthening the currency in circulation, as a necessary prerequisite for exercising its monopoly over emission; establishing operational norms for granting its loans and setting the interest rates which it would charge for them; and giving stability to international exchange, by defining the criteria for fixing the prices at which it would buy or sell bills of exchange on foreign banks.

Unifying and strengthening circulating money meant that the Bank had to withdraw from circulation the various currencies of different types that had circulated since 1923, so that only the Banco de la República bank note convertible into gold would have the role of money. Almost the whole of this task was done in a very short time, with notable benefits in terms of the transparency that now applied to the setting of prices, the absence of mistakes and the elimination of unwarranted advantage-taking in certain transactions. Above all, trustworthiness

Table 3

TYPES OF CURRENCY IN CIRCULATION IN JUNE OF THE YEARS* 1923 - 1933

Thousands of *pesos*

Type	1923	1924	1925	1926	1927	1928	1929	1930	1931	1932	1933
National Bank Notes	10.360	10.360	10.360	9.985	9.215	8.730	8.230	7.931	7.931	7.931	7.931
Silver Coins	9.779	9.780	9.778	9.778	9.778	9.778	9.778	9.778	9.551	9.551	6.611
Silver Certificates	-	-	-	-	-	-	-	-	-	-	4.940
Cupro-niquel Coins	2.000	2.000	2.006	2.000	2.000	2.000	2.000	2.000	2.000	2.000	2.000
Treasury Bills	3.214	999	242	86	43	32	28	26	25	26	24
Treasury Bonds	5.090	4.254	1.646	581	238	123	79	521	41	34	30
Bank Bonds	637	162	38	28	16	12	10	9	8	7	-
Mortage Certificates	4.096	3.163	1.938	906	285	52	32	25	22	19	-
Foreign Bank Notes	-	-	-	-	-	63	-	-	-	55	13
Bank notes of the Banco de la República	-	10.179	23.195	36.923	42.272	50.977	48.656	30.776	23.889	19.152	26.099
Total	35.176	40.897	49.203	60.287	63.847	71.767	68.813	51.066	43.522	38.733	47.635

*Include coins and bank notes in the vaults of the private banks and the vaults of the Banco de la república.
Source: *Primer informe del Gerente del Banco de la República a la Junta Directiva* ("First Report of the Governor of the Banco de la República to the Board of Directors") and Avella Gómez, Mauricio, op. cit., pages 389-390.

was given to the due compliance with contracts.

As may be seen in the figures in Table 3, by June, 1927 practically all of the *Cédulas de la Tesorería, Bonos del Tesoro* and *Cédulas Hipotecarias* had been withdrawn from circulation, thus leaving three kinds of currency in circulation: the bank notes of the Banco de la República, metal money and the national bank notes representative of gold issued in 1915.

From 1923 until 1931 the bank notes of the Banco de la República had the character of a fiduciary currency backed by gold, that is, the gold which the Bank kept in its vaults or in securities payable in gold, and convertibility between gold and bills was strictly maintained. The bills were printed and issued in denominations of one, two, five, ten, twenty, fifty, one hundred and five hundred *pesos*. These denominations dominated monetary circulation in the country until the second half of the twentieth century when, due to the inflationary process that began around 1973, they were replaced by higher denomination bills and coins, as shall be explained later on.

The amount of cupro-nickel and silver coins in circulation remained stationary between 1923 and 1930. Due to the fact that the government used the dividend paid to it by the Banco de la República to withdraw silver coins from circulation, their amount fell in 1931 and again in 1933, when bank notes representative of this metal were issued under the name of *Certificados de Plata* (Silver Certificates). The issuing of this currency was a response to the fall in the amount of money in circulation due to the world depression of the nineteen-thirties. It then became obvious that there was an excessive amount of metallic money in the hands of the public and the Banco de la República thus began to accumulate considerable amounts of silver coin in its vaults.

With the aim of returning these coins to the public, part of the stock of one *peso* bills was withdrawn from circulation and they were replaced with others of higher denomination. This decision increased the demand for silver coins and reduced the number held by the Bank, but it caused complaints among the public, which considered the change-over to be bothersome.

This situation led to the passing of law 82 of 1931, which authorized the Banco de la República to issue *Certificados de Plata*, with a 100% reserve requirement in silver. The issuing of these silver certificates in denominations of one and five *pesos* was fully accepted by the public, since by circulating indiscriminately with the Bank's gold-convertible bank notes they did away with the inconveniences that arose from the circulation of silver coins. Nevertheless, the Banco de la República, faithful to its commitment to unify the currency, showed some concern about the circulation of these certificates, insofar as they might serve as an encouragement to recur to emissions of silver that could lead to a de facto bimetallic system. This fear was not justified, since, after a slight rise in their circulation in the middle of the nineteen-forties, the silver certificates stopped circulating at the end of that decade: by the end of the nineteen-fifties only 122,000 *pesos* of them were registered in the balance of the Banco de la República.

The amount of national bank notes in circulation fell from 10,360,000 in June 1923 to 7,931,000 in June 1930, thanks to the fact that, semester after semester during this period, the government complied with the provisions of law 25 and used the dividends it received from the Bank to withdraw them from circulation. From 1931 onwards the Congress destined these dividends to other ends and the national bank notes representative of gold, placed into circulation to withdraw those that had been issued during the "War of the Thousand Days", only became partially amortized by the government in 1975.

Nevertheless, it is worth mentioning the following about the national bank notes. By around 1928 many of them were in a bad physical state, so in February of that year the government placed an order with the American Bank Note company for the fabrication and printing of 2 million bank notes to replace the deteriorated ones: 1.6 million 5 *pesos* notes (series F) and 400,000 10 *pesos* notes (series D). This contract roused fears of an unwarranted emission by the government and led to the intervention of the Council of State (*Consejo de Estado*, a Colombian administrative court), which wound up approving the measure, after receiving reassurances that the government would only issue these bills to re-

Below,
Political cartoon of the Banco de la República devouring the small banks. The private banks feared that the Banco de la República would dedicate itself to private credit, thus harming their business.

Right,
Political cartoon of Esteban Jaramillo reduced to poverty. In Fantoches, *1930. Finance Minister on four occasions between 1918 and 1934, Esteban Jaramillo was the most important financial expert in Colombia during the boom of the 1920's and the crisis of the 1930's.*

place the deteriorated ones. Towards this end it was decided that the bills would have the same seals and printing date as those that were originally produced through the *Junta de Conversión* in 1915.

As a result of this procedure, from 1929 onwards the national bank notes printed in that year circulated with the date of July 20, 1915. In addition, in 1938, by means of law 33, the government was authorized to order an edition of national bank notes with denominations of 5 *pesos* and 10 *pesos*, which were intended to replace those printed in 1928, a measure which was successfully carried out, so that by the end of the nineteen-forties only 369,075 *pesos* of the bills printed in 1928 still circulated. Finally decree 122 of 1948 ordered an edition of national bank notes of a half *peso* denomination to replace those of 5 *pesos* and 10 *pesos* which had been in circulation since 1938. These are the bank notes which are known to collectors as *"Lleritas"*, of which a last printing was made in 1953: they were jokingly named after former Finance Minister and future President Carlos Lleras Restrepo, who was short in stature. With the passage of time the Banco de la República withdrew these half *peso* bills from circulation and kept them in its vaults until 1975, when the government, with the dividends it received from the Banco de la República in that year, amortized 6,000,000 *pesos* of the 7,931,000 *pesos* that had been in circulation since 1930.

In addition to unifying and strengthening the currency, the Banco de la República dedicated its efforts to the establishment of clear operational rules on the expansion and contraction of circulating money, with the aim of giving it more elasticity, as the words of the first report of the Governor to the Board of Directors explain: "so that there may be at any moment a sufficient amount of money in circulation, without the occurrence of surpluses that may produce harmful inflations, nor excessive contractions that may lead to disastrous crises. Thus, it is necessary to have a regulatory authority for monetary circulation which, without endangering in any way the stability of the value of money, gives signals to the market about changes in the amount of money that transactions require and, when necessary, retires surplus amounts from the market". (Salazar, 1924, p. 18).

In other words, through the exercise of its rediscount policy the Banco de la República could stand up to the expansion or reduction of the demand for credit and for money in accordance with the volume of business transactions, as became evident on the occasion of the very long drought of 1926, which delayed the timely amortization of loans owed to the commercial banks, obliging these credit institutions to recur to the Banco de la República for rediscount resources.

To understand the Bank's role in stabilizing the exchange rate it is necessary to point out that, at the time it was founded, goods which were exported or imported were paid for with bills of exchange or cable orders on foreign banks.

In theory an excess of bills of exchange on foreign banks meant that the country had a favorable trade balance and such a surplus thus tended to produce a revaluation in the exchange rate. The opposite situation arose when these bills were in

Below, *One and two pesos bank notes of the Banco de la República. The bills of the latter denomination circulated between 1923 and 1977.*

short supply. But in the case of Colombia there was the additional factor of seasonal variations in the production and export of coffee, which caused fluctuations in the exchange rate. To control these fluctuations in the value of the bills of exchange, the Banco de la República was given the power to buy or sell them according to changes in the exchange rate.

To comply with this duty, the Banco de la República initially set the sale price of such bank drafts at the export price of gold, which was 1.0435 *pesos* per dollar, a price which was based on the intrinsic parity between the Colombian *peso* and the U.S. dollar (1.0275 *pesos* per dollar), plus the cost of shipping gold to New York, which was 1.6 *centavos* per dollar. The purchase price was fixed at the import price, that is, 1.0115 *pesos* per dollar, that is, the same intrinsic parity less the cost of importing gold. If the price of the dollar rose above the export price of gold, the Banco de la República sold bills of exchange or drafts on foreign banks, and if it fell below the import price it bought them. At that time there operated an exchange band whose width was the equiva-

lent of twice the cost of exporting or importing gold.

In accordance with these principles, in 1923 the Bank opened sales at 1.045 *pesos* per dollar, lowering the existing quotation, which was then 1.0615 *pesos* per dollar. Between June, 1924 and June, 1925 the Bank acted as a seller in the market for bills of exchange, since the price hovered round the export price for gold. Between July, 1925 and June, 1926, on the other hand, it bought drafts, since the price of the dollar was near the import price of gold.

After 1927 the width of the exchange band was brought into question because importers thought the sale price fixed by the Banco de la República was too high and exporters thought the purchase price was too low. This led the bank to set the sale price at 1.0275 *pesos* per dollar, equivalent to the intrinsic parity, and the purchase price between 1.015 and 1.0175 *pesos*.

In practice, the Banco de la República paid for the cost of shipping gold abroad or part of the cost of bringing gold to the country out of its earnings, so that it could help importers when it sold bills of exchange and exporters when it bought them. Within these narrower limits, the exchange rate was kept stable between 1927 and 1932, which led, in practice, to a revaluation of the real exchange rate, given that inflation was higher in Colombia in this period than in the countries it traded with.

As for the interest rate, taking into account the excess demand for its resources deriving from the liquidity crisis that coincided with its founding, the Banco de la República set the annual rediscount rate at 12%, which it then successively reduced to 10%, 9% and 7%. The latter rate was unmodified between May, 1924 and March, 1929. This significant early reduction of the rediscount rate was judged to be "artificial" by the then Governor of the Banco de la República, Felix Salazar, who held this office from January, 1924 until 1927.

The fall in the rediscount rate of the Bank was reflected in the interest rates charged by the commercial banks, though not in the expected proportion, because they continued to attract funds from the general public at a high interest rate and because the public sector placed considerable amounts of securities on the market, equivalent to nearly 40% of the credit managed by the private banks, with an annual interest rate of between 10-12%.

This private bank credit, which had only amounted to 30.5 million *pesos* in 1923, reached a peak of 95.4 million *pesos* in 1928, with an average annual growth rate over these five years of 21%. There is no doubt that this expansion was helped by the Banco de la República: by normalizing discount and rediscount operations, lowering bank costs, and centralizing the reserves of the banks, the Bank fostered the creation of

Below,
Bill of 5 pesos, *issue of 1923.*
The bills of this denomination circulated between 1923 and 1981.

Right,
10 pesos bill, issue of 1927, 10 pesos bill, issue of 1923. The bills of this denomination circulated between 1923 and 1981.

an interbank market and above all, made its policies a central guideline for the other banks.

In fact, by June 30, 1927 of the 26 banks that existed in the country, 23, which held more than 98% of the system's capital and reserves, were stockholders of the Banco de la República. The resources to fund this rapid growth of banking credit came from increases in current accounts, which grew from 14.2 million *pesos* in 1923 to 39.4 million *pesos* in 1929, and from the increase in the Banco de la República's credit, whose balance of discounts in 1923 was 2,516,000, a sum that rose to 18,134,000 *pesos* by the end of 1929.

This rapid expansion of banking credit coincided with the economic boom that took place between 1925 and 1929, which saw an average annual rise of Gross National Product per inhabitant of 5.2% during this period, led to a notable rise in the flow of foreign trade, provoked a rapid increase in public spending and produced a rise in the general level of prices.

Within the increase of foreign trade, imports more than doubled between 1923 and 1929, half of them going on consumer goods and the other half on raw materials and capital goods. Imports of consumer goods included heavy purchases of textiles and food, mostly in order to counteract the inflationary pressures of this period. Imports of raw materials went mainly for the expansion of the textile sector and the metallurgical industry, while those of capital goods had to do with the expansion of the transportation infrastructure.

The remarkable growth in the country's importing capacity was possible thanks to the growth of exports and of capital flows deriving from the indemnity for the loss of Panama and foreign loans to both the public and private sectors.

Right,
Bills of 20 and 50 pesos. The bills of the first denomination circulated between 1923 and 1983 and those of the second between 1923 and 1986.

Exports, which had an annual average of a bit more than 44 million dollars in the period 1915-1919, rose to nearly 64 million dollars annually between 1922-1924 and reached an average figure of 112 million dollars annually between 1925-1929. This very rapid expansion was due to increases in the volume of coffee that was exported and rises in the international price of the bean. As a result of the increased amount of exports, Colombia, which had been responsible for 3.5% of world coffee production in 1915, exported a little more than 11% of the world total by 1930. International prices of coffee, for their part, rose from 15.4 U.S. cents per pound in 1922 to 26.6 cents by 1928. In addition there was a rapid increase in the total amount of exports.

To the 25 million dollars which the country received as an indemnity for the Panama Canal, which was paid in annual installments of 5 million dollars between 1922-1926, was added a significant flow of capital to Colombia, as a consequence of a growing amount of foreign loans, the granting of which was facilitated by, among other reasons, the confidence shown by foreign lenders in the financial reforms carried out in 1923. Thus, the foreign debt of the country, which had been 24 million dollars in 1923, rose to 203.1 million dollars in 1928: the money went to the banking system and to the national, departmental and municipal governments.

This rapid indebtedness led to criticism by the opponents of the Conservative government in power, who were headed by Alfonso López Pumarejo and began to speak of a debt prosperity and point to the harmful effects of this unchecked borrowing in the form of inflation and the squandering of public funds.

Below, *The immobility of the Abadía administration, captured in this political cartoon by Rendón.*

Public spending rose from 38.9 million *pesos* in 1923 to 115 million *pesos* in 1928 and was financed both by foreign debt and an increase in public revenues.

To resume, greater coffee earnings within the context of a general export boom, added to the expansion of public spending and an increase in circulating money and banking credit, led to increases in demand that were reflected in the overall level of prices.

As was to be expected, this inflation gave rise to polemics about the policy followed by the Banco de la República and thus about the extent of its responsibility for the management of monetary policy. The upholders of the theory that the inflation had a monetary origin pointed to the passive role of the Bank and particularly, to the fact that the rediscount rate had remained unchanged between 1924 and 1929, when, in accordance with economic theory, this was the only instrument that the Bank wielded to check the creation of money which had led to an increase in international reserves: they rose from 7.5 million dollars at the end of 1923 to 64.7 million dollars by the end of 1928, as a consequence of the increased flow of foreign resources we have just referred to.

Those who did not share the monetary explanation of the inflationary process attributed the phenomenon to the fact that many people in rural areas were being employed in government public works programs, which had a negative effect on the supply of food and increased the cost of agricultural manpower.

From this brief account we may conclude that during the boom period of the nineteen-twenties the Banco de la República essentially operated in accordance with the rules established as its founding principles, in that it upheld the free convertibility of its bills into gold, maintained a stable exchange rate between the *peso* and the dollar based on the levels of parity, followed a policy of granting credit to the government within the restrictions of its original statutes and, for reasons of prudence, refused to grant credit to private individuals. However, it was not so successful in contracting the money in circulation when inflationary pressures arose, partly because the rules of the gold standard limited its powers in this field.

"GULLIVER SEGUIA DURMIENDO"

THE WORLD ECONOMIC CRISIS AND MONETARY ORTHODOXY

Opposite page,
Cover of the book Colombia Cafetera *("Coffee-growing Colombia") by Diego Monsalve, 1925. After the 1920's the international price of coffee and the earnings from coffee exports played a big role in the macroeconomic policies of Colombia.*

Right,
Line of unemployed people during the Great Depression of 1930, which had a devastating effect throughout the world, including Colombia.

The economic boom that marked most of the nineteen-twenties, which was described in general terms in the previous sections, began to slow down in the second half of 1928, when a fall in international coffee prices coincided with a paralysis in the international flow of capitals.

The effect of the second change is seen when we compare the nearly 70 million dollars that were lent to the country in the first half of 1928 with the 15.5 millions that entered Colombia between the second half of 1928 and the whole of 1929. According to José Antonio Ocampo and Santiago Montenegro, this sharp fall was due to the fact that "three separate factors merged to freeze foreign credit in the second half of 1928: the restrictive monetary policy that was adopted by the United States from July onwards, the firm attitude of the Colombian government towards foreign oil interests and growing doubts abroad about the fiscal situation of the country and the wisdom of the policy of public works". (Ocampo and Montenegro,1982, p. 42).

Everything seems to indicate that the last two factors were closely linked. In fact, in an attempt to put a brake on the accelerating foreign debt of the departments and municipalities the legislature passed law 6 of 1928, which subjected this indebtedness to the control of the President of Colombia and his Council of Ministers. This measure was used by the U.S. Commerce Department as a justification for circulating a warning about the possible risks involved in lending more money to Colombia.

Despite the government's attempts to rebut the arguments in the U.S. letter, which was relatively easy taking into account the relatively small importance which the servicing of the foreign debt had in terms of the national government's current income, the circular had a strong effect on the availability of foreign credit for Colombia, because at bottom it was not the country's financial situation that was under discussion; instead, it was a means of exerting pressure in favor of the U.S. oil companies which had openly questioned Colombia's policy in that field.

The closing off of foreign credit hit the mortgage banks particularly hard, because, since 1927, more than 60% of the mortgage certificates which they had issued had been placed in foreign markets. In addition, it should be pointed out that the short-term commercial credit granted by foreign banks to their Colombian branches to finance foreign trade operations practically disappeared during the crisis. Writing about this in the ninth annual report to the Board of Directors (for the financial year running from July 1, 1931 to June 30, 1932) the Governor of the Banco de la República, Julio Caro, who had been appointed in 1927 and held the post for 20 years, noted: "the foreign banks, especially the American ones, sent cables cancelling the credits

Right,
Police attacking a worker during a demonstration by car workers in Detroit, December, 1931.

which they had opened to Colombian institutions, some of them going to the incredible extreme of protesting about a bill of exchange from a respectable Colombian bank issued and drawn on an existing credit. It was a complete panic...." (Caro, 1932, p. 26).

The shutting off of foreign credit was aggravated, in the second half of 1928, by a fall in the international price of coffee, a phenomenon that became even more acute in 1929 because of the scarcity of banking finance caused by the world crisis, an exceptionally abundant harvest in Brazil and the inability of the Brazilian government to carry out a policy of warehousing surplus coffee stocks.

Due to the fall in coffee prices and the freeze in foreign credit, as well as the general world crisis that lowered prices for the rest of export goods, Colombia's import capacity, which had shown an average annual figure of 132.7 million dollars for the 1925-1929 period, fell to an average annual of 45.3 million dollars between 1930 and 1934.

Under the monetary scheme in effect at that time, such a contraction in the inflow of foreign resources had, of necessity, to be accompanied by a fall in international reserves, a contraction in the money supply and a decline in other monetary indicators. That this, in fact, was what happened is shown by the figures in Table 4.

This fall was especially severe in the years 1930 and 1931 and lasted until 1932 in the case of the international reserves and until 1934 in the case of the banking portfolio. The latter had to do with the restrictive monetary policy followed by the Banco de la República at the beginning of the crisis and the financial system's unwillingness to lend money - a response to the critical situation debtors were going through because of the rise in the real interest rate and the fall in the value of their collaterals as a consequence of the fall in the general price level.

Beyond this, the reduced capacity to import had a negative repercussion on customs revenues and in general on the fiscal resources of the government, so that by the end of 1930, that is, four months after the government of Enrique Olaya Herrera (1930-1934) had taken office, the fiscal deficit rose to 30,627,000 *pesos*,

Table 4

	MAIN MONETARY INDICATORS DURING THE RECESSION (Millions of pesos)								
Junio de cada año									
Year	Deposits in Current Account	Cash	Means of Payment	Monetary Base	Bank Reserves	Money Multiplier	Total Deposits	International Reserves (US$)	Bank* Portfolio
1927	34,2	56,3	9,05	68,6	12,3	1,32	61,7	42,0	67,3
1928	39,8	64,1	103,9	78,6	14,5	1,32	77,1	62,0	95,4
1929	36,0	62,2	98,2	76,1	13,9	1,29	80,4	55,0	83,5
1930	23,6	46,1	69,8	56,1	10,0	1,24	60,0	31,0	74,6
1931	20,2	38,1	59,1	48,6	9,7	1,22	57,7	21,0	55,3
1932	24,8	35,4	60,2	48,9	13,6	1,23	59,8	16,0	48,1
1933	30,3	44,0	74,3	59,9	15,9	1,24	64,2	18,0	44,1

* Amount at end of each year.
Source: the figures on total deposits are taken from Avella Gómez Mauricio, op. cit,. Page 304.

which was equivalent to 4.4% of the Gross Domestic Product. The logical consequence of this fiscal imbalance was the suspension of the program of public works, which had an adverse effect on the level of employment.

In this way the fall in private demand –caused among other factors by the decline in the price of coffee, which fell from around 27 U.S. cents per pound in 1928 to 11 cents per pound in 1932– joined with a fall in public spending, which caused a slowing down in agregate demand and economic growth. This led, in turn, to an open recession and falls in the general price level of around 17% annually for each of the years between 1929-1932.

This distressing situation repeated itself in almost all of the economies in the world, especially in the other countries of Latin America, which shared with Colombia the twin condition of having rapidly indebted themselves abroad before the crisis and of being exporters of agricultural goods and raw materials whose prices sharply fell in international markets.

Right, *Stamp depicting the Pedro A. López building. Vignette from a 5 pesos bill of 1953.*

Below, *Political cartoon about President Abadía's way of handling the economic crisis of the late 1920's.*

However, in contrast with many other Latin American countries where the economic crisis coincided with a political one, the recession took place in Colombia at a moment when, for the first time in half a century, the opposition forces represented by the Liberal party took over the presidency after an electoral campaign whose legitimacy was never in doubt.

EL RETRATO AL PRESIDENTE

El pintor López Mezquita — Suplico a su excelencia un momento de quietud.
Abadía — Pierda cuidado, maestro. Yo no me muevo nunca.

Above,
Three stamps on "Natural Treasures", printed in 1932: coffee, cattle and bananas.

Below,
On the occasion of the economic crisis of the 1930's, a new mission of foreign experts headed by Kemmerer visited the country, but they had a much less decisive influence on economic policy than in 1923.

Despite this political change, during its first months in office the administration of President Olaya Herrera managed the crisis with the same monetary orthodoxy based on the gold standard that had been employed before, because, among other reasons, the new president believed that if Colombia duly paid its foreign debt it would facilitate a new inflow of international capital, which would make it feasible to maintain the gold standard.

According to the theories that governed the monetary policy prevailing at that time, among the fruits of which were the institutions created by Kemmerer in 1923, the rediscount rate of the Banco de la República had to be raised, because, in the face of the imbalance in the foreign accounts this rise would accelerate the fall in the amount of money in circulation and produce a decline in internal prices, which would, in turn, make exports more competitive and imports more dear, thus restoring a favorable balance of payments and strengthening incomes and employment.

It was precisely these principles which guided the policy initially followed by the Banco de la República in dealing with the first symptoms of the crisis. In fact, in March, 1929, under the government of Miguel Abadía Méndez (1926-1930), the rediscount rate had been raised to 8% annually after having remained fixed at 7% annually since the beginning of 1924, as has already been noted.

The first rise in the rediscount rate produced the expected results, in the sense that during the following months the volume of banking rediscounts fell and gold reserves rose in relation to the bank notes and other monetary liabilities of the Banco de la República. This led to a reduction of the rediscount rate to 7% annually in July, 1929. The optimism on which this latter decision was based vanished very soon, however. In October, 1929, the rediscount rate once more rose to 8% annually and in November to 9% annually. It is worth noting that on the occasion of the decision in October, 1929 to raise the rediscount rate, an exception was made for the loans that had agricultural products as collateral and those which would be made to the government, and that the same thing happened when the rediscount rates were raised again in November, 1929, when a 1% differential was maintained between the common rediscount rate and that for preferential operations.

Thus was born the idea of preferential credit and the rediscount rate began to lose its condition of being an instrument used to guide monetary policy and was

Right, *President Enrique Olaya Herrera (1930-1934). To begin with, Olaya tried to maintain the gold standard, but international developments and the strong internal recession forced him to abandon monetary orthodoxy and undertake a vigorous anti-cyclical policy. Esteban Jaramillo at the wedding of his son Daniel, accompanied by Enrique Olaya Herrera and Miguel Abadía Méndez.*

employed to assign certain credits in a preferential way.

Contrary to what might have been expected under orthodox economic theory, the October and November, 1929 rises in the rediscount rate did not dissuade the banks from continuing to increase their demand for resources from the Banco de la República. On the contrary, during those months the rediscounts continued to grow until they reached the highest levels ever known in the history of the Banco de la República.

This situation, the policy of central banks in other countries and the repeated demands from representatives of different economic sectors for a reduction in interest rates led to a gradual abandonment of the use of the interest rate as the central instrument of monetary policy. In May, 1930 the rediscount rate was once more fixed at 8% for non-preferential credit and 7% for preferential credit and in September of the same year it was lowered by 1% for both types of credit.

Thus the rate of non-preferential interests returned to the level it had shown before the crisis. On this point, the Governor of the Banco de la República noted, in his report to the Board of Directors on the financial year from July 1, 1930 to June 30, 1931, that this policy had been adopted by taking into account "the considerable fall seen in the discount rates in the principal monetary markets of the world", (Caro, 1931, p. 31); it was also meant to show the Board of Directors' confidence in the financial policy of the new government. Nevertheless, it did not satisfy the different national economic sectors, which thought that further reductions were desirable.

These claims found an expression in the Congress, which, in one of the articles of law 82 of 1931, ordered the government "to obtain" further reductions. This order led Caro, the Governor of the Bank, to reject the idea in the following terms: "It is not possible to set the discount rates of a central bank through legislative orders. They depend on multiple and variable factors and considerations which the board of directors of the institution have to constantly study in order to guide their decisions in such matters without being upset by personal or political motives. Institutions of this kind cannot be managed by the opinions of the public, which generally has a very imperfect idea of their aims and functions and these institutions often have to go completely against what public opinion asks for, if they want to follow a wise policy in credit matters". (Caro, 1931, p. 14).

Despite the resistance of the Banco de la República, the rediscount rate continued to lose importance as an instrument of monetary management, since it fell to a 4% annual rate in 1934 and stayed fixed at that level during the following years, independent of the monetary, exchange or credit situations which faced the authorities from then onwards.

The measures adopted in the field of exchange policy also followed the postulates of the gold standard at the beginning of the crisis. In fact, up to May, 1929, the exchange rate fluctuated between the narrow limits fixed since 1927, that is a 1.0275 *pesos* per dollar sale price and a 1.0150 *pesos* per dollar buy price. In May, 1929 the first modification of the exchange rate was carried out, due to the fact that the Banco de la República, pressured by the high demand for bills of exchange, set the sale price for these bills at 1.0351 *pesos* per dollar. This rate was conserved until the beginning of 1931, when it was raised to 1.05 *pesos* per dollar, which remained in force until the beginning of 1932, as we shall explain in the following section.

To begin with, the government of Enrique Olaya Herrera decided that its fiscal policy would continue to uphold the principle of making timely payments of the service on the foreign debt. But it was difficult to uphold this commitment: the possibility of obtaining new or even re-negotiating existing debts of this kind was closed, customs revenues and the general sources of government income were depleted, the possibility of internal financing with the private sector was reduced to a minimum and the credit which the Banco de la República could grant to the government was kept by law within very strict limits. For the government there was no choice but to reduce its spending, which meant a reduction in the salaries of public officials and the paralysis of government investment, especially in public works programs. The austerity forced on public spending was, for the rest, in accordance with the principles of the gold standard, since, at a time when the Banco de la República had lost international reserves and the reserve ratio of its bank notes had fallen, it was impossible for it to issue money to finance public spending.

To resume, we might say that during the three-year period between the beginning of 1929 and the end of 1931, the fight against the economic recession was carried out in accordance with the principles and rules set forth by the orthodox view of economics that had governed the work of Kemmerer in 1923. But this orthodoxy was unable to reactivate the economy and its principles were gradually abandoned.

Below, *Export route of coffee, in the book* Colombia Cafetera *by Diego Monsalve, 1925.*

Opposite page, *"Producción", ilustración en el libro* Colombia Cafetera *de Diego Monsalve, 1925.*

THE ANTI-CYCLICAL POLICY

Opposite page, *The Colombian government appealed to the entire population for financial support for the War with Peru, as this poster shows. "National Defense Loan", publicity poster by Scandroglio.*

Right, *Coins of I, II and V* centavos *issued by the General Treasury of the Nation. Because it was impossible to import nickel during the Second World War, these coins were minted in nearly pure copper from the middle of the 1940's.*

The internal problems of the Colombian economy and the difficult international situation led, at the end of 1931, to a revision of the ideas that had guided economic policy in the country since the middle of 1923.

On the international front, the most outstanding event was the British government's decision to abandon the gold standard for the pound sterling in September, 1931. This measure, which affected the foreign exchange regime throughout the world, did not leave Colombia untouched: it led to a new fall in the country's already depleted international reserves, due to the panic that broke out among the bearers of the bank notes of the Banco de la República and depositors of all banks, who rushed to exchange these assets for gold.

On the internal front, pressure from different economic and political sectors, among them a Congressional study group, strengthened the movement that called for a less restrictive monetary policy.

Abandoning orthodoxy was not an easy task, since, as Mauricio Avella has correctly pointed out, "under the gold standard, the country had enjoyed an unprecedented period of booming commercial operations, monetary purity, an enlargement of credit resources and the building of infrastructure works. Given these conditions, to call for the dismounting of the prevailing monetary system might, in the best of cases, be regarded as eccentric". (Avella Gómez 1987, p. 210).

Avella's analysis reflects the concerns felt at that time by the President of Colombia, the Minister of Finance Esteban Jaramillo (who held the post for the fourth time between 1931 and 1934) and diverse representatives of the productive sectors. All of these political and economic forces profoundly feared the abandonment of free convertibility, remembering that this was the policy which had led to the indiscriminate emissions, without solid financial backing, which had taken place at the end of the nineteenth century and the beginning of the twentieth century. It was these scruples which were behind the consensus of opinion which believed that, while greater flexibility had to be given to the monetary system, it should not be completely dismantled. This is why many of the decisions taken in this period were justified by those who made them on the grounds that they were only temporary measures.

Faced by the need to deal with the new exchange regime of England, political opposition at home and a fall in the reserve ratio of bank notes, the government and the Board of Directors of the Banco de la República implemented two measures that marked a radical change in the course of economic policy. The first was the establishment of exchange and export controls and the second the issuing of norms that modified law 25 of 1923.

To give more flexibility to the management of the exchange rate, the Congress passed law 89 of September, 1931 and law 119 of November, 1931, which gave the executive branch wide powers to deal with the crisis. The powers were further developed through a government decree, no. 1683 of 1931, which suspended free trade in gold and established control over exchanges, which was to be initially handled by an autonomous board made up of the Bank Superintendent and two officials, one named by the President of Colombia and the other by the Board of Directors of the Central Bank.

A few days later the control of exchanges and exports was handed over to an office of the Banco de la República, which was to be advised by a committee whose members would be named by the Bank Superinten-

Above,
Enrique Olaya Herrera walking to the Capitol on the day of his inauguration. In the photo, from left to right: Jaime Jaramillo Arango and his wife, Alfonso López P., Alberto Pumarejo, María Londoño de Olaya, Alfonso Araujo, the new President, Francisco J. Chaux, Esteban Jaramillo and Eduardo Santos.

dent, the national government and the Bank, respectively.

Although these decisions were welcomed, it must be pointed out that exchange and export control was considered to be a temporary measure, as is made clear in the report of the Governor of the Banco de la República to the Board of Directors on the financial year from July 1, 1931 to June 30, 1932. In this report we read that, "while these measures of control have served to relieve the individual position of the more than thirty nations of Europe, the Americas and Asia which have had to recur to them because of the distressing period we are going through, they aggravate the general situation of the world, because of the checks and restrictions they place on international trade: for this reason they should not be maintained for a time longer than that which is absolutely demanded by the unavoidable necessities of each country". (Caro, 1932, p. 27). Despite this warning, the Office of Exchanges and Exports Control became a permanent institution in Colombia until it was finally disbanded sixty years later.

The functions of the Office of Exchanges and Exports Control included restricting or prohibiting the trade of bills of exchange in foreign currency, as well as the purchase and sale of foreign currency and gold. It was also in charge of granting permission, prior to the transaction itself, for carrying out international exchange operations that were destined for economically essential aims, especially the payment of imports and the service of the foreign debt. International exchange operations that did not correspond to the necessary movement of economic and financial activities were prohibited.

By assuming, in this way, a monopoly over operations for the purchase and sale of international exchanges, within what came to be called a "controlled" gold standard, the Banco de la República obtained more freedom in setting the nominal exchange rate.

Within the limits of this control, and still without renouncing the theory on setting the exchange rate, the authorities, as was pointed out before, devaluated this rate on January 12, 1932, upon establishing the sale price of the dollar as 1.05 *pesos*, a value which corresponded to the maximum intrinsic export

Below, *Cartoon about the imposition of exchange controls in 1931. Political cartoon by Rendón.*

price of gold. This devaluation did not satisfy the coffee-growers, who believed that exchange control was contrary to their interests and wanted exchange freedom.

Faced by this opposition, the government and the Banco de la República decided to award the coffee-growers an exchange rate premium of 10%, to be paid for a period of one year starting in March, 1932. This money was financed with resources of the national budget, by means of the emission of a government bond with a 6% annual interest that could be acquired by the Banco de la República through rediscounts.

This was a triple betrayal of the prevailing exchange, monetary and credit orthodoxy. In the first place, it established a differential exchange rate for the coffee-growers. In the second, it indirectly allowed the government to increase its borrowing from the Banco de la República by giving liquidity to these securities. And finally, for the first time in Colombia it established a forced investment because saving banks were obliged to use part of their deposits to buy the bonds which financed the coffee exchange rate premium.

In 1933, when the term of this de facto coffee subsidy had elapsed and in view of its high fiscal cost, the Banco de la República once again devalued the nominal exchange rate by fixing 1.16 *pesos* per dollar as the sale price and 1.13 *pesos* per dollar as the buy price for the dollar. An exception was made for the government, to whom the Bank would sell dollars at 1.05 *pesos*. With this decision, the fiscal cost of the exchange rate premium for coffee was eliminated, since from then on it would not be the Treasury who would pay the higher exchange rate but the importers and, above all, the consumers. Beyond this, the intrinsic parity between the dollar and the *peso* was abandoned as the main criterion for setting the exchange rate.

The trend towards devaluation was accentuated after the United States went off the gold standard in March, 1933. As a consequence, an excess demand for foreign currency was created, which pushed the nominal exchange rate above 1.16 *pesos* per dollar. The excess demand was evidenced by progressive delays in granting exchange licenses at the Office of Exchanges and Exports Control, which, together with pressures from the coffee-exporters, led to a new devaluation in September, 1933, when the buy price was set at 1.23 *pesos* per dollar and the sale price at 1.26 *pesos* per dollar.

Despite opposition from the importers, from then on a "semi-free" exchange system came into effect, which consisted of the right given to exporters to negotiate 85% of their foreign earnings on the stock exchange; the Banco de la República exchanged these earnings for Exchange Certificates, while the remaining 15% continued to be bought at 1.13 *pesos* per dollar. In this way the Bank was able to attend to the government's demand for foreign currency at this preferential rate without detriment to its own earnings and without producing harmful fiscal effects.

The "semi-free exchange" policy not only referred to the fact that part of the foreign currency earnings was bought at a fixed rate, but also to the situation of the importers, who could not freely dispose of the exchange certificates they purchased on the stock exchange since they had to use them for the purposes established by the Office of Exchanges and Exports Control. The exchange differential on the 15% of foreign earnings was known as the coffee industry differential (*diferencial cafetero*) and was

Sálvese quien pueda

the nucleus of the tax on coffee exports established in 1935.

Once this semi-free exchange system was decreed, the exchange rate of the certificates rose to 1.49 *pesos* per dollar at the beginning of 1934 and then to 1.75 *pesos* per dollar at the middle of that year. This price was maintained until 1948, as can be seen in Chart 1, and was used as the reference point for the devaluation of the *peso* against the dollar and against gold in 1938.

Right, *Stamp commemorating the 75th anniversary of the founding of the Colombian Society of Farmers. From the beginning of the 1930's, agricultural credit was given preferential treatment in the legislation governing the rediscount policy of the Banco de la República.*

This gold reference only had an accounting purpose, since, as José Antonio Ocampo and Santiago Montenegro point out, from April, 1933 onwards the Banco de la República began to stabilize the exchange rate with relation to the dollar, not gold.

Despite the internal inflation that arose after 1934, the nominal devaluation led to an improvement in the real exchange rate, which helped to neutralize the fall in the international prices of export goods and therefore, had a beneficial effect on economic recovery.

This was the same aim behind the increase of customs protection and the selective use of exchange controls, from 1934 onwards, which were intended to put up barriers against imports coming from countries which had restricted trade with Colombia or those goods which were imported from countries with which Colombia had an unfavorable trade balance.

As we have mentioned, exchange control and the overall policy of foreign trade was complemented with the passing of laws 73 and 82 of 1932, which introduced substantial reforms in the norms on the Banco de la República. Through these reforms, the composition of its Board of Directors was changed, the nature of its bank notes was modified, the credit that was potentially available to the government was enlarged, the minimum reserve requirement in gold for bills was reduced and the Bank was given more freedom over the way of maintaining and managing international reserves.

The number of directors who would serve on the Board of Directors of the Banco de la República was increased. To the ten who formerly sat on it were added one chosen by the National Federation of Coffee-Growers and another jointly elected by the Chambers of Commerce and the (Sociedad de Agricultores) Farmers Society. It was further established that the minister of Finance would be, in his own right, a member of the Board, as had in fact happened since 1923.

The first of these provisions was intended to strengthen the reform contained in law 17 of 1925, in the sense of giving the productive sectors the freedom to choose their own representatives on the Board of Directors of the Bank, instead of the original mechanism of 1923, which left this power to the shareholder banks, whether Colombian or foreign. The second was simply a legal

Chart 1

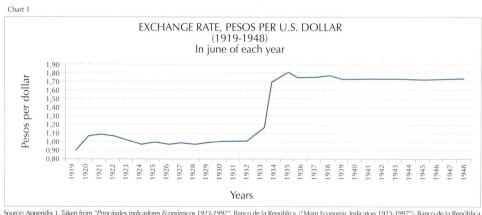

Source: Appendix 1. Taken from *"Principales indicadores Económicos 1923-1997"*. Banco de la República. ("Main Economic Indicators 1923-1997"). Banco de la República

Right,
National Defense Bond, issued November 1, 1932 and signed by Esteban Jaramillo, Finance Minister of Enrique Olaya Herrera.

recognition of the fact that, since 1923, the government had always included the minister of Finance among the three Directors it named.

The enlargement of the Board was not received with entire satisfaction by the Banco de la República and so, in 1933, the governing body of the institution was reduced to nine members, three to be named by the government, including the minister of Finance by right, two by the Colombian banks, one by the foreign banks, one by the private stockholders, one by the Coffee-Growers Federation and one by joint decision of the Chambers of Commerce and the 9Sociedad de Agricultores) Farmers Society.

The ratification of the direct naming of representatives by the economic sectors; the elimination of the condition that the bankers had to choose, as part of their representation, businessmen, farmers or professionals; and the permanent and institutional presence of the minister of Finance gave greater transparency to the membership of the Board of Directors of the Banco de la República. It expressly recognized the importance of the participation of the minister of Finance and the natural right of certain sectors of power to elect their own representatives.

The change in the nature of the bank notes of the Banco de la República meant that they were no longer representative of and convertible into a given amount of gold but became the national money, with an unlimited power to settle debts and as such, exercising the function of a legal means of payment.

The minimum gold reserve for the bank notes and other monetary liabilities of the Banco de la República was reduced from

Right,
Publicity for the subscription of bonds for the patriotic loan. Design by López, 1932.

Below,
Fighting in the region of Puerto Ospina, upper Putumayo. The Colombian army received support from German war veterans.

60% to 50% and the Bank was given complete freedom to maintain its reserves in its own vaults or deposit them abroad.

But without doubt the most substantial modifications had to do with the norms which governed the government's indebtedness to the Banco de la República. In fact, law 73 of 1931 authorized the Bank to make loans to the stockholder banks of up to 15% of its capital and reserves so long as the loans were guaranteed by government bonds and promissory notes. This implicitly enlarged the government's capacity of indebtedness with the Bank from 30% to 45%. In the first half of 1931, by virtue of this authorization the Bank bought 2 million *pesos* of Treasury promissory notes with a term of 4 and 5 years, an amount which the Bank tried to raise to 5 million *pesos* in the second half of the same year.

Despite its relative amplitude compared to what had been allowed under the norms of law 25 of 1923, the financial support which the Banco de la República now gave to the government was not enough and for this reason a contract was signed in 1931 which gave the Bank the right to exploit the government monopoly of the salt mines of Zipaquirá, Nemocón, Sesquilé and Tausa in exchange for an advance of 15.5 million *pesos* to the government. The credit thus granted was to be used to cancel the deficit of the General Treasury of the Nation, pay debts which the central government owed to the departments and municipalities, com-

plete the government's contribution to the capitalization of the *Caja de Crédito Agrario* (The Agricultural Credit Bank, a newly-created public institution that provided loans to farmers) and develop a three-year program of public works.

The advance received for the salt concession, the purchase of Treasury bonds in the first half of 1931 and the financing of the bonds issued to pay the coffee premium raised the government's debt to the Banco de la República from 4,047,000 *pesos* in June, 1930 to 22,027,000 *pesos* by June, 1932. An amount that would to continue to rise in the following years, due to the financing it had to grant to the government to cover the costs of the War with Peru, caused by the Peruvian invasion of Leticia, a Colombian town in the Amazon.

This increase of resources to the government was notable not only for the accelerated rate at which it grew, but also because it did away with the notion that the assets of the Banco de la República had to be kept in liquid form and implied a deliberate decision to use resources from emissions for the reactivation of the economy.

It is worth mentioning that since the term of the salt concession was initially fixed at 13 years, to run from January 1, 1932, the contract with the government explicitly recognized that the legal existence of the Banco de la República would have to go beyond the limit laid down in law 25 of 1923, which set its life at 20 years. For this reason, when this contract was signed it was agreed to prolong the legal existence of the Bank for another ten years, that is, up to 1953, and along with it the length of its monopoly over the emission of bank notes. For the rest, the Banco de la República administered the salt mines until the end of the nineteen sixties, when, by virtue of different legal norms, its administration was placed in the hands of the *Instituto de Fomento Industrial* (IFI - the Institute of Industrial Promotion).

Returning to the main theme, we should point out that the adopting of less orthodox policies by the Banco de la República with respect to government financing also applied to its handling of credit to the private sector. In fact, in the Board of Directors meeting of October 1, 1931, it was decided that the Bank,

Below, *Colombian army at Güepí, with armament seized from Peruvian troops.*

for the first time since its foundation, would grant direct credits to the general public, through the granting of loans backed by bonds representative of agricultural goods in bonded warehouses. As well as seeking to increase circulating currency, this measure was clearly intended to ease credits for the agricultural sector, which was judged to be of vital importance for the Colombian economy.

To begin with, as there were no bonded warehouses for general merchandise and these loans were granted against bonds issued by coffee and tobacco storehouses, this measure was not important in quantitative terms. But as general bonded warehouses gradually came into existence, this kind of credit became one of the sources of primary expansion for the Banco de la República. This was clearly seen in 1937, when, with the aim of upholding the internal price of coffee, the National Federation of Coffee-Growers was obliged to ask for financial resources through this mechanism.

Although it was willing to cooperate in the aim of economic recovery, the Banco de la República always recommended prudence and was vehemently opposed to exorbitant emissions, as was made clear in the Governor's report to Board of Directors for the financial year from July 1, 1930 to June 30, 1931. There we read: "The nation must continue granting its decided support to the government for the development of measures which the government considers the most effective to deal with the difficulties that confront us, trying not to create others with the understandable impatience of those who demand immediate solutions to their personal problems, which in many cases are insoluble, or come up with ill-thought out plans that often, when they are discussed in the parliament or the press, only serve to upset public opinion and aggravate distrust... Most of these plans are based on the emission of papers that would circulate as money, their authors believing, in their simplistic way, that the profound problem may be reduced to a mere matter of printing money and that the artificial increase of mediums of exchange will solve the crisis". (Caro, 1931, p. 39-40).

At the same time that credit to the national government and private individuals was extended, the Bank's loans to the financial system began to fall after November, 1931. From a maximum level of 19.5 million *pesos* in the second half of that year they fell to 8.5 million *pesos* in June, 1932 and continued to descend, almost without interruption, until 1937.

This was due to the fact that the funds granted by the Bank to the government, which were meant to circulate through the financial system and reactivate the economy, were, because of the poor state of business and the banking portfolio, ultimately used by the commercial banks to pay their debts to the Banco de la República

Thus, while the primary expansion of money which resulted from the monetary policy adopted in support of fiscal expansion entered into circulation, the Bank found itself obliged to restrict its operations with the private banks, because these institutions did not wish to expand their credit operations due to the evident deterioration in the

Above,
Stamp publicizing the coffee industry, 1947. Tobacco stamp, 1939.

Below,
First headquarters of the Banco Central Hipotecario in Bogotá, founded in the early nineteen-thirties, with a 50% capital contribution by the Banco de la República.

quality of the loans that had been granted during the phase of expansion. These loans were an especially heavy burden on the borrowers at a time when there was a marked fall in real estate prices and a high real interest rate.

To solve the problem of private debts the government reduced the interest rate on debts, limited the interests on arrears, extended the terms originally agreed on and allowed for a partial payment with mortgage certificates, credit instruments which had a reduced value in the market but were received at par value by the mortgage banks by virtue of an agreement with the government. These measures were complemented by the creation of the *Banco Central Hipotecario* (The Central Mortgage Bank), with a capital of 20 million *pesos*, half of which was supplied by the Banco de la República, and by the foundation of the *Corporación Colombiana de Crédito* (The Colombian Credit Corporation), which was authorized to issue bonds with which it bought bad loans from the commercial banks.

Since, in addition to refusing to expand their primary operations with the Banco de la República, the commercial banks maintained excess reserves during the crisis, it was natural that private credit would suffer, for which reason the sectors linked to coffee made an effort to persuade the government to found a credit institution that would dedicate itself to farm loans. This resulted in law 52 of 1931, which authorized the creation of the *Caja de Crédito Agrario*, which, as we have pointed out, the Bank partly capitalized through the advances granted to the government for the salt concession.

To sum up, the monetary contraction that took place between 1929 and 1931 was

Above and below, *Stamps depicting the foundation of the Instituto de Crédito Territorial (Institute of Property Credit) and the Caja de Crédito Agrario (Agricultural Credit Bank).*

halted in 1932 and reverted, in an accelerated way, to its prior state in 1933-1934 as the result of an expansive fiscal policy financed by a primary emission of the Banco de la República and a great expansion of emission towards the private sector. All this took place within the context of the great wariness of the commercial banks, which wound up having adverse effects on the volume of credit and the general level of financial intermediation.

The 1928 level of deposits in current account was only reached again in 1934 and from that year onwards showed a high growth, reaching the point, around the middle nineteen-forties, when, for the first time, these deposits surpassed the amount of cash in the hands of the public.

The decision of the U. S. government to keep part of its metal reserves in silver caused a rise in the price of this metal and stimulated its export from Colombia. For this reason silver coins, which were then minted at a standard of 0.900, became scarce. This forced the Banco de la República to place half *peso* bills into circulation in 1935 and the government, for fiscal reasons, set out to withdraw silver coins from circulation. This program of financial intermediation included a prohibition on exporting or melting down silver coins and their compulsory surrender to the Banco de la República in exchange for bills or cupro-nickel coins.

Finally, we should point out that the expansive policy put into effect towards the end of 1931 with the aim of reactivating the economy showed results, since from 1932 onwards the shrinkage of the economy was reversed and an expansion began which lifted the Gross Domestic Product to an average annual growth level of 6% between 1932 and 1934.

MONETARY POLICY BETWEEN 1935 AND 1950

Opposite page, *Alfonso López Pumarejo (1934-1938; 1942-1945) led a broad political reform which culminated in the modification of the Constitution. He was also responsible for an agrarian and tax reform and the consolidation of the country's internal debt with the Banco de la República.*

Below, *Eduardo Santos (1938-1942). During the administration of Santos the country's monetary unit was redefined, which permitted the Banco de la República to hand over resources to the government for the cancellation of the internal debt, the creation of a special exchange account and the financing of the ordinary expenses of the government.*

The economic recovery we have just mentioned was accompanied by a growth of the inflation rate between 1934 and 1935, at the same time that the *peso* was devalued with respect to the dollar and also to gold, as we have said. This juncture of events made the nation recall the epoch of the big expansion of the money supply and led to a more conservative macro-economic policy from the year 1935 onwards, the beginning of a period which can be clearly divided into three intervals: the first one between 1935 and 1939, the one coinciding with the Second World War, and the one which began with the end of the war and ended with a new reform in the institutional framework of the Banco de la República in 1951.

Law 7 of February, 1935 approved a number of contracts signed at the end of 1934 between the national government and the Banco de la República, which dealt with:

• the consolidation of the debts deriving from the financing of the war with Peru, an expansion of their term and the freezing of interest payments;

• the freeing of the collaterals that backed these debts;

• an explicit agreement on the part of the Banco de la República to transfer to the government the earnings that the Bank might obtain through the passing of a law that reduced the gold content of the monetary unit;

• the government's decision to use these earnings to pay the debts covered

Below, *First page of the Constitutional Reform of 1936, legislative Act number 1 of that year.*

by the contract and if it became feasible, employ the rest for the establishment of a fund for the stabilization of the public debt; and

- the establishment of a special account which would register the profits or losses resulting from exchange control, an account that would be liquidated when the reduction of the gold content of the monetary unit came into effect.

These contracts moderated the fiscal cost of the government's debt with the Banco de la República. The first administration of Alfonso López Pumarejo (1934-1938) also carried out a reform which included the establishment of taxes on coffee exports, income, inherited wealth and excess profits.

This tax reform had the clear aim of redistributing wealth and was part of a broader social policy that included reforms of the agrarian laws and the strengthening of the social sectors represented by the trades union movement. Its application had beneficial effects, given that there was a tendency towards a fiscal surplus between 1935 and 1939, which made it unnecessary for the government to ask for new credits from the Banco de la República. In fact, these credits were reduced in 1939 when, as a consequence of the contracts authorized under law 7 of 1935, the government was able to cancel the credits it had obtained from the Banco de la República to finance the War with Peru.

Towards this end, in November, 1938, on the initiative of Carlos Lleras Restrepo, Finance Minister during the government of Eduardo Santos (1938-1942), law 167 on monetary stabilization was passed. This new measure reduced the gold content of the monetary unit from 1.5976 grams at a standard of 0.91666, as had been established in the Fiscal Code of 1912, to 0.56424 grams at a standard of 0.900. The new weight and precious metal content of the monetary unit meant that the intrinsic parity of the U.S. dollar would be the equivalent of 1.75 Colombian *pesos*, the exchange rate between these two currencies then prevailing in the market.

In accordance with this norm and other agreements later signed between the central government and the Banco de la República, the Bank transferred earnings of 17.3 million *pesos* to the government. These earnings were used to amortize the government's debt with the Bank (8 million *pesos*), finance the ordinary expenses of the government (5 million *pesos*), establish the Stablization Fund for the public debt (3 million *pesos*) and increase the Special Exchange Account (1.3 million *pesos*), instead of liquidating it.

The fiscal stability brought by the above measures was complemented by an untroubled exchange situation. The lack of foreign loans –among other reasons, because a moratorium on the payment of foreign debt had been decreed in 1935– and the decision to maintain

Right, *Lauchlin Currie, who, from the time of his arrival in the country in 1949, had a notable influence on the design of Colombian economic policy and the teaching of economics. His theory on the leading sectors of economic development won international acclaim and was the basis of the system of savings and house loans created in 1972.*

the exchange rate of the *peso* against the dollar forced the authorities to seek a balance in external accounts through the establishment of quantitative controls, as became evident in 1937-38 and 1939-40, when the reduction of the external price of coffee led to stricter controls on imports and the establishment of a system of prior deposits in the Banco de la República as a requisite for obtaining the respective import licenses.

The reduced financing of the government by the Banco de la República, the small importance of the credit granted by the Bank to the private sector, with the above-noted exception of 1937, and the tendency towards a slight surplus in external accounts led to a moderate growth of the means of payment between the years 1939 and 1940, when they expanded at an average annual rate of 8.1%, nearly 90% of which was due to the increase in primary money, considering the relative insignificance of secondary money and therefore of the money multiplier.

Nevertheless, from 1938 there began a stage of rapid expansion of secondary money, as can be seen in Chart 2, where the difference between the means of payment and the monetary base is a measure of the secondary expansion of

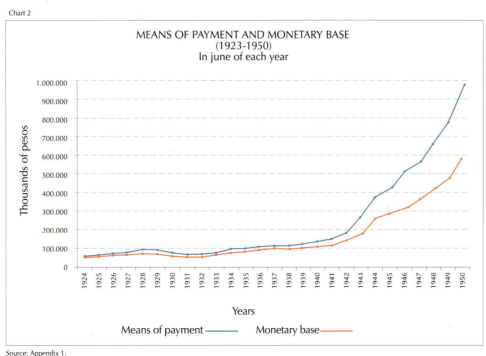

Chart 2

MEANS OF PAYMENT AND MONETARY BASE (1923-1950) In june of each year

Source: Appendix 1.

Above, *López Pumarejo and Plinio Mendoza. As a representative of the political movement headed by Gaitán, the latter proposed a law for the radical reform of the Banco de la República in 1947, but it was not accepted by the Congress.*

Right, *March in support of the policies of Alfonso López Pumarejo during the crisis of his second term, ca. 1943.*

grew and more depth was given to the financial system.

This growth in the secondary expansion of money could have been more accelerated if it had not been for the banks maintaining more reserves than the legally-required minimum; this was a result of the conservative credit policy and of the way the financial intermediaries managed liquidity in this period.

The macro-economic stability of the period 1935-1939 was seen in a growth of the Gross Domestic Product, which grew on average by more than 5% annually, with the exception of 1937, which was a particularly difficult year because of the unfortunate fall in coffee prices. It was also a period of low inflation, when the annual growth rate in prices was around 5%.

The economic growth and relative stability of prices which the country had achieved in the second half of the nineteen-thirties were greatly upset by the outbreak of the Second World War in 1939. In the following five years the country would once more witness a rapid ac-

money by the banking system. This was due to the fact that, once the effects of the crisis of the nineteen-thirties were left behind, the number of bank branches

Alfonso López Pumarejo (1886 - 1959), political cartoon by Rendón. Liberal politician and statesman, twice President of Colombia (1934 - 1938 and 1942 - 1945). He was active as a politician, banker, diplomat and journalist and played a big role in his party's return to power after many years in the wilderness. As President, he proposed to carry out an "Ongoing Revolution" that would reform the constitution and, in his own words, he changed "the organization of the Republic, its institutions and laws". He reformed public education, the tax system and the economy in general, with wide public support. His second administration was made difficult by the opposition of the Conservatives and the restrictions imposed by the Second World War.

cumulation of its international reserves but, in contrast with what happened in the nineteen-twenties, economic growth slowed down during the war.

This accumulation of international reserves was produced, in part, by a new foreign indebtedness but it was essentially the result of a rapid rise in the value of export and a dramatic fall in imports, which in the period between 1942-1944 fell below the level of 1939.

The increase of exports was due to the success of coffee during the war, as a consequence of the signing of the world pact on national coffee quotas in 1940, which led the price of the bean to stabilize around 15 U.S. cents per pound: the amounts exported rose because of the increase of the Colombian quota under the Pact, which was further enlarged when Brazilian exports faced difficulties caused by the war.

The opposite was true of imports. Once the United States entered the war there was a notable fall in imports, which, together with the rise in exports, created an accelerated accumulation of international reserves, which rose from 24 million dollars in 1940 to 176 million dollars by the end of 1945. This surplus of foreign earnings, under a fixed exchange regime, gave rise to a rapid expansion of the means of payment at a time when there was a simultaneous contraction of the supply of goods because of the shortage of raw materials, components and capital equipment. This slowing down of economic growth and the trend towards a rise in the general level of prices created conditions for the carrying out of an economic policy of a highly interventionist character.

Resolved to keep a fixed level in the nominal exchange rate, the authorities eased exchange controls in a way that mirrored the rigor applied in the years when there was a shortage of foreign earnings.

On the fiscal front, the consequent fall in customs revenues and a tendency to increase public spending produced a new fiscal deficit, which was financed through new taxes, foreign loans and loans from the Colombian private sector. The credit granted by the Banco de la República kept stable, even though short term obligations with the Bank were restructured and their terms extended. The most significant of these financing measures was the emission of a National Defense bond, which was obligatorily subscribed by the payers of income tax, savings banks, insurance companies, the National Coffee Fund and industrial companies. Next in importance was the renewal of the foreign debt, in that the government was able to obtain credits of 20 million dollars between 1941 and 1943 from the Import and Export Bank of the United States.

Monetary policy was pressured in 1941 by the financing granted to the coffee sector after the signing of the coffee

Right,
One peso *bill of the Banco de la República, commemorating the fourth centenary in 1938 of the founding of Bogotá.*

Below,
Stamp dedicated to the coffee industry, with an overseal showing the faces of Stalin, Roosevelt and Churchill to celebrate the end of the Second World War, 1945.

pact in 1940 and the creation of the National Coffee Fund as a mechanism to regulate the supply of the bean. In order to avoid a big expansion of the means of payment a series of different kinds of ad-hoc decisions were taken.

To begin with, for the first time since the foundation of the Banco de la República and in line with law 7 of 1943, the reserve requirement ratio for the banks was raised with the aim of restricting the supply of money. In second place, the Banco de la República issued a security for the express purpose of withdrawing some of the money in circulation. This security, which was called a Deposit Certificate, took the form of a forced investment by companies for an amount equivalent to 20% of their profits and 50% of the value of the depreciation of their equipment. By the same token, the main purpose of the import deposits at this time was to withdraw money from circulation, rather than to discourage imports by making them more expensive; on the contrary, imports were also stimulated by different measures in order to reactivate the economy but also in order to check the growth of the means of payment.

Despite its evident originality, the stabilization plan adopted during the Second World War had little success in controlling inflation and it was only from 1944 onwards, when imports began to increase a bit, that it was possible to recover the growth rate of the economy.

The shortage of imports during the war had repercussions for all economic activities in the country and the Banco de la República was not exempt from them. Given, on the one hand, the withdrawal from circulation of the silver coins with a high content of precious metal, which was probably the result of the measure that took effect in 1935, and, on the other, the impossibility of importing bank notes or coins of any kind, in 1942 and 1943 the Bank was forced to cut in half and put a new seal on the one *peso* bills, so that they could circulate as substitutes for the fifty *centavos* coin and half-*peso* bills. Collectors refer to this currency as a split half-*peso* (*medio peso partido*).

But since it was not possible to import nickel either, the coins made with alloys of this metal stopped being produced and coins of a nearly pure copper content began to circulate: they continued to be issued and to circulate until

the end of the nineteen-seventies, when they began to be replaced by other alloys or were simply withdrawn from circulation because of their depreciated value.

In 1944, at a time when economic growth accelerated, inflation reached a figure of more than 20%, the highest rate since 1923. During 1945 and 1946 the economy expanded at a rate of nearly 15%, while average annual inflation was 10%. It seemed, therefore, that the economic process that had taken place during the Second World War had reversed itself, since there was an increase in imports, a fall in international reserves, a restricted growth in the means of payment, a lessening of inflation and a spurt of economic growth.

To begin with, the Conservative government of Mariano Ospina Pérez (1946-1950) committed itself to strengthen these trends. It advocated a plan of fiscal adjustment that increased taxes and initially put a strict limit on the emission of public debt, whether by the nation, the departments or the municipalities.

In addition, since the government and the Central Bank were aware that the increased pace of economic activity might lead the commercial banks to strongly increase their demand for resources from the Banco de la República and did not contemplate using an increase in the rediscount rate as a coercive measure against this excess demand, the government introduced a novel policy in 1946: a scheme to control the portfolio of banks though the imposition of quantitative growth limits by the Bank Superintendency.

This control turned out to be completely ineffective because the general quantitative limits were soon raised and, in addition, different kinds of exceptions were introduced.

The government's inability to control the credit granted by the Banco de la

Left,
At the beginning of his administration Mariano Ospina Pérez undertook a macro-economic stabilization plan that, upon being abandoned, gave rise to the first annual inflation rate of more than 20% since the foundation of the Banco de la República.

Below,
The "split" half-peso bill. Due to the scarcity of fractional money and the fact that new half-peso bills could not be imported because of the Second World War, the government split the 1 peso notes in half, stamped a new seal on the halves and placed them in circulation as the equivalent of 50 centavos.

Left,
Tramcar on fire in front of the Governor's Office of Cundinamarca in Bogotá, during the riots following the assassination of Gaitán on April 9, 1948. In the background is the Hotel Granada, the site of the future headquarters of the Banco de la República.

Below,
Jorge Eliécer Gaitán (1898 - 1948), Commemorative coin. Lawyer and Liberal politician, he had the widest popular following during the first half of the 20th century. His assassination changed the course of modern Colombian history.

República to the banks and its reluctance to impose a policy of fiscal austerity meant that the fall in international reserves, with its negative effect on the primary expansion of money, was more than compensated for by the internal credit granted by the Banco de la República to the banks, the government and the general public.

The growth of primary money was enlarged with the increase in the emission of secondary money due to the growth of the money multiplier, which rose from 1.48 in 1945 to 1.60 in 1950, as a result in the fall in the reserve requirement ratio. That is, the private banks began to meet some of the new demand for credit by reducing the excess reserves that they had maintained during a long period.

The growth of the means of payment in circulation once again caused a rise in inflation in the years 1947 and 1948 and particulary in 1950, when, for the second time since 1923, the annual rise in the general price level broke the 20% barrier. In view of this problem and the very grave political situation that was provoked by the assassination of the Liberal leader Jorge Eliécer Gaitán in April, 1948, the monetary authority, towards the end of 1950, got the bankers to enter into a gentlemen's agreement to curb the growth of the banking portfolio and the means of payment.

This pact showed its results in 1951, a year when the amount of money in circulation fell in absolute terms, although it had adverse effects upon the economic activity.

It is curious that the Board of Directors of the Banco de la República, instead of using the power to manage the reserve requirement ratio for monetary ends that had been given to the Bank for the first time since its foundation in 1923, had chosen, instead, to promote an agreement on self-

regulation by the banks themselves of the banking portfolio and the means of payment.

In exchange matters, the maintenance of a fixed nominal exchange rate, together with the inflation that took place during the nineteen-forties, led to a revaluation of the real exchange rate, since internal inflation was higher than the rise of prices in the international market. During the first half of this decade, given the excess supply of foreign earnings, such behavior could be considered normal. But when the process of accumulating international reserves was reversed after 1945, it was no longer possible to sustain the nominal exchange rate. This led, under law 90, to a nominal devaluation of 11% in December, 1948, when the exchange rate rose from 1.75 *pesos* per dollar to 1.95 *pesos* per dollar.

But this nominal devaluation meant little for the real exchange rate, given the inflation of the following years. This nominal devaluation was followed by another, in April, 1951, when the exchange rate rose from 1.95 *pesos* per dollar to 2.51 *pesos* per dollar. Both devaluations introduced, by means of different mechanisms, multiple exchange rate schemes.

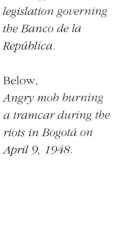

Right,
Jorge Eliécer Gaitán. In 1947 his followers made an unsuccessful attempt to modify the legislation governing the Banco de la República.

Below,
Angry mob burning a tramcar during the riots in Bogotá on April 9, 1948.

THE REFORM OF 1951 AND THE VICISSITUDES OF COFFEE

Opposite page, *Detail of a 1 peso bill, the first printed on the presses of the Banco de la República, 1959. Until 1957 the bills that circulated in the country were imported; since then almost all have been produced in Colombia.*

Below, *Roberto Urdaneta, Mariano Ospina Pérez, Alfonso López Pumarejo, Alberto Lleras Camargo, a member of the government of Venezuela, Eduardo Santos and Darío Echandía, at the inauguration of Alberto Lleras Camargo, August 7, 1958.*

At the end of 1949, Carlos Villaveces, a then member of the Board of Directors of the Banco de la República, prepared a study that was presented to the Second Meeting of Specialists of the Central Banks of the Americas, held in Santiago, Chile.

In an theoretical way, this study set forth the possibility of cushioning economic cycles through an anti-cyclical policy and pointed to the convenience of developing it through the central banks, by giving them sufficient powers to control the emission of money, guide credit and regulate foreign trade operations.

Specifically, these powers would have to include the authority to regulate banking reserves, determine the terms of credits, control interest rates, set exchange rates, establish discounts to affiliated banks and intervene in the open market through the purchase and sale of government securities.

By presenting this work, Villaveces hoped that his ideas would be adopted and serve as the foundation of a system which would allow "the central banks to encounter the best way of controlling the phenomena that result from economic cycles" (Villaveces, 1949, p. 1269), on the basis of a legislation that would, as far as possible, be uniform, given the peculiarities of each country. Without doubt, a vision of the central banks that was different to that of Kemmerer and oriented more to a Keynesian, development-minded point of view had begun to put down roots.

This outlook was also seen in the draft of a legislative bill on the role of bank

Right,
*Luis Ángel Arango, Governor of the Banco de la República, October, 1947 - January, 1957. Undated and unsigned oil painting.
Ignacio Copete Lizarralde, Governor of the Banco de la República, June, 1957 - February, 1960. Oil painting by Hector Osuna, 1990.*

Below,
Carlos Villaveces, who, together with Manuel Mejía, Bernardo Restrepo Ochoa, Manuel Casabianca and Luis Ángel Arango, formed part of the commission that proposed substantial reforms in the functions of the Banco de la República, many of which were adopted under decree 756 of 1951.

credit in the economy, which was presented to the Colombian Congress in 1949 by the then Minister of Finance, Hernán Jaramillo Ocampo. Among the arguments presented to support the measure, he wrote: "its general outlines accept the widely published and discussed ideas about the importance of exercising monetary control to stop inflations or curb deflations. And with regard to credit, it establishes a system of intervention through rediscounts and the fixing of differential credit rates, in accordance with the policy of development that it is best to follow at a given time". (Jaramillo Ocampo, 1949, p. 1270).

Since the Congress was closed by order of the executive branch in 1949, the above bill was not passed, but the ideas found in it, like those set forth by Villaveces in Santiago, Chile, gave rise to the issuing of two norms that represented a sharp break with the institutional management of money and credit that had been in force up to that time.

With the aim of encouraging the development of the national economy, channeling credit towards productive activities and guaranteeing full employment, as well as stimulating agricultural and industrial production, decree 384 of 1950 authorized the commercial banks to grant credits with a term of up to five years, provided they were exclusively used for the construction or enlargement of development works.

This marked the death of the banking legislation of 1923, in that this legislation had decreed that the commercial banks could not grant credits with a term longer than two years, nor destine resources to investments in industrial companies or real estate, except when such investments were the product of credits that had been previously granted.

In a complementary way, decree 384 of 1950 sought to stimulate long-term credit by stipulating that, as a requisite for obtaining import licenses, importers would

Right,
Two coins of 1952: one of 2 centavos *with the effigy of Liberty and another of 10* centavos *with the effigy of the* cacique *(indigenous chief)* Calarcá.

Below,
Present headquarters of the Banco de la República, vignette from bank note. 5 pesos, 1960.

be obliged to place deposits of up to 40% of the value of each license in the Stabilization Fund that had been created by virtue of law 167 of 1938 and that this Fund could invest these resources in "societies or companies in which the State holds shares so long as they are used to finance works of economic development and have a term no longer than five years and an interest rate no higher than 6% annually".

Decree 384 was followed by another measure along the same lines. After ample discussions held during eight sessions that took place throughout January, 1951, a commission of the Board of Directors of the Banco de República agreed on the outlines of a decree, finally drafted by Roberto García Paredes in his condition of Deputy Governor of the Bank, which on being accepted by the full Board, became decree 756 of 1951.

The commission was made up of Manuel Mejía, Bernardo Restrepo Ochoa and Carlos Villaveces, with the periodical assistance of García Paredes, the Bank's lawyer, Manuel Casabianca, and its Governor, Luis Ángel Arango, who had been named to succeed Julio Caro in 1947 and stayed in office until the end of 1956.

By virtue of decree 756 of 1951, which was issued by the government of Laureano Gómez (1950-1953), the Banco de la República was given the power to carry out a monetary, credit and exchange policy designed to stimulate conditions that would be favorable to the orderly development of the Colombian economy. Towards that aim, with the ratifying vote of the minister of Finance, it could:

- fix quotas for its affiliated banks in their ordinary loan and discount operations;
- establish a special quota of credit for discount operations intended for agricultural, industrial and commercial activities, being able to establish within this quota the percentage for each of these ends;
- establish emergency quotas of a temporary nature;
- set and vary the interest rates that the Banco de la República would charge for its operations of loans, discounts and rediscounts;
- establish and alter the reserve requirement ratio for commercial banks and savings banks, within limits of 10%-30% in the case of sight deposits and 5%-20% for the rest;
- set marginal reserve requirements up to 100% and establish their use to finance public indebtedness or to execute

loans or operations favorable to the development of the national economy.

At the same time, decree 756 of 1951 authorized the Banco de la República to raise the government's credit limit with the Bank to 8% of the revenues collected during the previous year, for which the government might issue promissory notes with an interest rate of 4% annually, payable within the respective fiscal year and to be used by the Banco de la República, at its discretion, to carry out open market operations.

The remaining provisions of Decree 756 of 1951 referred to the minimum reserve requirement ratio for the Banco de la República, which was set at 25% for its bills and 15% for other monetary liabilities. They also dealt with the way of maintaining this reserve; the government's obligation to deposit its liquid funds in the Banco de la República; and the Bank's right to redeposit them in credit institutions which had made a prior agreement with the Bank to use them as loans for the development of the country's production. Finally, it was established that the government and the Bank would mutually agree to the corresponding reform of the Bank's statutes, which would include the creation of an agency dependent on the Board of Directors that would be in charge of studying the monetary, credit and exchange measures needed for the proper development of the country's economy.

In furtherance of this last matter decree 2057, October 2, 1951, authorized the government to sign a contract with the Banco de la República whose aim was to extend the life of the Bank and ratify its right to issue bank notes for a further twenty years, as from July 20, 1953. The same decree also authorized private stockholders to sell their stocks to the Stabilization Fund and allowed for the sale of the government's stocks in the open market, without this giving rise to the loss of any of its rights and prerogatives over the Bank, including its participation in the Board of Directors, whose membership and procedure for naming members was also defined in it.

Thus, the Board of Directors of the Banco de la República was made up of the minister of Finance and Public Credit, two directors named by the government, three directors jointly and simultaneously named by the national and foreign stockholder banks, the manager of the Coffee-Growers Federation, a director proposed by the Farmers and Cattle-Raisers Societies and finally, a director proposed by the Chambers of Commerce.

The last two directors were named by the government from a list of those who had obtained the highest number of votes in the elections of their respective trade associations.

Even though several analysts have stated that it was only on the basis of Decree 2057 of 1951 that the minister of Finance began to have a vote in the Board of Directors of the Banco de la República, the truth is that he had always had this right, as can be inferred from a reading of law 25 of 1923. In reality, what the minister of Finance did have after decree 2057 of 1951 was veto power.

Right, *Captain (retired) Eduardo Torres Roldán, founder of the printing house for the bank notes of the Banco de la República, which formally began operations on October 23, 1959.*

Below, *Bills of 1 (1959) and 5 pesos (1961) from the first issue printed on the presses of the Banco de la República.*

It is necessary to emphasize that Decree 756 of 1951 considerably broadened the right of the Banco de la República to intervene in monetary and credit matters. It is also clear that, in contrast with the original legislation, the rediscount of operations in the Banco de la República would no longer be granted on the understanding that banks would want to pay the price fixed by the Board of Directors of the Bank, but on the condition that the resources thus obtained, by the banks and the end-users of the credits, would be destined for certain aims. For the rest, the reserve requirement ratio was established as a specific instrument of monetary control, but the ratio could also be used to guide credit towards certain activities.

When we analyze the paper on anticyclical policy presented by Carlos Villaveces and the arguments he put to the commission which the Board of Directors had assigned to study changes in the institution, it becomes clear that he and Luis Ángel Arango were the real mentors of the 1951 reform.

This conclusion differs from the traditional interpretations, which emphasize the marked influence on the adoption of these reforms of the leaders of the political movement headed by Liberal party leader Jorge Eliécer Gaitán, who had proposed a reform of the Central Bank in the Congress in 1947, or give the credit for the reforms to a number of foreign experts who worked in the country at this time.

The project proposed by Gaitán's followers, which was elaborated by Guillermo Hernández Rodríguez and Antonio García, among others and put before the Senate by Plinio Mendoza Neira, Francisco de P. Vargas and Antonio José Lemos Guzmán, proposed, among other changes, that the Bank have direct operations with the general public "whenever the banking institutions apply a policy of restriction of credit opposite to the orientations of the Central Bank"; that it be authorized to finance co-operatives, which would considered to be affiliated institutions in their own right; that it would spread the use of credit among different regions and a variety of economic activities; that the Bank be represented, by right, on the boards of directors of the affiliated institutions; that the private banks would be obliged to consider and grant credits in the chronological order of applications for them and also to explain to applicants the reasons for denying a credit. It was evident, of course, that these ideas, which might have been welcomed in a socialist economy, were not to the liking of the bankers who sat on the Board of Directors of the Banco de la República in 1951 and for this reason none of these reforms was included in decree 756 of that year. This was confirmed by Antonio García in his criticism of the banking reform of 1951, found in his book "Problemas de la Nación Colombiana" ("Problems of the Colombian Nation".)

References to the influence of the recommendations made by foreign experts have to do with a mission sponsored by the International Bank for Reconstruction and Development, headed by Lauchlin Currie, who arrived in the country in 1949. He was the author of two studies, entitled "Bases of a Development Program for Colombia" ("Bases de un Programa de Fomento para Colombia") and "Reorganization of the Executive Branch of the Colombian Government" ("Reorganización de la Rama Ejecutiva del Gobierno de Colombia".) In both reports he dealt with the organization of the Banco de la República and with the financial system in general, for which he proposed diverse reforms.

Right, *Alberto Lleras (1945-1946; 1958-1962), first President under the "National Front" agreement for alternating the rule of the two major parties: he is signing the agrarian reform law of 1961.*

Below, *Half*-peso *bill issued in 1948 by the Republic of Colombia, not by the Banco de la República. These bills were used to replace and withdraw from circulation the bills originally issued in 1915, which, in turn, had served the same purpose for the bills issued during the War of the Thousand Days. Collectors refer to these bills as "Lleritas".*

In particular, he was enthusiastic about the idea that the commercial banks be allowed to give long-term loans, in view of the near absence of a capital market in Colombia and taking into account that "the solidity of the banking system does not depend, in the end, on the term of maturity of a bank's assets but on the solidity of the economy in general". (Currie, 1951, p. 348).

Currie's support for this idea has led to confusion among some analysts, who believe that, by favoring a policy of long-term banking credit, he was one of the creators of the banking reform of 1951, in particular decree 756 of that year. What Currie did in fact propose was to use discount policy as the main instrument of monetary policy, in view of the impossibility of utilizing open market operations, the technical difficulties involved in continually shifting the reserve requirement ratio and the uselessness of the discount rate. Currie was emphatic about not using the Bank's credits for inflationary purposes when directing some of its resources to long-term projects, writing that "to suggest limited investments by the banks in certain assets, we do not wish to suggest the financing of long-term development projects by means of inflation... The objective is not to obtain a bigger formation of capital by means of inflation but to improve the direction of the capital flow. Similarly, the objective is not to increase the volume of existing credit but to guide a part of this volume towards development ends". (Currie, 1951, p. 666).

Ideas very similar to those of Currie were advanced by another foreign expert who visited the country at this time, David Grove, an official of the U.S. Federal Reserve Board, who, with the assistance of Gerald Alter, acted as a consultant for the Banco de la República in 1949. In his first memorandum, entitled "Deficiencies in the Structure of the Colombian Central Bank", Grove wrote that "a monetary policy intended to establish quantitative limits on the expansion of circulating currency is also essential if selective credit controls have to be employed. In reality, any system of selective credit control would fail when the volume of banking credit expands without taking inflationary effects into account. Therefore it appears to be essential to concentrate on quantitative controls for the moment. As the new monetary policy comes into effect it would be important to consider the way in which the selective controls could be used to channel the lending capacity of the affiliated banks and official credit institutions into the most productive forms of private investment". (Grove, 1988, p. 24-25)

Thus we can see that it was not the ideas of Currie or Grove which led the Banco de la República to adopt a long-term credit scheme independent of the monetary situation, nor did they advocate trying to use primary emission to expand capital formation.

In this respect Jaime Mz. Recaman is perfectly correct when, in his "Legal History of the Banco de la República", he states that the financial reform of 1951 was more

Below, *Manuel Mejía Jaramillo (1887-1958) on stamps of 5 and 10 pesos, dedicated to the exportation of coffee. Manager of the Coffee-Growers Federation for many years, who played an influential role in the design of the country's macro-economic policies up to the end of the 1950's.*

the brain-child of the Board of Directors of the Banco de la República than the product of the advice given by the foreign specialists, many of whose substantial recommendations were not adopted, such as those relating to the membership and election of the Board of Directors, the authority to be in charge of issuing metallic money and the supervision of banking.

Nevertheless, some of Groves' recommendations were successful: the authorization for the sale of the government's stocks; the creation of an agency with top technical skills, dependent on the Board of Directors of the Bank, to formulate measures of monetary control; and the transfer of control of the Stabilization Fund to the Bank's Board of Directors.

The reforms found in decrees 384 of 1959 and 756 of 1951, which, as we have said, were intended to expand the terms of banking credit and finance the formation of capital for certain economic activities with the Bank's resources, were strengthened in the 1950's by the emergence of new public institutions of credit. In 1959, the Banco Popular was created, followed by the Banco Cafetero (Coffee-Growers Bank) in 1953 and the Banco Ganadero (Cattle-Raisers Bank) in 1956, each meant to satisfy the demand of specific economic sectors. These institutions joined the list of the official credit agencies established in the nineteen-thirties and nineteen-forties, like the Banco Central Hipotecario, the Caja de Crédito Agrario, the Instituto de Crédito Territorial (the Institute of Property Credit) and the Instituto de Fomento Industrial.

Despite its undoubted importance, the new scheme for monetary and credit institutions created in 1950-1951 did not immediately have a decisive impact on the design of macro-economic policy. Rather, this resulted from the enormous influence which the coffee sector gradually exercised over the management of economic policy.

In 1945, the country exported a bit more than 5 million 60-kilo sacks, for which it received 104.5 million dollars. In 1950, a bit under 4.5 million 60-kilo sacks earned 307.4 million dollars for Colombia. In other words, during the five years following the end of the Second World War, the price of coffee more than tripled. This phenomenon was accentuated in the years 1953 and 1954, when the country earned 492.2 and 550.2 million dollars, respectively, on coffee exports. Beginning in 1955 international coffee prices began to fall, with the result that in 1963 the value of coffee exports only rose to 310.2 million dollars, even though the amount exported in that year was 6.6% higher than that exported in 1954, the year which saw the highest-ever prices in world markets up to that time.

While the boom in prices was due to such international economic factors as the end of the Second World War, the outbreak of hostilities in Korea and adverse climatic conditions in Brazil in the middle of 1953, the fall that began in 1955 had to do with surplus production on a world level and the absence of mechanisms to control the supply of coffee to international markets.

These vicissitudes in the price of coffee, a product which came to account for

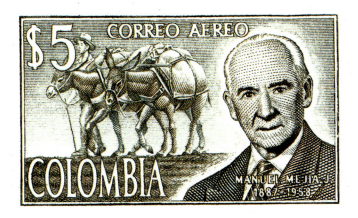

Below, *Gustavo Rojas Pinilla (1953-1957), who overthrew President Laureano Gómez in 1953. His administration benefited from high coffee prices and, for a while, a period of economic growth and moderate inflation. When he was deposed in May, 1957 there was an enormous macro-economic imbalance.*

90% of total Colombian exports at this time, governed the country's import capacity after 1950: coffee exports played a very dynamic role in expanding its economic activities but when prices fell, they were by the same token a major limitation on growth.

The period between 1952-1955 - at the height of the coffee boom - was a period of high growth (a more than 5.5% average annual increase in the Gross Domestic Product) and low inflation (less than 4% annually), with a tendency towards an equilibrium in public finances, a relatively moderate expansion of the means of payment and a rapid increase in imports.

The rapid growth of imports was due to an easing of quantitative controls, to the point where the list of prohibited imports practically disappeared in 1954, a situation that was unprecedented since the beginning of the nineteen-thirties.

These decisions helped control inflation in two ways. On the one hand, the supply of imported goods grew and on the other, they prevented an accumulation of international reserves. The latter effect was reflected in the low expansion of primary money. Nor did it grow in response to the credits granted to the government by the Banco de la República, thanks to the prevailing fiscal stability. Furthermore, when international reserves temporarily forced the creation of primary money in 1954, the Board of Directors of the Banco de la República established increasing reserve requirement ratios, making use of the powers given to it under the reform of 1951.

This situation of relative macro-economic stability began to reverse itself in 1955 with the beginning of a fall in the price of coffee, the existence of an overvalued exchange rate and the appearance of a fiscal deficit in 1955 and 1956 that was financed, in good part, by the placing of government securities in the Banco de la República.

Faced by the adverse result in the accounts of the external sector, the authorities tried, between the beginning of 1955 and the middle of 1957, to maintain the

nominal exchange rate through a set of restrictive measures on imports which included the temporary freezing of import licenses, the creation once more of import lists and the establishment of stamp taxes, increasing import deposits in accordance with what the government judged to be the necessity or convenience of different import goods. In addition to this, in May, 1955 a free exchange rate for non-essential imports was established, which rose from 3.93 *pesos* per dollar in this month to 7.00 *pesos* per dollar in April, 1957.

By the end of 1956 it had become evident that the exchange regime could not be sustained, especially when, despite all of these restrictions, it had not been possible to make timely payments of the short-term foreign trade debt, which rose from 249 million dollars in 1956 to 386 million dollars in 1957. This non-fulfillment caused a grave paralysis of foreign purchases in the first half of 1957.

It was this exchange situation and strong inflationary pressures which the military government which replaced General Gustavo Rojas Pinilla (President, through a military coup, from 1953-1957) had to face when it came to power in 1957. After a month in office, the new government, through decree 107 of June, 1957, set in march a stabilization program designed to simplify the multiple exchange system, control imports, normalize the payment of the foreign debt, balance the fiscal accounts and restrict monetary expansion.

On the exchange front, decree 107 of 1957 created two markets, one for exchange certificates, where the rate rose from the 2.50 *pesos* per dollar established in 1951 to 4.80 *pesos* per dollar, and the other a free capital market, where the initial rate was 5.90 *pesos* per dollar. The certificate market was financed by the main exports of goods and was used to pay for imports, the service on the foreign debt and government services abroad. The free market was financed by other exports and covered the payment of private services and non-registered capital. These two markets lasted until

Below,
Three members of the Military Junta that took over the government on May 10, 1957: Rear Admiral Rubén Piedrahita, General Rafael Navas Pardo and General Luis E. Ordoñez. General Gabriel Paris and General Deogracias Fonseca are absent.

Opposite page, *Demonstration to celebrate the fall of Rojas Pinilla. In the background is seen the construction work on the present headquarters of the Banco de la República.*

Right, *Alberto Lleras Camargo. At the beginning of his second term in 1958 a stabilization policy was carried out, which had a beneficial effect on economic growth, the control of inflation and the external account. This program was abandoned at the end of his government and gave rise to the traumatic devaluation of 1962.*

1966. The rate for exchange certificates rose from 6.10 *pesos* per dollar in March, 1958 to 6.70 *pesos* in June, 1960 and then to 9.00 *pesos* in November, 1962.

In the matter of import controls, the stabilization program instituted by the military government (May 1957-August 1958), which was overseen by the Finance Minister Antonio Alvarez Restrepo, was based on the establishment of lists of prior-consent licenses and prohibited imports, which together with the nominal devaluation helped to adjust the trade balance in 1957. When we further take into account that the payment of the foreign debt was normalized through the establishment of one tax on coffee exports, another on bills of exchange, and resources from foreign credits, there is no doubt that the 1957 stabilization program was successful on the external front.

The same may be said of the fiscal policy, where the heavy deficits of 1955 and 1956 gave way to a modest surplus in 1957. Where the policy did not have a great success was in the field of monetary control, for reasons which we will summarize below.

The first Minister of Finance during the second term of Alberto Lleras (1958-1962) was Hernando Agudelo Villa, who had consistently called for an anti-inflationary policy since the end of the nineteen-forties and now followed a policy of austerity in economic and financial matters, in line with the 1957 stabilization plan. The

Left, *Guillermo León Valencia, with some members of his cabinet: José Antonio Montalvo, Héctor Charry Samper and Marco Alzate Avendaño.*

key objective of Agudelo's policy was to stop the devaluation of the currency, through the elimination of inflationary pressures.

Despite a large number of economic and political difficulties the stabilization program was maintained, with the result that between 1958 and 1960 there was a fiscal surplus; the equilibrium in the trade balance was maintained; inflation was controlled –the average annual rate did not surpass 8% after having risen to more than 20% in 1957–; high growth rates were reached and monetary growth was controlled, keeping to an average annual rate of 14.4% in these years. The last accomplishment was the result of a decision to stabilize the money supply, despite two difficult circumstances.

The first was an adjustment of quotas in the world coffee pact at the end of 1957, which forced the National Coffee Fund to retain coffee that might have been exported and thus finance stocks held in inventory. To do this it made an abundant use of credits from the Banco de la República, to the extent that this indebtedness rose from 93 million *pesos* in July, 1957 to 614 million *pesos* in July, 1958, which was the equivalent of 40.8% of the monetary base.

The second had to do with the administration of the Stabilization Fund, as laid down in decree 107 of 1957. Under this norm, it was managed by the Banco de la República and import deposits were directly placed in the Bank, not in the Fund. Consequently, the Fund was forced to borrow from the Bank to reimburse the deposits, since its financial resources were tied up in long-term loans to build oil pipelines, grain silos for the National Institute of Provisions (*Instituto Nacional de Abastecimiento*), railways and hydroelectric plants. The emissions for the Stabilization Fund reached an amount equivalent to 10% of the monetary base in 1958.

To curb this rise in the monetary base the Board of Directors of the Banco de la República had to recur to successive rises in the reserve requirement ratio of the banks and also raise the prior import deposits. However, from then on it became customary to reduce the reserve requirement when banking loans were used for certain purposes, which weakened this instrument of monetary control and meant that credit was oriented towards certain sectors of the economy but not to others. This last policy was strengthened with the passing of law 26 of 1959, which ordered that 15% of the banking portfolio should be directed towards agricultural activities at preferential interest rates.

In the midst of a period that was particularly turbulent –because of the boom and decline in coffee prices; very acute exchange problems, especially after 1957; fiscal imbalances; and the use of ad-hoc monetary measures to control the expansion of money– one thing had stood out since the beginning of the nineteen-fifties: rediscount policy would not be used to guide monetary policy but to orient credit. This decision was strengthened with the issuing of a norm in 1957 through which the ordinary and special quotas of credit destined for the commercial banks by the Banco de la República since 1951 were converted in a single one, of which 60% would be used to finance industrial, agricultural and cattle-raising activities.

In September, 1961, when Misael Pastrana Borrero became Minister of Finance, the stablization program was abandoned, with a very rapid dismounting of credit, exchange and fiscal controls, which resulted in a heavy fiscal deficit, an excessive growth of the government's debt with the Banco de la República and a rapid monetary expansion. Thus, the seeds were sown for the traumatic devaluation of 1962.

When the government of President Guillermo León Valencia (1962-1966) took office in August, 1962, the macro-economic situation was characterized by a high fiscal deficit, a shortage of foreign exchange, an imbalance in the current account of the balance of payments and a high growth of the money supply. An attempt was made to correct this macro-economic imbalance through the devaluation of the exchange rate certificates –which rose from 6.90 *pesos* per dollar to 9.00 *pesos* per dollar in November, 1962–, and improvements in tax collection to balance the fiscal accounts and avoid the contracting of more debts with the Banco de la República.

Nevertheless, this attempt turned out to be pretty ineffective. In 1963 the country suffered the highest annual inflation in its history, 32.6%. In the following years there were new exchange imbalances. Among the reasons for its failure there were the three months of open debate in the Congress about the convenience of a devaluation and how it should be carried out; the precarious fiscal situation and a new financing of the government by the Bank; the increase of credit from the Bank that was destined to finance the purchase and retention of coffee by the National Coffee-Growers Federation; a general rise in nominal salaries which included a six-monthly revision; and the government's general lack of credibility.

The inflation of 1963, its negative effect on the real exchange rate and the persistent external imbalance gave rise to the establishment, in September, 1965, of a complex system of exchange rates: a rate of 9.00 *pesos* per dollar was fixed for preferential imports; 13.50 *pesos* per dollar for the intermediate market; and one that fluctuated around 18 *pesos* per dollar for the free market, which was maintained. This measure was complemented by a new attempt to free imports in September, 1965, after a severe restriction during the first nine months of that year.

In the midst of this erratic and in a certain sense, chaotic management of the exchange rates, monetary policy followed a course similar to the one of the preceding years, that is, the reserve requirement ratio was used to try to neutralize primary expansion every time that such expansion threatened to become excessive but allowances were made for credits that stimulated economic growth.

Below,
Coffee-harvesters in the 1960's.

INSTITUTIONAL CHANGES IN THE NINETEEN-SIXTIES. THE MONETARY BOARD AND DECREE 444 OF 1967

Opposite page, *Guillermo León Valencia (1962-1966). His government faced fiscal and exchange imbalances which led, in 1963, to the highest annual inflation since the founding of the Banco de la República. With the creation of the Monetary Board in that year, the State reasserted its right to guide money and credit.*

Right, *Carlos Sanz de Santamaría, Minister of Finance under President Valencia, responsible for the measures that originated the Monetary Board.*

The ideas of Professors Currie and Grove on the creation of an institution that would act as the monetary authority without having representatives from the private sector were only taken up 12 years after they had been proposed and then only in a partial way.

In fact, it was not until 1963, by virtue of article 5 of law 21 of August 20 of that year, that a Monetary Board was created for the purpose of "studying and adopting monetary, exchange and credit measures which, in accordance with the current norms, are the responsibility of the Banco de la República" and "exercising other complementary functions which the government assigns to it". The same law gave the government the power to determine its organization and composition.

This authorization was formalized through law decree 2206 of September 20, 1963, signed by President Guillermo Leon Valencia and his Minister of Finance Carlos Sanz de Santamaría. Article 1 ordered that the Monetary Board be made up of the ministers of Finance, Agriculture and Development, the Governor of the Banco de la República and the Director of the National Planning Department. In 1968 the Director of the Colombian Institute of Foreign Trade was added to the Board and the Bank Superintendent and Economic Secretary of the Presidency of Colombia joined it as non-voting members.

The membership of this monetary authority corresponded, in part, to the proposals made by Currie and Grove, in that private-sector representatives did not sit on it, but it departed from them in authorizing the participation of two cabinet ministers, apart from the minister of Finance, instead of having a rotating system of non-

political officials sitting on the Board for fixed periods.

The system of membership did not satisfy the hopes of Alfonso Palacio Rudas either, a journalist and Liberal politician who, like Currie and Grove, was an advocate of making the Board a technical body named by the President of Colombia but clearly independent of the government. Palacio Rudas made this point in June, 1971, when he noted: "no legal or economic expert counsels... giving the control of money and credit to a body of novice and popularity-seeking ministers, instead of entrusting it to a monetary board or magistracy of a high academic level which, representing the public interest, will not yield to the pressure of insatiable budgets". (Cited by Avella, 2000, p. 125).

Independent of the criticisms about its membership, by creating the Monetary

Right,
Eduardo Arias Robledo, Governor of the Banco de la República between, 1961-1970.

Board the State did reclaim its right to fully exercise sovereignty over monetary matters, that is, the power to regulate everything related to money and especially, its issue and withdrawal from circulation.

In this way it gave up delegating the formulation of monetary, exchange and credit policy to the Board of Directors of the Banco de la República, a power which the Board had exercised since 1923 and especially, after the reforms introduced in 1951. As a result, the Board of Directors of the Banco de la República came to carry out the administrative functions of that institution and was responsible for ensuring that the rulings of the Monetary Board were faithfully carried out.

Law decree 2206 of 1963 took up another recommendation made by the foreign missions which visited the country in the early nineteen-fifties by ordering the Monetary Board to name two experts who would permanently advise it on the fulfillment of its functions, who would take part in but not vote at its deliberations.

This law-decree not only conferred on the Monetary Board those functions which had been previously assigned, by decree 756 of 1951, to the Board of Directors of the Banco de la República, but it also gave it additional ones.

These included the right to:
- fix limits on the volume of loans or investments made by credit institutions;
- establish the growth rate for the totality of assets of these institutions, with the power to fix different rates for different institutions;
- determine the interest or discount rates which credit institutions might charge to their clients;
- set terms for the loans and discounts realized by these institutions;
- prohibit credit institutions to carry out operations that implied grave risks;
- authorize the Banco de la República to buy, amortize or sell its own securities issued or guaranteed by the national government, with the aim of regulating the monetary market;
- order the minting of coins, whose emission would continue to be in the hands of the General Treasury of the Nation. In addition, it was given the right to carry out controls over foreign exchange and foreign trade that had been granted to the Board of Directors of the Banco de la República under law 1 of 1959 and law 83 of 1962.

There is no doubt that this multiplicity of faculties and instruments gave the Monetary Board full powers to carry out monetary, exchange and credit policy, for which it had to rely on the close support of the Banco de la República and its management.

During the period from 1956 to 1960, the tenure of the Bank's Governors was relatively short, by its own standards: Ignacio Copete Lizarralde served from September, 1956 to February, 1960 and Jorge Cortés Boshell from February to December, 1960. From then on the customary longer tenure held true. Eduardo Arias Robledo served from January, 1961 to October, 1969, folllowed by Germán Botero de los Ríos (October, 1969 to August, 1978), Rafael Gama (August, 1978 to August, 1982), Hugo Palacios Mejía (September, 1982 to September, 1985), Francisco Ortega (October, 1985 to February, 1993) and finally, the Governor at the time of writing, Miguel Urrutia, who has held the post since the beginning of 1993.

The other institutional change that was important for monetary and exchange management derived from decree 444 of 1967, which returned to exchange controls, in that it ordered that the negotiation of gold and foreign exchange must be done through the Banco de la República. It established a crawling peg regime, that is, a continual, not sudden, modification of the exchange rate, which meant that the idea of maintaining a nominal fixed parity for money over long periods was dropped. It also sought to unify exchange rates by eliminating exchange markets with differential rates; created a system of promoting non-traditional exports; established controls on foreign investment, the remittance abroad of profits and the payment of royalties; and gave the Monetary Board new powers in the exchange field.

Exchange unification was accomplished in june, 1968, when the rate of the exchange certificate, which had been set at 13.50 *pesos* per dollar in March, 1967, reached the rate obtaining in the capital market that had replaced the free market. Both rates were placed at 16.30 *pesos* per dollar and from that time onwards the country once more had, for the first time since 1948, a single exchange rate.

But in addition to eliminating the multiple exchange rate, the rules of the game for exchange were made stable again through decree 444 of 1967, which had been created by President Carlos Lleras Restrepo (1966-1970) and his Minister of Finance, Abdón Espinosa Valderrama. This made possible a rapid growth of non-traditional exports, which facilitated foreign indebtedness and a strengthening of the balance of payments, as demonstrated by the accumulation of net international reserves. After having been negative between the middle of 1961 and the beginning of 1968, these reserves thereafter showed a continual growth, reaching 429 million dollars by the end of 1974. For the rest, despite a variety of external circumstances, Colombia did not face any balance of payments crisis and was the only Latin American country that did not restructure its foreign debt in the 1980's.

According to Eduardo Wiesner the new exchange policy amounted to a revolution, in that "the attitude that exchange stability per se was correct had been overcome. It was recognized, at least implicitly, that the monetary or fiscal stability needed to guarantee a stable parity did not exist. Finally, it was admitted that the only way of managing devaluation from a political point of view, both on a domestic and foreign level, was to do it in a gradual and constant way. In this manner the new policy managed to: reduce the controversy over devaluation; lessen the problems deriving from delays in the payment of foreign debt; and avoid compensatory salary adjustments and counter-productive monetary emissions. In short, it managed to prevent devaluations becoming the cause of abrupt disturbances and of both economic- and political-type difficulties. For all of these reasons the new exchange regime was an undoubted advance". (Wiesner, 1978, p. 182).

Below, *Joaquín Vallejo, Minister of Finance at the end of the government of President Valencia and Abdón Espinosa, who held that post during the presidencies of Carlos Lleras Restrepo and López Michelsen.*

Above, *Political cartoon by Osuna, parodying the famous comic strip by Quino, "Mafalda". Manolito, the son of a shopkeeper, dreams not of of being Rockefeller but Abdón Espinosa Valderrama, Finance Minister under President Carlos Lleras and then under Alfonso López Michelsen.*

Stamp portraying the Flota Mercante Grancolombiana, the merchant fleet belonging to Colombia, Ecuador and Venezuela.

THE AGE OF INFLATION

Opposite page,
Four Governors of the Banco de la República: the present Governor, Miguel Urrutia Montoya, who took office on February 22, 1993; Rafael Gama Quijano, August, 1978 to August, 1982; Hugo Palacios Mejía, August, 1982 to September, 1985; and Germán Botero de los Ríos, February, 1970 to August, 1978. Oil painting by Antonio Roda, 1995. Detail.

Right,
Francisco Ortega, Governor of the Banco de la República between 1985 and 1992. Oil painting by Antonio Roda, 1995. Detail.

Under the new institutional framework for monetary and exchange affairs, the quarter century which ran from the authorization of the exchange statute at the beginning of 1967 to the adoption of a new constitution for the country in 1991 was a period in which the Colombian economy grew in a continual way, despite its slowing down at the beginning of the 1980's. It was subjected to external shocks that caused ups and downs in fiscal, monetary and credit policy and it witnessed a diversification and modernization of the financial system, marked by the creation of new credit institutions and the emergence of new instruments for carrying out economic transactions.

Despite the uneven rhythm of economic growth in some periods, and the different macro-economic policies that were pursued by the authorities, in the monetary field the distinctive characteristic of the period following 1973 was the emergence and consolidation of an inflation process that led the general price level to grow at an average annual rate of more than 20%.

In the period between 1973-1997 there was only one year when the annual inflation rate fell to 17%, a figure which contrasts with what happened in the fifty years between 1923 and 1972, when there were only four years in which the annual inflation rate surpassed this level and the overall inflation rate was only a bit higher than 7% annually on average.

The inflation in Colombia since the 1970's has, of course, been moderate compared to that suffered by a number of Latin American countries in which, especially in the 1980's, annual inflation rates of 5,000% or even higher were reached. The particularity of Colombian inflation did not lie, therefore, in its high level but in the

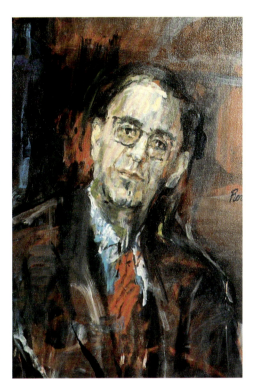

long-lasting, moderate and stable way in which it persisted. No other country has had an inflation rate fluctuating around 23-25% annually for more than 20 consecutive years.

Three factors help to explain the persistence and stability of inflation in Colombia during the period in question. To begin with, the ruling classes worked out an implicit social pact which, by means of credit financed with the primary emission of money at subsidized interest rates, apportioned the inflationary tax among certain sectors and in this way diminished the negative effects of inflation on these sectors.

In second place, a regime of inflation-linked salary adjustments was established, which allowed the purchasing power which had been lost in the course of the prior year to be restored to salaries and other incomes at the beginning of the new year.

The result of this has been that the inflationary process has not had a significant effect on the purchasing power of salary income and thus the labor movement did not strongly object to the inflationary process or the policies that sustained it.

Finally the accomodating behavior of the monetary authority, through a wide expansion of the means of payment, systematically validated this index-linked salary system and tacit social pact, to the point where it was only when annual inflation threatened to pass the 30% threshold that monetary policy became truly restrictive.

The close relationship between an excess in the creation of money, which may be defined as the difference between the growth in the means of payment and the growth of the Gross Domestic Product, and inflation may be observed in Chart 3.

The appropriation of the inflationary tax by certain economic and social sectors materialized as the Banco de la República and monetary policy in general gradually found themselves trapped, after the nineteen-seventies, by the need to administer a long list of credit lines destined for special purposes and at preferential interest rates, in accordance with the ideas contained in the reform of 1951.

The commitments that successively emerged included: the Fund of Private Investments (FIP - *Fondo de Inversiones Privadas*), created by resolution 11 of 1963 for the purpose of promoting the industries dedicated to exports or import substitution; the Industrial Financing Fund (FFI - *Fondo Financiero Industrial*), established by resolution 54 of 1968, whose objective was to provide financing to small and medium industries; the Financial Fund for Urban Development (FFDU - *Fondo Financiero de Desarrollo Urbano*), created by resolution 63 of 1968 to finance investment projects, mostly in medium-sized cities; the Agrarian Financial Fund (*Fondo Financiero Agrario*), which emerged as a result of resolution 23 of 1966 and was later converted, under law 5 of 1973, into the *Fondo Financiero Agropecuario* (FFAP), whose general purpose was to increase the production of food and raw materials in the countryside; the Fund for Public Works Contractors (FCOP - *Fondo de Contrastistas de Obras Públicas*), designed to relieve the liquidity crisis in the Ministry of Public Works; the Export Promotion Fund (Proexpo - *Fondo de Promoción de Exportaciones*), created through decree 444 of 1967 and oriented towards the financing of non-traditional exports; and later on, the Fund for Electricity Development (FDE - *Fondo de Desarrollo Eléctrico*), created in 1976 to lend financial support to electrical energy enterprises and the Fund for Business Capitalization (FCE - *Fondo de Capitalización Empresarial*), established in 1983.

Almost of all these funds initially lacked resources to rediscount their operations and had to recur to foreign credit, emissions of the Banco de la República or the use of special resources from the regime of bank reserves. This, together with the policy of

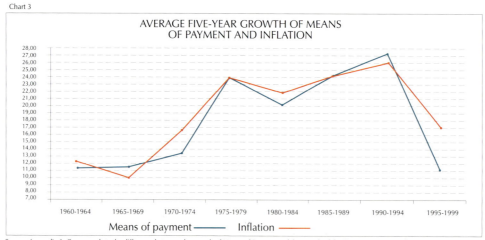

Chart 3

AVERAGE FIVE-YEAR GROWTH OF MEANS OF PAYMENT AND INFLATION

Source: Appendix 1. Corresponds to the difference between the growth of Means of Payment and the growth of the Gross Domestic Product.

Below, *President Carlos Lleras Restrepo (1966-1970). During his administration macro-economic stability was recovered, inflation was reduced and a process of export diversification was initiated, based on the exchange norms found in decree 444 of 1967.*

establishing preferential interest rates, caused all transparency to be lost in the management of credit subsidies.

By administering and, in one way or another, financing all of these credit lines the Banco de la República, originally conceived as a Central Bank for the emission and control of the money supply, turned into a credit bank which selected and financed projects for private investment in a manner similar to that of the financial intermediaries which have neither the responsibility nor the prerogative to make primary issues of money.

The Special Credit Funds rediscounted operations of the private and public commercial banks, the Caja Agraria, the Banco Central Hipotecario and the Financial Corporations that began to be founded in 1959 and rapidly expanded in number after the issuing of decree 2369 of 1960, so that 29 of these financial intermediaries were operating by 1978.

The purpose of these Corporations was to promote the creation, transformation and reorganization of manufacturing, agricultural or mining companies, for which end they could own stocks in or grant them credits. They mostly opted for the second alternative by acting as intermediaries for credits, which they rediscounted in the Special Credit Funds administered by the Banco de la República.

In September, 1972 the savings and housing-loans corporations (CAVS - *corporaciones de ahorro y vivienda*) began operations, in accordance with the authorization given by decree 678 of May of that year. The function of these institutions was to gather savings from the public with the aim of using them for the financing of construction, on the basis of the principle of constant value.

This new system sought to encourage savers to conserve the purchasing power of their savings and avoid the eroding effect

Above, *The government of President Misael Pastrana Borrero (1974-1978) created the "Four Strategies" plan, based on making construction the leading sector of the economy. The moderate but persistent inflation which has characterized the Colombian economy since the 1970's began during his administration.*

with the founding of the CAVS and the creation of the Units of Constant Purchasing Power (UPACs -*Unidades de Poder Adquisitivo Constante*), during the government of Misael Pastrana Borrero (1970-1974). The savings and housing loans corporation began operations on September 15, 1972, when the value of the UPAC was set at 100 *pesos*. By the beginning of 1974 ten of these institutions were operating, seven with private capital and three with public capital.

Due to the fact that the savings and housing loans system was in a privileged position for a number of years, in that it remunerated sight savings with higher interest rates than those paid for the same resources by other financial intermediaries, the UPAC system operated with success, despite complaints from some sectors of the borrowers. It was also successful because, in general terms, nominal salaries rose more than housing loan installments and the price of housing rose more quickly than the due balance of the debts. By 1997 the UPACs had come to represent 25% of the total portfolio of the banking system.

of long-term inflation. To achieve this, the remuneration for the resources thus deposited would be based on two principles: monetary correction, intended to make up for the loss of the purchasing power of money as a result of inflation, and a real interest rate that constituted the true remuneration for the savers.

Furthermore, since the debtors would not pay for the monetary correction on a month-by-month basis, as the latter was accumulated so that it could be amortized as their nominal incomes rose, the system facilitated the paying off of loans through low installments, which was supposed to increase the demand for credit and housing.

In a certain sense, this was the essential aim of the new systems of savings and housing loans, which regarded the construction of houses as an activity with an effective and growing latent demand, the exploitation of which would stimulate a high growth in the economy as a whole.

This theory was developed by Professor Lauchlin Currie and came into being

Below, *Misael Pastrana Borrero. Cartoon by Héctor Osuna, which refers to the economic emergency decree issued by his government.*

Right,
The administration of President Alfonso López Michelsen (1974-1978) was marked by a rise in coffee prices and the accumulation of foreign reserves. These phenomena led to the taking of ad-hoc monetary policies that impeded the full development of the financial reform undertaken at the start of his administration.

In 1998 a sharp fall in housing prices, as a result of a reverse in the cycle of construction and a pronounced rise in the interest rate, which had affected the calculation of the monetary correction since 1994, wound up affecting the payment capacity of the borrowers and led the system of home finance into a profound crisis, from which, at the time of writing (mid-2001) it has still not recovered.

The crisis was further accentuated by legal ambiguities deriving from a number of decisions by the Constitutional Court which led to the abolishment of the existing UPAC system and the restoration of a scheme that had in fact a greater resemblance to the one originally thought up by Professor Lauchlin Currie, that is, the interest rate was now detached from the calculation of the monetary correction and a new unit of constant purchasing power was created, which was known as the Unit of Real Value (UVR - *Unidad de Valor Real*).

During the same period of the nineteen-seventies, the creation of the financial corporations and the savings and housing loans institutions was followed by a measure which subjected the institutions then known as non-banking or extra-banking financial intermediaries to the control of the Bank Superintendency. These institutions would later give rise to the Commercial Finance Companies (*Compañías de Financiamiento Comercial*).

As we shall see later on, this process of diversification in financial institutions gave more depth to the financial system and took place around the same time that the Banco de la República was nationalized through law 7 of 1973.

Through this measure and the consequent contract signed between the government and the Banco de la República, it was agreed that:

• as from July 20, 1973, the state authority to issue money would be non-delegated and exercised by the State through the Banco de la República;

• the life of this institution would be prolonged for 99 years as from July, 1973, along with its faculty to issue bank notes;

• the government would acquire the

stocks in the power of the banks, except for one for each banking establishment, which would not give it the right to vote or receive dividends. With the measure and a complementary one, decree 2617, December 15, 1973, which corrected some legal flaws in law 7, the participation of private capital in the Banco de la República came to an end, after having been in force since 1923;

• the membership of the Board of Directors was modified.

The 10-member composition of the Board was restored. It was to be made up of three members named by the national government, one of them being the minister of Finance in his own right; three elected by the banks affiliated to the Banking Association; the manager of the National Federation of Coffee-Growers; and three more, representing consumers, producers and exporters (apart from coffee exporters), respectively.

The latter three would be chosen by the government from lists of five names presented by the respective trade associations.

Above, *Stamp commemorating the 50th anniversary of the founding of the National Coffee-Growers Federation, with a picture of Juan Valdés, the personification of Colombian coffee.*

Below, *Uncle Sam and the "devaluation rate" of coffeee, cartoon by Merino (a play on the word "taza", (cup) and "tasa" (rate). El Tiempo, March 3, 1971.*

In the midst of this process of diversifying and giving more depth to the financial system and the above-mentioned change in the institutional framework of the Banco de la República, monetary policy was subjected to strong fluctuations.

Between 1967 and 1970 there were heavy expansionist pressures on the means of payment because the increase in international reserves was strengthened by the granting of larger credits by the Bank to the commercial banks and Special Credit Funds. The reduction of the Bank's credit to the government and the repayment of some loans by the Coffee-Growers Federation did not serve to fully moderate the expansion of primary money, whose increase in this period, except in 1967, was higher than 30% annually. Instead, raising the reserve requirement ratio became the mechanism of monetary restriction: the reserve requirement ratio practically doubled between 1967 and 1970. This restrained monetary growth, so that the annual average inflation rate between 1967 and 1970 was only 7.3%.

In the following two years the fall in international reserves –the result of falls in the international prices of coffee and a rapid increase in imports and thus a lesser expansion of primary money– led to a reduction of the reserve requirement coefficients. Within this context the growth in the means of payment was relatively moderate in 1971 and 1972.

These would be the last two years of moderate expansions of the monetary supply, since between 1973 and 1995 the

means of payment grew at a more than 20% annual rate, independent of the situation in the foreign sector or the circumstances surrounding public finances.

On the external front, beginning in July, 1975, the price of coffee, which had been around 58 U.S. cents per pound in the first half of the nineteen seventies, began to rise and during the 1976-1980 period reached an average price of 1.76 dollars per pound, with a peak of 3 dollars per pound in April, 1977. Such a bonanza led to a great inflow of foreign earnings that raised gross international reserves from 396 million dollars in June, 1975 to more than 5.6 billion dollars in 1981.

Faced with such an abundance of foreign exchange and resolved to not float the exchange rate for fear of revaluation, the monetary authorities were subjected to strong pressures. Despite a variety of corrective measures, the means of payment expanded, on average, at an annual rate of nearly 20% between 1976 and 1981. These measures included elevating the reserve requirement ratio, enlarging the liberation of imports, reducing the pace of nominal devaluation and ingenious attempts to find new mechanisms to contract primary money, which included speeding up foreign payments, restricting private foreign debt and emitting Banco de la República securities. Naturally, this monetary expansion, which was aggravated by adverse climatic conditions in 1976 and 1977, accelerated inflation, which rose from an annual average of 16.8% in 1970-74 to an annual average of 23.9% between 1975-79, despite a significant fall of nearly 10 percentage points in 1978 from the 28% annual rate seen in 1977.

One of the consequences of the inflationary process that began in 1973 and intensified with the coffee boom of the mid-1970's was that monetary policy put a stop to the attempt at financial liberation that had been initiated during the administration of president Alfonso López Michelsen (1974-1978). In the second half of 1974 a financial reform was undertaken with the central aims of restoring a more active role to the banking system in the assignation of credit and eliminating many of the limitations and regulations which the financial sector faced. To achieve these aims, it was thought that the market should play a more decisive role in the setting of active and passive interest rates on assets and liabilities. However, the monetary expansion deriving from the accumulation of international reserves and ad-hoc measures taken by the authorities to curb it made it impossible to carry out most of these reforms.

In the midst of a quickening inflation, the growth rate of the Gross Domestic Product showed an average annual rate of 5% between 1975-1979, which was below that of the period of 1970-1974 (6.5%) but much higher than that of 1980-1985 (2.4%), a period in which the Colombian economy faced a new external imbalance, a growing fiscal deficit and a profound financial crisis.

Despite the fact that Colombia did not contract excess debt, due in part to the coffee boom, and showed a timely compliance with its foreign debt payments,

Below, *President Julio César Turbay Ayala (1978-1982). International coffee prices declined at the end of his government and a new imbalance in public finances became evident.*

Right,
Bogotá Stock Exchange, 1973.

Below,
The massive use of credit cards that began in the 1970's reduced the demand for cash and helped to modernize the system of payments in Colombia.

the international crisis at the beginning of the nineteen-eighties caused a fall in the flow of foreign capitals. This, together with high imports and a reduction in the value of exports resulting from falling coffee prices, led to deficits in the trade balance and the current account, a situation which, because of the rapid depletion of foreign reserves, brought the country near to a balance of payments crisis in 1982 and 1983.

To check this fall the economic authorities eased the rigid controls on foreign indebtedness imposed during the epoch of high coffee prices and the Banco de la República followed a general credit policy that sought to restore to the economy the liquidity that had been lost as a result of the fall in international reserves. This granting of credit resources increased in 1982, when there was a crisis of confidence that had to do with doubts about the solvency and liquidity of many financial institutions: this was curbed by the Bank's exercise of its powers as the lender of last resort.

This financial crisis, which was the result of imprudent and illegal credit prac-

tices by some financial intermediaries, led the Bank Superintendent to intervene in the operations of a growing number of them between June and September, 1982: in the end, most were taken over by the government.

If we add the secondary expansions caused by reductions in the minimum reserve requirements to the increase of the primary money in circulation, we observe a moderate growth in the means of payment compared to the period of the coffee boom, but in any case it was close to 20% annually between 1982 and 1984, a period when the average annual inflation was slightly below this level.

When, in October, 1984, the gross international reserves of the Banco de la República barely surpassed 1.5 billion dollars, the government of President Belisario Betancur (1982-1986), under the guidance of the Minister of Finance Roberto Junguito, designed an adjustment plan intended to correct the imbalance in foreign exchange and the fiscal deficit and achieve a complete recuperation of the financial sector.

On the external front, the measures were intended to reestablish the international flow of capital, through a macro-economic stability program that was overseen by the International Monetary Fund and supported by the World Bank. Beyond this, actions were taken to correct the backwardness of the exchange rate. For the latter purpose nominal devaluation was sped up: it was 28% in 1984 and 51% in 1985. In the fiscal field the charging of a valued added tax was established, the government's debt with the Banco de la República was refinanced at low interest rates, the gasoline tax was increased and a rigid control of government spending was applied. Taken as a whole, the measures that were adopted produced a devaluation of the real exchange rate.

The macro-economic effects of this program were strengthened by the rise in the international prices of coffee in 1986, a year in which the country obtained, for the first time since 1980, a surplus in the current account of the balance of payments. This phenomenon was controlled by a non-inflationary accumulation of foreign reserves, through an intensification

Left, *The government of President Betancur (1982-1986) confronted the fall in international coffee prices and the international crisis at the beginning of the 1980's. Half-way through his administration a program of macro-economic stabilization was undertaken, which once again corrected the fiscal and external imbalances.*

Left, *"The decrees fall down", cartoon by Héctor Osuna in* El Espectador, *on the occasion when the emergency economic decrees issued by the government of Belisario Betancur were judged to be unconstitutional.*

of open market operations by the Banco de la República and the speeding up of the payment of the short-term foreign debt of public sector institutions and the National Federation of Coffee-Growers.

However, the mini-boom in coffee of 1986 did not last long, since the prices of coffee began to fall again in 1987. Paradoxically this fall created a tendency towards monetary expansion, due to the fact that, to maintain the internal price, the National Federation of Coffee-Growers began to spend some of the funds which had been frozen from a monetary point of view on the occasion of the rise in prices. Faced with this situation, the monetary authorities, as had been usual in such cases since 1960, recurred to rises in the reserve requirement ratio.

This measure was complemented, during the administration of Virgilio Barco (1986-1990), with norms that tended to more strictly regulate the factors relating to the solvency of the financial institutions. Nevertheless, it should be pointed out that by the end of the Barco administration, with a view towards creating conditions which would allow the Colombian economy to open itself up to international market forces, the process of nominal devaluation was accelerated. This, together with a rapid expansion of the means of payment, had adverse effects on inflation, which reached an average annual rate of 28% between 1988 and 1990.

In the midst of the persistent growth of the means of payment and the accelerating inflation, the bank notes which the Banco de la República had issued since 1923 progressively disappeared from circulation, since bills were replaced by metal coins, as may be seen in Table 5.

For the rest, the printing of the seventh edition of the two thousand *pesos* bill in 1993 did away with the anachronistic legend which indicated the amount of gold that the Banco de la República would pay to the bearer of these bank notes. The legend had been meaningless

Right, *Virgilio Barco (1986-1990). During his presidential term, the first steps were taken to open the economy to world markets. Inflation accelerated at the end of his administration.*

Table 5

BANK NOTES THAT WERE WITHDRAW FROM CIRCULATION AND REPLACED BY COINS IN THE PERIOD 1974 - 1996		
Type of Bank Note	Period of Circulation	Replaced by
One peso bank note	1923 - 1974	Nickel coins 6.8 grams
Two pesos bank note	1923 - 1977	Copper coins 7.9 grams
Five pesos bank note	1923 - 1981	Copper coins 9.0 grams
Ten pesos bank note	1923 - 1980	Nickel coins 10.0 grams
Twenty pesos bank note	1927 - 1983	Copper coins 6.0 grams
Fiftty pesos bank note	1923 - 1986	Nickel coins 8.4 grams
One hundred pesos bank note	1928 - 1992	Copper coins 5.3 grams
Two hundred pesos bank note	1974 - 1992	Nickel coins 7.08 grams
Five hundred pesos bank note	1923 - 1993	Bimetallic coins 7.4 grams
One thousand pesos bank note	1979 - 1996	Copper coins 7.3 grams

Source: Hernández, Pedro Pablo. "Catálogo de Billetes de Colombia".

Above,
Coins of different alloys which, beginning in the mid-1970's, have replaced the bank notes issued by the Banco de la República since 1923.

since the beginning of the nineteen-thirties, when the convertibility of bank notes into gold was eliminated.

The inflationary process that began in 1973 did not, however, prevent the financial system from acquiring more depth, as may be observed in graph 4, which shows the rapid growth of bank liabilities in relation to the size of the economy since the 1970's.

One of the most notable signs of this process of greater depth and modernization in finances and the system of payments in general was a rapid expansion in the use of credit cards for economic transactions. Though this new instrument of credit and payment had been introduced to the country with the Diners card in the nineteen sixties, it only began to have a wider use in 1970, when the Banco de Bogotá obtained a license from the Bank of America to operate the Credibanco card. The name was changed to Credibanco Visa in 1979, when the Bank of America, owner of the rights to issue the Bank Americard, ceded them to Visa International. In later years, other services, like Mastercard, Credencial and Bic joined Credibanco and Diners in providing facilities for financing and payment through credit cards.

The popularity of the Credibanco cards as an instrument for the purchase of consumer goods was due to the fact that, in contrast with the first Diners cards, their holders were able to delay the payment of their purchases through the credit that was granted to them by the financial institutions which issued this mechanism of payment.

Restricted at first to only financing purchases made in Colombia, with the exchange liberalization established in 1990 it now became possible to acquire goods from abroad with credit cards. Another innovation came in 1992, when the system became more modern and widened its services to include the debit card, which allowed holders to transfer funds from current or savings accounts to the commercial establishments in which they purchased goods. The massive adoption of credit cards has meant that the demand for cash has decreased and it has therefore allowed for more flexibility in the payment system.

Chart 4

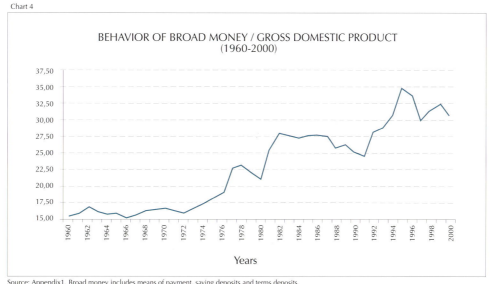

Source: Appendix 1. Broad money includes means of payment, saving deposits and terms deposits.

THE REFORM OF 1991

Opposite page,
Picture of the Constituent Assembly that drafted the new Constitution. Oil painting by Beatriz González, 1991. Detail.

Right,
Stamp commemorating the 1991 Constitution.

The moderate but long-lasting inflation, the repeated monetary financing of the fiscal deficit, especially during the nineteen eighties, the apportioning of the inflationary tax through mechanisms that went beyond tax and budget norms and a consensus of opinion in the international ambit (both technical and ideological) meant that the monetary authority could not avoid the influence of the multiple changes made to Colombian institutions by the country's new Political Constitution of 1991.

The first frank and open expression of dissatisfaction with the way that the benefits of seigniorage and the inflationary tax were granted to certain private-sector institutions and inflation unfairly affected other social sectors, going beyond tax legislation, went back to the middle of 1973, when Professor Lauchlin Currie and some of his collaborators in the National Planning Department published four articles in the Department's journal criticizing the inflationary tendency of the institutions responsible for monetary management in Colombia at that time. This viewpoint was shared by Alfonso Palacio Rudas, who criticized the monetary authority's proclivity to design policies that gave more importance to the sharing out of the credit pie than keeping prices stable.

Within the institutional framework that existed then, it was to be expected that an authority invested with an autonomous power to hand out subsidies at its own discretion, through the setting of interest rates lower than those existing in the free market, would cause distrust. Rudolf Hommes, economic analyst and future Finance Minister, made this point in the late nineteen-eighties when he wrote about the need for reform, arguing that the Banco de la República, through the Monetary

Board, was vulnerable to certain temptations and opportunities for personal and bureaucratic aggrandizement, since there were no mechanisms to control the actions of its officials.

On the international front the technocratic thinking of the multilateral agencies had reached a consensus on the need for wide reforms, which included a new set of rules for central banks. Specifically, it was felt that when the executive and legislative branches of a government monopolize monetary control they may sacrifice price stability in the name of fleeting and transitory benefits in the field of economic growth. This temptation is especially common in democratic regimes in pre-election periods, when, with a view to holding onto power, certain political groups may adopt monetary policies that cause economic cycles to become more acute.

Although the officials of the Banco de la República did not initially accept criticisms of its institutional structure, attributing inflation to causes other than monetary

Left, *Proclamation of the new Constitution of Colombia, July 4, 1991: Antonio Navarro Wolf, Ana Milena Muñoz de Gaviria, Cesar Gaviria Trujillo, Horacio Serpa Uribe and Alvaro Gómez Hurtado.*

management instead, they wound up becoming convinced of the need for reform.

Under the leadership of the then Governor of the Bank, Francisco Ortega, officials of the institution prepared a document entitled "A Proposal for the Monetary Regime in the Constitutional Reform", which became the basis for discussions during sessions held in the first half of 1991 by the National Constituent Assembly, the elected body in charge of drafting the new constitution.

This proposal differed in several respect from that originally presented by the administration of President César Gaviria (1990-1994), but it was actively supported by a number of Assembly members who were knowledgeable about the matter, among them, Alfonso Palacio Rudas, Carlos Lleras de la Fuente, Carlos Lemos, Guillermo Perry, Rodrigo Lloreda and Carlos Ossa. After extensive debates, the Constitution of 1991 established that the Banco de la República would be independent of the government, by decreeing that it would exercise the functions pertinent to a central bank "as a legal entity of public law, with juridical, financial and technical autonomy, subject to its own legal regime".

By virtue of this constitutional mandate the Bank has the functions of regulating money, international exchanges and credit; issuing legal currency; administering international reserves; being the lender of last resort and banker to the banking system; and acting as the fiscal agent of the government. The Bank must exercise these functions in coordination with the country's general economic policy.

The Constitution established that the Board of Directors of the Banco de la República is the monetary, exchange and credit authority and would have seven members, including the minister of Finance, who is chairman of the Board. The Governor of the Bank, elected by the Board itself, is also a member. In 1993, the President of Colombia chose, as his own right, the other five members, for a term of four years, which may be renewed. When this first period came to an end, the succeeding presidents could only replace two of them during their respective administrations.

Under the administrations of Presidents César Gaviria, Ernesto Samper Pizano (1994-1998) and Andrés Pastrana (1998-2002), the following served on the Board of Directors of the Banco de La República: Miguel Urrutia, María Mercedes Cuellar, Roberto Junguito, Carlos Ossa Escobar, Nestor Humberto Martínez, Salomón Kalmanovitz, Oscar Marulanda, Hernando José Gómez, Antonio Hernández Gamarra, Luis Bernardo Florez, Leonardo Villar, Sergio Clavijo, Carlos Caballero and Fernando Tenjo. The large number shows that there was a higher turn-over than was expected, due to the resignation, before the end of their terms, of Carlos Ossa, María Mercedes Cuellar and Roberto Junguito, the latter in his second term.

Since the 1991 reform, the ministers of Finance who have acted as chairmen of the Board have been Rudolf Hommes, Guillermo Perry, José Antonio Ocampo, Antonio Urdinola, Juan Camilo Restrepo and Juan Manuel Santos. During the same

Below, *Members of the Board of Directors of the Banco de la República appointed by President Cesar Gaviria.*

period, the Governors of the Banco de la República have been Francisco Ortega, who assumed office before 1991, and Miguel Urrutia, who took over at the beginning of 1993.

In pursuance of this constitutional mandate the main function of the Bank is the defense of the purchasing power of money; it is prohibited to establish quotas of credit or grant collaterals for the private sector, except in the case of the intermediation of external credit for its placement through credit establishments or liquidity support for the same; and the credit may only be granted to the government with the unanimous approval of Board members. In addition, the Constitution prohibited the Congress from ordering the Banco de la República to grant credit in favor of the State or the private sector.

In this way triumphed the ideas of those who, with a view towards reducing inflation, wanted the Banco de la República to return to its original functions as a central bank of monetary emission and control and to distance it from the supply of credit to specific sectors of the national economy. To achieve this aim, it was foreseen that the Special Credit Funds would no longer be administered by the Banco de la República, a policy which started in 1982 when the National Electricity Fund (FEN - *Financiera Eléctrica Nacional*) was created as an autonomous agency that replaced the Electricity Financing Fund (*Fondo Financiero Eléctrico*). A similar change occurred in 1990, when FINAGRO replaced the *Fondo Financiero Agropecuario* as the agricultural financial fund.

To resume, in response to international trends, the Constitution of 1991 established the Bank's independence of the government and guaranteed it a financial, instrumental and technical autonomy. In line with the Constitution, the law ordered the Bank to establish yearly targets to reduce inflation. This provision was found in law

Above, *Members of the Board of Directors of the Banco de la República: Leonardo Villar, Salomón Kalmanovitz, Luis Fernando Flórez, Antonio Hernández Gamarra.*

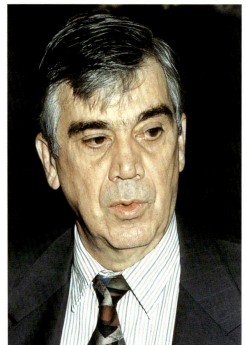

21 of 1992, which set forth the norms to which the Banco de la República has to subject itself in performing its functions, which was recently declared unconstitutional by the Constitutional Court because it was judged to limit the Bank's autonomy over this important matter.

The reform of the monetary institutions in Colombia took place within the framework of the technical and ideological consensus we have referred to. In this view, the public sector in Latin America had pursued too many objectives and had over-regulated economic activity, all of which produced negative effects on the continent's welfare and economic growth. In the nineteen-nineties, on the basis of this diagnosis, the Colombian government, like those of other Latin American countries, carried out a series of reforms to redefine the functions of state institutions with regard to their impact on economic activity.

Below, *Members of Board of Directors of the Banco de la República: Néstor Humberto Martínez, Carlos Caballero Argáez, Carlos Ossa Escobar.*

With the object of encouraging efficiency and competitiveness, what became known as the "opening" (*la apertura*) of the economy essentially sought to let market forces play a bigger role in the assigning of resources, for which reason the reforms emphasized the liberalization of the exchange market, foreign trade and the financial market, while it also called for more flexibility in the labor market and a stronger degree of decentralization.

In providing orientation for the financial sector, the reforms, in addition to creating a new structure for the Board of Directors of the Bank, set out to eliminate the assigning of credit to different sectors, suppress nearly all forced investments, establish multi-purpose banks instead of specialized ones, and reduce reserve requirement ratios. At the same time it was decided to privatize a good part of the banks that had been nationalized during the financial crisis of the mid-nineteen-eighties.

The reforms did away with the Bank's monopoly over the purchase and sale of foreign exchange, substantially modified exchange control and determined that the fixing of exchange rate should be done through a system of exchange bands, which remained in force until the end of September, 1999.

The system of exchange bands had been established at the beginning of 1994, when the exchange scheme based on continual nominal devaluation, in force since 1967, was dropped. This decision, which was more in tune with the objective of lowering inflation, was taken in order to eliminate the issuing of exchange certificates that had been going on since the beginning of the nineteen-nineties. Its aim was to stop the monetization of the enormous flow of foreign exchange that entered the country as a result of a government amnesty on Colombians holding such capital abroad and, in a more general way, give more freedom to the exchange regime.

These exchange certificates were issued to pay for foreign exchange and in this way delay their monetization for a time. When the certificates began to mature it became impossible to maintain this system and it was then decided to allow the exchange rate to fluctuate within a band, which was a way of ensuring that the Bank did not intervene so much in the exchange market, thus giving greater autonomy to monetary management.

The parameters of the band –that is, its central parity, width and slope– were periodically adjusted by the Board of Directors of the Bank as a way of giving clear

Above,
Stamp commemorating coffee and the reconstruction of the coffee zone after the recent earthquake.

Below,
Ernesto Samper (1994-1998). His government was opposed to the policy for a revaluation of the exchange rate which the Board of Directors of the Banco de la República had begun in the early 1990's.

signals to the market on the exchange rate, so that the rate would not jeopardize the inflation goals nor the sustainability of the balance of payments.

At the end of 1994 the nominal exchange rate was revalued by 7%, by reducing the central parity of the exchange band in force at that time. This decision gave rise to a public debate between the Board of Directors and the recently-installed government of President Ernesto Samper Pizano, since the executive branch did not look favorably upon a measure which accentuated the process of a real revaluation of the exchange rate which had begun in 1991 and only ended in the middle of 1997.

For the rest, before it was abandoned in 1999 the exchange band suffered two shifts: a 9% devaluation on September 2, 1998 and another 9% on June 27, 1999. On the latter occasion it was decided to broaden the band from 14% to 20%.

At the time that the exchange scheme was abandoned, the Board of Directors of the Banco de la República explained the decision in the following way: "the decision to abandon the commitment to defend the limits of exchange band was taken on the basis of a series of considerations that allowed us to foresee a smoother transition to a regime of a floating exchange rate. Among these stand out the reduction in the deficit in the current account of the balance of payments, which fell from around 8% of the Gross Domestic Product in the first quarter of 1998 to less than 2% of the Gross Domestic Product at the end of the first half of 1999; the 25 percentage points of real devaluation registered in the past two years; the strengthening of the financial system through programs of capitalization and debt-restructuring; the reduction of inflation to a single-digit rate; and the agreement with the International Monetary Fund. By offering guarantees to national and international markets that the country will carry out the reforms needed to place its economy on the path of sustained growth, this agreement facilitates access to international credit resources and reduces to an important extent the risks which floating the exchange rate might have caused in other circumstances". (Junta Directiva, 1999, p.8).

Below, *Meeting of the Board of Directors of the Banco de la República, 1998. From left to right: Antonio Hernández Gamarra; Juan Camilo Restrepo; Roberto Junguito; Sara Ordóñez, Bank Superintendent; Gerardo Hernández Correa, Secretary of the Board; Salomón Kalmanovitz; Luis Bernardo Flórez, Leonardo Villar and Miguel Urrutia.*

In analyzing the evolution of monetary management since the establishment in 1991 of the Bank's Board of Directors as the country's monetary, exchange and credit authority, it is convenient to divide the period into two parts: 1991-1994 and 1995-early 2001.

The first was characterized by strong increases in the means of payment (31.3% annually on average), deriving from the initial decision to maintain the exchange rate and the above-mentioned inflow of foreign exchange, which raised gross international reserves from 3,949 million dollars in December, 1990 to 8,060 million dollars in December, 1994.

The second has been characterized by a much more moderate monetary growth (an average annual rate of 16.4%) and a simplification of the process for making decisions about the carrying out of monetary policy.

The latter had to do with the measures taken to unify, reduce and stabilize the coefficients of the minimum reserve ratio and acquire a more exact knowledge of the demand for banking reserves. Other factors were the decision which led to the simplification of and greater technical sophistication behind the obligatory investments which the banks have to make in FINAGRO securities and the flexibility and automatization in shoring up the liquidity of the financial intermediaries, with a view towards ensuring an adequate functioning of the system of payments. All this meant that in the years 2000-2001 the most important instrument for supplying or removing liquidity from the economy have been open market operations, through the purchase or sale of government securities in the inter-bank market.

In order to control inflation, in late 1996 the Board of Directors of the Banco de la República chose the monetary base as the intermediate goal of its policy. Towards this end it created a corridor of 3% more or

Chart 5

**INFLATION RATE
(1990-2001)**

Source: Appendix 1.

Abajo,
*José Antonio
Ocampo, head of the
National Planning
Department and
Finance Minister
during the
government of
Ernesto Samper.*

Opposite page,
*Three recent bills
issued by the Banco
de la República.*

less for the path of growth of this monetary aggregate. This decision assumed that there was a predictable relationship between the monetary base and broader monetary aggregates. Or to put it in another way, what lay behind the intermediate goal of establishing a corridor for the monetary base was the growth of cash in the hands of the public and the banking reserve, together with the multiplier of the latter with respect to the liabilities subject to the reserve requirement.

For this reason there never existed a commitment to blindly correct deviations of the monetary base with regard to the corridor. On the contrary, deviations of the enumerated variables that were significant in terms of their projections gave rise to changes in the corridor of the monetary base, independent of the inflationary situation. All of this shows that Colombian monetary policy in the second half of the nineteen-nineties did not follow a strictly monetary target, either in terms of the monetary base or wider aggregates.

Faced by an unstable demand for cash, a more flexible exchange management and a notable reduction in both observed and expected inflation, the Board of Directors of the Banco de la República, in the session held on October 13, 2000, wanted to make their strategy for monetary policy more explicit, with the aim of giving more transparency to decision-making and making the policy more comprehensible to the different economic agents.

As a consequence of this determination, the Board of the Bank issued a press release on this date which explained to the public that from that time onwards the fundamental elements in the management of monetary policy would be the inflation target, the general state of the economy and the supply of money.

This policy was set forth in an editorial in the October, 2000 edition of the Bank's

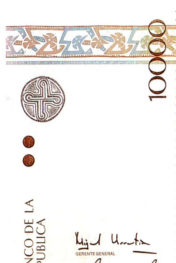

Right,
50,000 pesos bill issued by the Banco de la República, in homage to Jorge Isaacs.

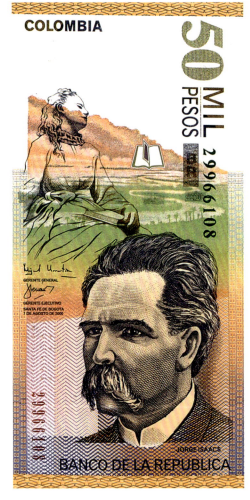

journal, the *Revista del Banco de la República*: "the first two elements are based on inflation targeting and the reference value of the monetary aggregate is based on the strategy of setting a monetary goal. Inflation targeting makes a direct communication with the public possible, creates incentives for the Central Bank to fulfill its objectives, makes the policy transparent and facilitates an external monitoring and evaluation of policy. In turn, the reference value of the monetary aggregate sends early signals about the appropriateness or not of the policy which is applied, signals which are of great importance because of the existence of variable lags between the actions of the Central Bank and the final result of inflation". (Urrutia, 2000, p. 10).

If the task of the Board were to be judged only in terms of the lowering of inflation, there would be no doubt that this policy has been completely successful, as may be seen in Graph 5, which shows the annual inflation rate from December, 1990 until the middle of the year 2001. The 32.4% inflation rate registered in 1990 fell to less than 8% in June, 2001, an achievement that stands out even more when we consider that it was only in 1996 that the annual inflation rate did not descend with respect to the previous year and also remember that between 1999 and the first half of the year 2001 inflation has been less than 10%, a figure not seen in Colombia since 1969.

Unfortunately, the reduction of inflation took place in the midst of a rapid slowing down of economic growth. The growth rate of the Gross Domestic Product, which reached an average annual figure of a little more than 5% between 1992 and 1995, fell on average to a bit less than 2% between 1996 and 1998 and showed a rate of -4.2% in 1999. In the year 2000 the Gross Domestic Product grew at a rate of 2.8%, well below the potential capacity of the economy and the long-term average of previous periods.

Some analysts attribute the weakness of economic activity to the monetary policy and especially, to the rise in the real interest rate that took place in the second half of 1998. Nevertheless, more complete analyses emphasize that the macro-economic stability of Colombia was jeopardized by the excess of public and private spending that arose at the beginning of the nineteen-nineties.

Since it was financed with foreign indebtedness, this excessive spending caused a revaluation of the real exchange rate and a non-sustainable increase in the prices of assets, especially real estate. This, added to the boom in the placing of internal credit, was expressed in a marked deterioration of the quality and repayment of loans from the financial system to diverse economic sectors, especially housing loans.

In this state of macro-economic imbalance and a vulnerable financial system, the Colombian economy had to face up to the international crisis of 1998, which together with the defense of the *peso*'s stability, led to a rise in the real interest rate in that year, with negative effects on growth and employment.

Oposite page,
César Gaviria (1990-1994). He intensified the opening up of the economy in the midst of a strong revaluation of the exchange rate. The 1991 Constitution enshrined the Banco de la República's autonomy with regard to the government.

Andrés Pastrana (1998-2002) with Juan Manuel Santos, Finance Minister. The search for macroeconomic equilibrium has guided the main economic decisions of his administration.

In any case, from a historical perspective perhaps it is too early to come up with a detailed and well-thought out analysis of the complex factors that led the Colombian economy to suffer the only decline in its Gross Domestic Product since the beginning of the nineteen thirties.

Independently of this judgement, it is clear that many of the macro-imbalances which the Colombian economy suffered in the nineteen-nineties had been corrected by the middle of the year 2001. This should help to achieve a higher and more stable economic growth, a reduction of unemployment and the maintenance of low inflation rates.

And it is precisely within this context of a low and stable inflation that we find a congressional initiative to change the monetary unit. If a Senate bill which is now (mid-2001) being considered by the legislature is passed (it only lacks two statutory House of Representative debates for its final approval) by the end of the year 2002 the monetary unit of Colombia will be the new *peso*, equivalent to one thousand *pesos* in present currency. If, as is expected, the project becomes law, within a short time the present types of money in circulation will become a thing of the past, since they will be replaced, without any real effect, by the new *pesos* of a smaller denomination. Thus a new chapter in the history of Colombian money would begin.

Appendix

MAIN MONETARY INDICATORS.
GROWTH OF THE GROSS DOMESTIC PRODUCT AND ANUAL INFLATION
1924-2000 (Millions of pesos)
In June of each year

* Broad money includes means of payment, savings deposits and term deposits.

** Millions of dollars.

*** *Pesos* per dollar.

n.d.a. : no data available.

Source: Banco de la República. *"Principales Indicadores Económicos 1923 - 1997"*. Journals of the Banco de la República: October, 1999 and August, 2000. National Planning Dpt. *"Estadísticas Históricas de Colombia"* Vol. I. GRECO. *"El Desempeño Macroeconómico Colombiano - Series Estadísticas (1905-1997)."* Segunda versión. Borradores de Economía. No.21.

Note 1: The data on broad money, cash and money base between 1924 and 1935 are taken from Avella, Mauricio. *"Pensamiento y Política Monetaria en Colombia 1886 - 1945"* Pag. 304.

Note 2: The data on broad money and bank portfolio from 1923 to 1931 correspond to the values at the end of each year.

Note 3: The data on the exchange rate correspond to the official exchange rate..

Year	Means of Payment	Deposits in Current Account	Cash	Monetary Base	Broad money*	Bank Portfolio	Gross International Reserves**	Exchange Rate ***	Growth of GDP %	Inflation %
1924	50,9	15,9	35,0	44,3	58,9	40,5	14,0	1,01	n.d.	9,00
1925	61,2	19,5	41,7	52.1	74,8	42,9	26,0	1,03	n.d.	10,09
1926	81,9	28,5	53,4	64,4	92,4	55,3	38,0	1,01	9,6	12,50
1927	90,5	34,2	56,3	68,6	99,1	67,3	42,0	1,03	9,0	11,85
1928	103,9	39,8	64,1	78,6	118,2	95,4	62,0	1,02	7,3	7,28
1929	98,2	36,0	62,2	76,1	90,4	83,5	55,0	1,04	3,6	-11,73
1930	69,8	23,6	46,1	56,1	74,0	74,6	31,0	1,04	-8,6	-21,68
1931	59,1	20,2	38,9	48,6	67,0	55,4	21,0	1,04	-1,6	-13,39
1932	60,2	24,8	35,4	48,9	71,7	53,7	16,0	1,05	6,6	-19,59
1933	74,3	30,3	44,0	59,9	83,7	47,7	18,0	1,16	5,6	-1,28
1934	102,0	40,3	61,7	78,2	107,3	42,5	18,0	1,73	6,3	16,88
1935	98,9	38,4	60,5	79,9	109,9	47,0	17,0	1,84	2,4	-2,22
1936	108,4	45,2	63,2	3,1	121,1	62,4	19,0	1,76	5,3	10,23
1937	128,4	54,5	73,9	9,3	143,0	76,4	25,0	1,76	1,6	12,37
1938	130,3	55,5	74,8	966	146,6	86,4	24,0	1,80	6,5	0,92
1939	146,5	65,1	81,4	106,	164,9	96,0	24,0	1,75	6,1	4,41
1940	149,4	74,0	75,4	109,9	169,9	95,2	24,0	1,75	2,2	-3,13
1941	172,8	85,9	86,9	118,5	196,6	106,7	30,0	1,76	1,7	-1,40
1942	192,8	93,4	99,4	136,0	218,0	112,1	38,0	1,75	0,2	8,67
1943	272,2	148,1	124,1	183,6	305,1	143,9	88,0	1,75	0,4	15,88
1944	374,2	195,6	178,6	248,7	424,9	162,9	147,0	1,75	6,8	20,31
1945	431,2	236,4	194,8	286,6	500,1	216,5	158,0	1,75	4,7	11,33
1946	521,6	295,8	225,8	316,6	603,9	314,6	172,0	1,76	9,6	9,29
1947	570,3	314,2	256,1	352,1	666,1	390,5	132,0	1,75	3,9	18,19
1948	683,3	369,3	314,0	418,5	783,2	474,8	108,0	1,75	2,8	16,41
1949	787,1	432,2	354,9	476,2	896,1	538,1	91,0	1,96	8,8	6,66
1950	982,7	536,4	446,3	571,7	1.087,3	669,2	109,0	1,96	1,1	20,12
1951	950,1	529,1	421,0	533,8	1.068,8	758,1	109,0	2,51	3,1	9,34
1952	1.175,8	682,7	493,1	640,6	1.333,6	926,0	127,0	2,51	6,3	-2,37
1953	1.334,6	798,2	536,4	739,4	1.522,5	1.120,0	187,0	2,51	6,1	7,37
1954	1.698,6	1.034,9	663,7	979,0	1.930,0	1.399,2	265,0	2,51	6,9	8,67
1955	1.781,2	1.154,6	626,6	968,0	2.073,5	1.758,3	154,0	2,51	3,9	2,21
1956	2.103,9	1.397,8	706,1	976,4	2.437,2	2.139,4	152,0	2,51	4,1	7,82
1957	2.681,9	1.766,5	915,4	1.365,9	3.058,9	2.419,5	166,0	2,96	2,2	20,23
1958	2.964,9	1.964,7	1.000,2	1.504,5	3.433,9	2.500,6	122,0	6,82	2,5	8,10
1959	3.579,9	2.466,0	1.113,9	1.828,2	4.129,0	2.866,2	206,0	6,40	7,2	7,86
1960	3.645,2	2.508,0	1.137,0	1.724,3	4.262,1	3.217,7	214,0	6,70	4,3	7,22
1961	4.271,2	2.970,4	1.300,8	1.972,8	4.942,3	3.914,7	153,0	6,70	5,1	5,90
1962	5.078,3	3.612,8	1.465,5	2.344,0	5.901,6	4.702,9	175,0	6,70	5,4	6,41
1963	6.235,1	4.391,6	1.843,5	2.615,4	7.202,8	5.382,7	147,0	9,00	3,3	32,56
1964	7.563,7	5.419,6	2.144,1	3.079,8	8.712,3	7.307,9	141,0	9,00	6,2	8,92
1965	8.558,7	6.199,6	2.359,1	3.603,8	9.788,2	7.812,7	104,0	9,00	3,6	14,55
1966	9.924,2	7.145,9	2.778,3	4.428,7	11.447,5	8.955,8	109,0	9,00	5,2	12,98
1967	11.632,8	8.660,6	2.972,2	4.970,7	13.433,9	10.558,0	142,0	13,50	4,1	7,30
1968	14.019,5	10.477,4	3.542,1	6.636,9	16.104,2	12.572,4	163,0	1631	5,9	6,55
1969	16.120,3	12.097,6	4.022,7	8.907,8	18.700,0	21.503,0	212,0	17,7	6,1	8,60
1970	19.569,0	14.348,0	5.221,0	11.663,3	22.700,0	27.779,0	317,0	18,3	6,2	6,78
1971	22.028,0	16.352,0	5.676,0	12.277,0	25.900,0	35.334,0	320,0	19,80	6,0	13,62
1972	25.488,0	18.805,0	6.683,0	14.154,0	30.300,0	45.357,0	286,0	21,82	7,7	14,01
1973	32.662,0	24.300,0	8.362,0	19.441,0	41.600,0	55.889,0	510,0	23,47	6,7	23,53
1974	40.015,0	30.742,0	9.273,0	23.235,0	57.500,0	72.346,0	537,0	25,58	5,7	26,04
1975	48.285,4	36.821,0	11.464,4	30.407,5	76.400,0	101.542,0	396,0	30,82	2,3	17,70
1976	62.734,4	47.443,0	15.291,4	43.565,9	104.500,0	125.052,0	813,0	34,65	4,7	25,68
1977	90.433,5	69.536,0	20.897,5	66.471,5	167.500,0	163.086,9	1.683,0	36,50	4,2	28,37
1978	113.518,0	84.903,0	28.615,0	87.481,6	215.200,0	217.935,5	2.113,0	38,81	8,5	18,77
1979	141.922,1	103.838,0	38.084,1	109.908,0	265.300,0	268.449,1	3.401,0	42,69	5,4	28,80
1980	175.566,0	127.704,0	47.862,0	144.325,0	339.600,0	359.683,9	4.616,0	47,10	4,1	25,96
1981	222.631,0	156.916,0	65.715,0	178.988,0	519.500,0	531.159,0	5.374,0	53,90	2,3	26,35
1982	275.574,0	194.545,0	81.029,0	217.294,0	719.600,0	730.001,6	5.316,0	63,52	0,9	24,03
1983	317.548,0	218.401,0	99.147,0	234.201,0	865.500,0	930.541,7	3.948,0	77,78	1,6	16,64
1984	386.568,0	267.130,0	119.438,0	262.107,0	1.071.600,0	1.213.726,6	2.086,0	99,40	3,4	18,28
1985	472.874,0	317.982,0	154.892,0	310.496,0	1.399.100,0	1.564.989,7	1.931,0	140,73	3,1	22,45
1986	652.135,0	447.687,0	204.448,0	427.010,0	1.914.400,0	1.983.347,5	2.494,0	192,35	5,8	20,95
1987	829.933,0	574.450,0	255.483,0	586.789,0	2.464.800,0	2.499.568,7	3.348,0	241,39	5,4	24,02
1988	1.063.423,0	712.280,0	351.143,0	701.240,0	3.086.700,0	3.222.648,4	4.008,0	296,36	4,1	28,12
1989	1.353.268,0	926.269,0	426.999,0	933.077,0	4.026.700,0	4.294.670,7	3.391,0	377,92	3,4	26,12
1990	1.705.146,0	1.157.680,0	547.466,0	1.121.187,0	5.153.300,0	5.736.407,1	3.949,0	497,31	4,3	32,37
1991	2.140.751,0	1.439.375,0	701.376,0	1.412.522,0	6.499.700,0	7.195.064,2	5.197,0	623,33	2,0	26,82
1992	3.084.441,0	2.135.433,0	949.008,0	2.604.939,0	9.589.200,0	9.118.731,9	7.449,0	675,79	4,0	25,14
1993	4.022.728,0	2.793.228,0	1.229.500,0	3.492.878,0	12.847.200,0	13.279.679,4	8.232,0	784,24	5,4	22,61
1994	5.246.122,0	3.554.287,0	1.691.835,0	4.535.048,0	18.218.600,0	18.867.184,9	8.060,0	830,94	5,8	22,60
1995	6.186.154,0	4.057.431,0	2.128.723,0	5.559.744,0	25.922.200,0	26.778.928,4	8.667,0	874,86	5,7	19,47
1996	7.150.296,0	4.625.780,0	2.524.516,0	5.928.295,0	30.189.900,0	35.006.630,8	8.030,0	1.071,96	2,0	21,64
1997	8.762.585,0	5.605.748,0	3.156.837,0	6.784.896,0	37.016.100,0	43.046.031,0	10.332,0	1.082,37	3,2	17,68
1998	8.952.700,0	5.417.200,0	3.535.500,0	7.339.000,0	45.428.400,0	51.246.800,0	9.075,0	1.386,61	0,6	16,70
1999	9.518.200,0	4.942.600,0	4.575.600,0	7.203.200,0	49.771.500,0	50.630.000,0	8.393,0	1.693,99	-4,2	9,23
2000	12.766.100,0	7.237.800,0	5.528.300,0	8.369.000,0	53.086.400,0	46.029.400,0	8.355,4	2.120,17	2,8	8,75

Main Features of Metallic Money that has Circulated since 1821

OCHO REALES
Law of 1821

Minting material	Weight in grams	Monetary unit	Standard
Silver	24.00	Ocho reales (Silver *peso*)	0.666

Description of the seal

Obverse: On the obverse there is a picture of an indigenous woman who wears a feather crown on her head. On the circumference the words "REPÚBLICA DE COLOMBIA" and towards the lower edge the year the coin was minted. This coin was known as the "china", a term used in Santa Fe, the capital of Colombia, for the women of indigenous origin who worked as domestic servants.

Reverse: On the reverse there is a pomegranate. To its right the denomination of the coin is shown in Arabic numerals and to the left, the letter "R", which stands for the word "*Real*". On the circumference the place and year in which the coin was minted and the initials of the assayers are inscribed.

DOS REALES
Law of 1821

Minting material	Weight in grams	Monetary unit	Standard
Silver	6.50	Dos reales (La peseta)	0.583

Description of the seal

Obverse: On the obverse there is a picture of an indigenous woman who wears a feather crown on her head. On the circumference the words "REPÚBLICA DE COLOMBIA" and towards the lower edge the year the coin was minted. This coin was known as the "china", a term used in Santa Fe, the capital of Colombia, for the women of indigenous origin who worked as domestic servants.

Reverse: On the reverse there is a pomegranate. To its right the denomination of the coin is shown in Arabic numerals and to the left, the letter "R", which stands for the word "*Real*." On the circumference the place and year in which the coin was minted and the initials of the assayers are inscribed.

UN REAL
Law of 1821

Minting material	Weight in grams	Monetary unit	Standard
Silver	3.00	El real	0.666

Description of the seal

Obverse: On the obverse there is a picture of an indigenous woman who wears a feather crown on her head. On the circumference the words "REPÚBLICA DE COLOMBIA" and towards the lower edge the year the coin was minted. This coin was known as the "china", a term used in Santa Fe, the capital of Colombia, for the women of indigenous origin who worked as domestic servants.

Reverse: On the reverse there is a pomegranate. To its right the denomination of the coin is shown in Arabic numerals and to the left, the letter "R", which stands for the word "*Real*." On the circumference the place and year in which the coin was minted and the initials of the assayers are inscribed.

Minting material	Weight in grams	Monetary unit	Standard
Silver	1.50	Medio real	0.583

Description of the seal

Obverse: On the obverse there is a picture of an indigenous woman who wears a feather crown on her head. On the circumference the words "REPÚBLICA DE COLOMBIA" and towards the lower edge the year the coin was minted. This coin was known as the "china", a term used in Santa Fe, the capital of Colombia, for the women of indigenous origin who worked as domestic servants.

Reverse: On the reverse there is a pomegranate. To its right the denomination of the coin is shown in Arabic numerals and to the left, the letter "R", which stands for the word "*Real*." On the circumference the place and year in which the coin was minted and the initials of the assayers are inscribed.

MEDIO REAL
Law of 1821

Minting material	Weight in grams	Monetary unit	Standard
Silver	0.60	Cuarto de real	0.583

Description of the seal

Obverse: On the obverse stands out the main figure of the Phrygian Cap, a symbol of liberty, with the number 1 engraved on its left side and the number 4 on the right. In the lower part the year in which the coin was minted is shown.

Reverse: On the reverse there is a pomegranate.

CUARTO DE REAL
Law of 1821

Minting material	Weight in grams	Monetary unit	Standard
Gold	27.00	Ocho escudos (Onza)	0.875

Description of the seal

Obverse: On the obverse there is a bust of a figure symbolizing liberty. She wears a headband bearing the word "Libertad". On the circumference, towards the upper edge the words "REPÚBLICA DE COLOMBIA" are inscribed and near the lower edge the year of minting.

Reverse: On the reverse there is the coat of arms of the Republic. Two cornucopias spilling forth fruits and flowers stand out on the reverse. Within the circumference formed by the cornucopias there is a sheaf of lances with crossed bows and arrows. On the circumference the place and year in which the coin was minted and the initials of the assayers are inscribed.

OCHO ESCUDOS
Law of 1821

DOS ESCUDOS
Law of 1821

Minting material	Weight in grams	Monetary unit	Standard
Gold	6.80	Dos escudos (Doblón)	0.875

Description of the seal

Obverse: On the obverse there is a bust of a figure symbolizing liberty. She wears a headband bearing the word "Libertad". On the circumference the words "REPÚBLICA DE COLOMBIA" are inscribed and near the lower edge the year of minting.

Reverse: On the reverse there is the coat of arms of the Republic. Two cornucopias spilling forth fruits and flowers stand out on the reverse. Within the circumference formed by the cornucopias there is a sheaf of lances with crossed bows and arrows. On the circumference the place and year in which the coin was minted and the initials of the assayers are inscribed.

ESCUDO
Law of 1821

Minting material	Weight in grams	Monetary unit	Standard
Gold	3.75	Escudo (Dos pesos)	0.875

Description of the seal

Obverse: On the obverse there is a bust of a figure symbolizing liberty. She wears a headband bearing the word "Libertad". On the circumference the words "REPÚBLICA DE COLOMBIA" are inscribed and near the lower edge the year of minting.

Reverse: On the reverse there is the coat of arms of the Republic. Two cornucopias spilling forth fruits and flowers stand out on the reverse. Within the circumference formed by the cornucopias there is a sheaf of lances with crossed bows and arrows. On the circumference the place and year in which the coin was minted and the initials of the assayers are inscribed.

UN REAL
Law of 1826

Minting material	Weight in grams	Monetary unit	Standard
Silver	3.3842	Un real	0.885

Description of the seal

Obverse: On the obverse, the one *peso* and half, quarter, eighth and sixteenth of a *peso* coins display the coat of arms of the Republic. On the circumference, below the coat of arms, the year in which the coin was minted is engraved in Arabic numerals and in the upper part there is the inscription "REPÚBLICA DE COLOMBIA".

Reverse: On the reverse there is an infula with the word "Libertad" engraved in relief, surrounded by two olive branches that entwine at the base. The value of the coin is stated in the center: "1 REAL", with the initials of the assayers below and the initial of the place in which the coin was minted above.

Minting material	Weight in grams	Monetary unit	Standard
Silver	1.6921	Medio real (Dieciseisavo de peso)	0.885

Description of the seal

Obverse: On the obverse, the one *peso* and half, quarter, eighth and sixteenth of a *peso* coins display the coat of arms of the Republic. On the circumference, below the coat of arms, the year in which the coin was minted is engraved in Arabic numerals and in the upper part there is the inscription "REPÚBLICA DE COLOMBIA".

Reverse: On the reverse there is an infula with the word "Libertad" engraved in relief, surrounded by two olive branches that entwine at the base. The value of the coin is stated in the center: "1/2 REAL", with the initials of the assayers below and the initial of the place in which the coin was minted above

MEDIO REAL
Law of 1826

Minting material	Weight in grams	Monetary unit	Standard
Silver	0.8460	Cuarto real (Treinta y dosavo)	0.885

Description of the seal

Obverse: On the obverse there is a cornucopia spilling forth fruits and below it is inscribed the year in which the coin was minted.

Reverse: On the reverse, within the border of laurel, the value of the coin is stated by the fraction "1/4" in Arabic numerals. On either side of this fraction the initials of the assayers are stated and above it is the initial of the place where the coin was minted.

CUARTO DE REAL
Law of 1826

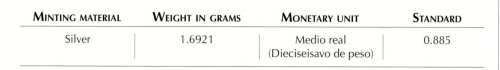

Minting material	Weight in grams	Monetary unit	Standard
Gold	27.0732	Ocho escudos (Onza)	0.875

Description of the seal

Obverse: On the obverse there is a bust of a figure symbolizing liberty. She wears a headband bearing the word "Libertad". On the circumference the words "REPÚBLICA DE COLOMBIA" are inscribed and near the lower edge the year of minting.

Reverse: On the reverse there is the coat of arms of the Republic. Two cornucopias spilling forth fruits and flowers stand out on the reverse. Within the circumference formed by the cornucopias there is a sheaf of lances with crossed bows and arrows. On the circumference the place and year in which the coin was minted and the initials of the assayers are inscribed.

OCHO ESCUDOS
Law of 1826

UN ESCUDO
Law of 1826

Minting material	Weight in grams	Monetary unit	Standard
Gold	3.3842	(Escudo) (Octavo de onza)	0.875

Description of the seal

Obverse: On the obverse there is a bust of a figure symbolizing liberty. She wears a headband bearing the word "Libertad". On the circumference the words "REPÚBLICA DE COLOMBIA" are inscribed and near the lower edge the year of minting.

Reverse: On the reverse there is the coat of arms of the Republic. Two cornucopias spilling forth fruits and flowers stand out on the reverse. Within the circumference formed by the cornucopias there is a sheaf of lances with crossed bows and arrows. On the circumference the place and year in which the coin was minted and the initials of the assayers are inscribed.

UN PESO
Law of 1826

Minting material	Weight in grams	Monetary unit	Standard
Gold	1.6921	Peso (Dieciseisavo de onza)	0.875

Description of the seal

Obverse: On the obverse there is a bust of a figure symbolizing liberty. She wears a headband bearing the word "Libertad". On the circumference the words "REPÚBLICA DE COLOMBIA" are inscribed and near the lower edge the year of minting.

Reverse: On the reverse there is the coat of arms of the Republic. Two cornucopias spilling forth fruits and flowers stand out on the reverse. Within the circumference formed by the cornucopias there is a sheaf of lances with crossed bows and arrows. On the circumference the place and year in which the coin was minted and the initials of the assayers are inscribed.

OCHO REALES
Law of 1834

Minting material	Weight in grams	Monetary unit	Standard
Silver	27.0732	Ocho reales (El colombiano)	0.885

Description of the seal

Obverse: On the obverse there is the coat of arms of the Republic. On the circumference, the year in which the coin was minted and the inscription "REPÚBLICA DE COLOMBIA".

Reverse: On the reverse there is an infula with the word "Libertad" engraved in relief, surrounded by two olive branches that entwine at the base. The value of the coin is stated in the center: "COLOMBIANO OCHO REALES", with the initials of the assayers below and the initial of the place in which the coin was minted above.

Minting material	Weight in grams	Monetary unit	Standard
Silver	0.8460	Cuarto de real (Treinta y dosavo)	0.885

Description of the seal

Obverse: On the obverse there is a cornucopia spilling forth fruits and below it is inscribed the year in which the coin was minted.

Reverse: On the reverse there is the value of the coin stated in the center: "1/4 DE REAL". On the upper part, the place in which the coin was minted.

CUARTO DE REAL
Law of 1836

Minting material	Weight in grams	Monetary unit	Standard
Gold	27.073	Ocho escudos (Onza)	0.875

Description of the seal

Obverse: On the obverse there is a bust of a figure symbolizing liberty. She wears a headband bearing the word "Libertad". On the circumference the words "REPÚBLICA DE COLOMBIA" are inscribed and near the lower edge the year of minting.

Reverse: On the reverse there is the coat of arms of the Republic. Two cornucopias spilling forth fruits and flowers stand out on the reverse. Within the circumference formed by the cornucopias there is a sheaf of lances with crossed bows and arrows. On the circumference the place and year in which the coin was minted and the initials of the last names of the assayers are inscribed.

OCHO ESCUDOS
Law of 1836

Minting material	Weight in grams	Monetary unit	Standard
Gold	3.3842	Escudo (Octavo de onza)	0.875

Description of the seal

Obverse: On the obverse there is a bust of a figure symbolizing liberty. She wears a headband bearing the word "Libertad". On the circumference the words "REPÚBLICA DE COLOMBIA" are inscribed and near the lower edge the year of minting.

Reverse: On the reverse there is the coat of arms of the Republic. Two cornucopias spilling forth fruits and flowers stand out on the reverse. Within the circumference formed by the cornucopias there is a sheaf of lances with crossed bows and arrows. On the circumference the place and year in which the coin was minted and the initials of the last names of the assayers are inscribed.

UN ESCUDO
Law of 1836

Minting material	Weight in grams	Monetary unit	Standard
Silver	27.073	Ocho reales (Granadino)	0.885

Description of the seal

Obverse: On the obverse there is the coat of arms of the Republic. On the circumference, the year in which the coin was minted and the inscription "REPÚBLICA DE LA NUEVA GRANADA".

Reverse: On the reverse, a laurel crown is found; within it the value of the coin is written in Arabic numerals and below is found the word "*reales*". On the circumference the place in which the coin was minted and the initials of the assayers are inscribed.

OCHO REALES
Law of 1837

Minting material	Weight in grams	Monetary unit	Standard
Silver	3.3842	Octavo de peso (Real)	0.885

Description of the seal

Obverse: On the obverse of the *real* and *medio real* are seen the pomegranate and two cornucopias. Towards the lower edge of the pomegranate the year in which the coin was minted is inscribed and on the circumference the words "REPÚBLICA DE LA NUEVA GRANADA" are engraved.

Reverse: On the reverse, a laurel crown is found; within it the value of the coin is written in Arabic numerals and below is found the word "*real*". On the circumference the place in which the coin was minted and the initials of the assayers are inscribed.

OCTAVO DE PESO
Law of 1837

Minting material	Weight in grams	Monetary unit	Standard
Silver	1.6921	Medio real (Dieciseisavo de peso)	0.885

Description of the seal

Obverse: On the obverse of the *real* and *medio real* are seen the pomegranate and two cornucopias. Towards the lower edge of the pomegranate the year in which the coin was minted is inscribed and on the circumference the words "REPÚBLICA DE LA NUEVA GRANADA" are engraved.

Reverse: On the reverse, a laurel crown is found; within it the value of the coin is written in Arabic numerals and below is found the word "*real*". On the circumference the place in which the coin was minted and the initials of the assayers are inscribed.

MEDIO REAL
Law of 1838

OCHO REALES
Law of 1846

Minting material	Weight in grams	Monetary unit	Standard
Silver	20.00	Ocho reales (pesos)	0.900

Description of the seal

Obverse: These coins have the coat of arms of the Republic, without pedestal or seal, on the obverse. The coat of arms is surrounded by two branches of laurel and olive, which cross at the lower part of the coat of arms. On the circumference the words "REPÚBLICA DE LA NUEVA GRANADA" and the year of minting are engraved.

Reverse: On the reverse, a laurel crown is found; within it the value of the coin is written "*ocho reales*". On the circumference the place in which the coin was minted and the standard are inscribed.

MEDIO REAL
Law of 1846

Minting material	Weight in grams	Monetary unit	Standard
Silver	1.25	Medio real	0.900

Description of the seal

Obverse: On the obverse the pomegranate and two cornucopias. Towards the lower edge of the pomegranate the year in which the coin was minted is inscribed and on the circumference the words "REPÚBLICA DE LA NUEVA GRANADA" are engraved.

Reverse: On the reverse, a laurel crown is found; within it the value of the coin is written in Arabic numerals and below is found the word "*real*". On the circumference the place in which the coin was minted and the initials of the assayers are inscribed.

DIECISEIS PESOS
Law of 1846

Minting material	Weight in grams	Monetary unit	Standard
Gold	25.800	Dieciseis pesos (Onza)	0.900

Description of the seal

Obverse: On the obverse of the *onza* and *cóndor* there is a bust of a figure symbolizing liberty. She wears a headband bearing the word "Libertad". On the circumference the words "REPÚBLICA DE LA NUEVA GRANADA" are inscribed and near the lower edge the year of minting.

Reverse: On the reverse there is the coat of arms of the Republic adorned with the national flags and with the standing condor of the seal. On the circumference, the value of the coin, the place in which the coin was minted and the initials of the assayers are inscribed.

Minting material	Weight in grams	Monetary unit	Standard
Gold	3.225	Dos pesos (Escudo)	0.900

Description of the seal

Obverse: On the obverse of the *onza* and *cóndor* there is a bust of a figure symbolizing liberty. She wears a headband bearing the word "Libertad". On the circumference the words "REPÚBLICA DE LA NUEVA GRANADA" are inscribed and near the lower edge the year of minting.

Reverse: On the reverse there is the coat of arms of the Republic adorned with the national flags and with the standing condor of the seal. On the circumference, the value of the coin, the place in which the coin was minted and the initials of the assayers are inscribed.

DOS PESOS
Law of 1846

Minting material	Weight in grams	Monetary unit	Standard
Silver	25.00	Diez reales (Peso fuerte)	0.900

Description of the seal

Obverse: The main figure On the obverse there is the national coat of arms adorned with the national flags and with the standing condor of the seal. In the lower part the year in which the coin was minted is shown in numbers and in the perimeter, the inscription "REPÚBLICA DE LA NUEVA GRANADA".

Reverse: On the reverse, a laurel crown is found; within it the value of the coin is written "*diez reales*". On the lower part the standard is inscribed.

DIEZ REALES
Law of 1847

Minting material	Weight in grams	Monetary unit	Standard
Silver	20.00	Ocho reales	0.900

Description of the seal

Obverse: These coins have the coat of arms of the Republic, without pedestal or seal, on the obverse. The coat of arms is surrounded by two branches of laurel and olive, which cross at the lower part of the coat of arms. On the circumference the words "REPÚBLICA DE LA NUEVA GRANADA" and the year of minting are engraved.

Reverse: On the reverse, a laurel crown is found; within it the value of the coin is written "*ocho reales*". On the circumference the place in which the coin was minted and the standard are inscribed.

OCHO REALES
Law of 1847

DOS REALES
Law of 1847

Minting material	Weight in grams	Monetary unit	Standard
Silver	20.00	Dos reales (1 peseta)	0.900

Description of the seal

Obverse: These coins have the coat of arms of the Republic, without pedestal or seal, on the obverse. The coat of arms is surrounded by two branches of laurel and olive, which cross at the lower part of the coat of arms. On the circumference the words "REPÚBLICA DE LA NUEVA GRANADA" and the year of minting are engraved.

Reverse: On the reverse, a laurel crown is found; within it the value of the coin is written "*dos reales*". On the circumference the place in which the coin was minted and the standard are inscribed.

DÉCIMO DE REAL
Law of 1847

Minting material	Weight in grams	Monetary unit	Standard
Copper	10.18	Décimo de real	

Description of the seal

Obverse: The law of April 27, 1847, changed the obverse of the *décimo de real* and *medio décimo de real*, in that it stipulated that the central sash of the coat of arms should be stamped with a radiant aureole surrounding it. On the circumference, the words "REPÚBLICA DE LA NUEVA GRANADA" and the year of minting are inscribed.

Reverse: On the reverse the same law ordered that the inscription stating the value of the coin would be surrounded by a garland of pomegranate leaves, flowers and fruits.

MEDIO DÉCIMO DE REAL
Law of 1847

Minting material	Weight in grams	Monetary unit	Standard
Copper	5.09	Medio décimo de real	

Description of the seal

Obverse: The law of April 27, 1847, changed the obverse of the *décimo de real* and *medio décimo de real*, in that it stipulated that the central sash of the coat of arms should be stamped with a radiant aureole surrounding it. On the circumference, the words "REPÚBLICA DE LA NUEVA GRANADA" and the year of minting are inscribed.

Reverse: On the reverse the same law ordered that the inscription stating the value of the coin would be surrounded by a garland of pomegranate leaves, flowers and fruits.

Minting material	Weight in grams	Monetary unit	Standard
Silver	25.00	Peso	0.900

Description of the seal

Obverse: The law of May 30, 1853 established that the monetary unit of the republic of Nueva Granada would be the *Peso*. On the obverse there is the national coat of arms adorned with the national flags and with the standing condor of the seal. On the circumference the words "REPÚBLICA DE LA NUEVA GRANADA" and the year of minting are engraved.

Reverse: On the reverse there is the value of the coin stated in letters and surrounded by an olive crown. On the circumference the place in which the coin was minted and the standard are inscribed.

UN PESO
Law of 1853

Minting material	Weight in grams	Monetary unit	Standard
Silver	2.5	Décimo de peso	0.900

Description of the seal

Obverse: The coins that, in accordance with the law of June 2, 1846, had been known as *reales* were to be named *décimos de peso* after the passing of the law of May 30, 1853. On the obverse the pomegranate and two cornucopias. On the circumference the words "REPÚBLICA DE LA NUEVA GRANADA" and the year of minting are engraved.

Reverse: On the reverse there is the value of the coin stated in letters and surrounded by an olive crown. On the circumference the place in which the coin was minted and the standard are inscribed.

DÉCIMO
Law of 1853

Minting material	Weight in grams	Monetary unit	Standard
Gold	16.400	Cóndor (Diez pesos)	0.900

Description of the seal

Obverse: On the obverse there is a bust of a figure symbolizing liberty. She wears a headband bearing the word "Libertad". On the circumference, towards the upper edge the words "REPÚBLICA DE LA NUEVA GRANADA" are inscribed and near the lower edge the year of minting. The denomination of the coin, equivalent to ten *pesos*, is not given.

Reverse: On the reverse there is the coat of arms of the Republic adorned with the national flags and with the standing condor of the seal. On the circumference, the value, the place in which the coin was minted, the weight, and the standard of the coin are inscribed.

CÓNDOR
Law of 1853

Minting material	Weight in grams	Monetary unit	Standard
Silver	5.00	Dos décimos	0.900

Description of the seal

Obverse: In the center of the obverse is found the coat of arms of the Republic, which is surrounded by an olive crown. On the circumference the inscription "REPÚBLICA DE LA NUEVA GRANADA" and the year of minting are engraved.

Reverse: On the reverse there is the value of the coin stated in letters and surrounded by an olive crown. On the circumference the place in which the coin was minted and the standard are inscribed.

DOS DÉCIMOS
Law of 1856

Minting material	Weight in grams	Monetary unit	Standard
Silver	25.00	Un peso	0.900

Description of the seal

Obverse: The law of May 30, 1853 established that the monetary unit of the republic of Nueva Granada would be the *Peso*. On the obverse there is the national coat of arms adorned with the national flags and with the standing condor of the seal. On the circumference the words "REPÚBLICA DE LA NUEVA GRANADA" and the year of minting are engraved.

Reverse: On the reverse there is the value of the coin stated in letters and surrounded by an olive crown. On the circumference the place in which the coin was minted and the standard are inscribed.

UN PESO
Law of 1857

Minting material	Weight in grams	Monetary unit	Standard
Silver	5.00	Dos décimos	0.900

Description of the seal

Obverse: These coins have the coat of arms of the Republic, without pedestal or seal, on the obverse. The coat of arms is surrounded by two branches of laurel and olive, which cross at the lower part of the coat of arms. On the circumference the words "REPÚBLICA DE LA NUEVA GRANADA" and the year of minting are engraved.

Reverse: On the reverse there is the value of the coin stated in letters and surrounded by an olive crown. On the circumference the place in which the coin was minted and the standard are inscribed.

DOS DÉCIMOS
Law of 1857

Minting material	Weight in grams	Monetary unit	Standard
Silver	2.50	El décimo	0.900

Description of the seal

Obverse: On the obverse the pomegranate and two cornucopias. Towards the lower edge of the pomegranate the year in which the coin was minted is inscribed and on the circumference the words "NUEVA GRANADA" are engraved.

Reverse: On the reverse there is the value of the coin stated in letters and surrounded by an olive crown. On the circumference the place in which the coin was minted and the standard are inscribed.

DÉCIMO
Law of 1857

Minting material	Weight in grams	Monetary unit	Standard
Silver	2.50	Medio décimo	0.900

Description of the seal

Obverse: On the obverse the pomegranate and two cornucopias. Towards the lower edge of the pomegranate the year in which the coin was minted is inscribed and on the circumference the words "NUEVA GRANADA" are engraved.

Reverse: On the reverse there is the value of the coin stated in letters and surrounded by an olive crown. On the circumference the place in which the coin was minted and the standard are inscribed.

MEDIO DÉCIMO
Law of 1857

Minting material	Weight in grams	Monetary unit	Standard
Silver	0.813	Décimo de peso	0.666

Description of the seal

Obverse: On the obverse there is the pomegranate of the coat of arms, with the year of minting on the lower part of the coin.

Reverse: On the reverse there is the value of the coin, expressed by inscription "1/4". On the circumference the place in which the coin was minted and nine stars.

CUARTO DE DÉCIMO
Law of 1857

Minting material	Weight in grams	Monetary unit	Standard
Gold	16.129	Diez pesos (Cóndor)	0.900

Description of the seal

Obverse: On the obverse there is a bust of a figure symbolizing liberty. She wears a headband bearing the word "Libertad". On the circumference the words "REPÚBLICA DE LA NUEVA GRANADA" are inscribed and near the lower edge the year of minting.

Reverse: On the reverse there is the coat of arms of the Republic adorned with the national flags and with the standing condor of the seal. On the circumference, the value, the place in which the coin was minted, the weight, and the standard of the coin are inscribed.

DIEZ PESOS
Law of 1857

Minting material	Weight in grams	Monetary unit	Standard
Gold	3.225	Dos pesos (Quinto de Cóndor)	0.900

Description of the seal

Obverse: On the obverse there is a bust of a figure symbolizing liberty. She wears a headband bearing the word "Libertad". On the circumference the words "NUEVA GRANADA" are inscribed and near the lower edge the year of minting.

Reverse: On the reverse there is a horizontal oval medallion on which the value of the coin is engraved. On the circumference the initial of the place where the minting was done and the standard and weight of the coin.

DOS PESOS
Law of 1857

Minting material	Weight in grams	Monetary unit	Standard
Silver	5.00	Dos décimos	0.835

Description of the seal

Obverse: On the obverse the inscription "ESTADOS UNIDOS DE COLOMBIA" and the nine stars that represent the States of the Union.

Reverse: On the reverse there is the value of the coin in letters and the year of minting surrounded by an olive crown. On the circumference the place in which the coin was minted and the standard are inscribed.

DOS DÉCIMOS
Law of 1867

DÉCIMO
Law of 1867

Minting material	Weight in grams	Monetary unit	Standard
Silver	2.500	El décimo	0.835

Description of the seal

Obverse: On the obverse the bust of liberty with an infula on her head that bears the word "Libertad" in relief. The year in which the coin was minted is found beneath the bust. On the circumference the words "ESTADOS UNIDOS DE COLOMBIA" and the nine stars that represent the States of the Union.

Reverse: On the reverse there is the coat of arms of the Republic adorned with the national flags and with the standing condor of the seal. On the circumference, the value, the place in which the coin was minted, the weight, and the standard of the coin are inscribed.

MEDIO DÉCIMO
Law of 1867

Minting material	Weight in grams	Monetary unit	Standard
Silver	1.250	Medio décimo	0.666

Description of the seal

Obverse: On the obverse the bust of liberty with an infula on her head that bears the word "Libertad" in relief. The year in which the coin was minted is found beneath the bust. On the circumference the words "ESTADOS UNIDOS DE COLOMBIA" and the nine stars that represent the States of the Union.

Reverse: On the reverse there is the coat of arms of the Republic adorned with the national flags and with the standing condor of the seal. On the circumference, the value, the place in which the coin was minted, the weight, and the standard of the coin are inscribed.

VEINTE PESOS
Law of 1867

Minting material	Weight in grams	Monetary unit	Standard
Gold	32.258	Veinte pesos (Doble Cóndor)	0.900

Description of the seal

Obverse: On the obverse the bust of liberty with an infula on her head that bears the word "Libertad" in relief. The year in which the coin was minted is found beneath the bust. On the circumference the words "ESTADOS UNIDOS DE COLOMBIA" and the nine stars that represent the States of the Union.

Reverse: On the reverse there is the coat of arms of the Republic adorned with the national flags and with the standing condor of the seal. On the circumference, the value, the place in which the coin was minted, the weight, and the standard of the coin are inscribed.

DIEZ PESOS
Law of 1867

Minting material	Weight in grams	Monetary unit	Standard
Gold	16.129	Diez pesos (Cóndor)	0.900

Description of the seal

Obverse: On the obverse the bust of liberty with an infula on her head that bears the word "Libertad" in relief. The year in which the coin was minted is found beneath the bust. On the circumference the words "ESTADOS UNIDOS DE COLOMBIA" and the nine stars that represent the States of the Union.

Reverse: On the reverse there is the coat of arms of the Republic adorned with the national flags and with the standing condor of the seal. On the circumference, the value, the place in which the coin was minted, the weight, and the standard of the coin are inscribed.

DOS PESOS
Law of 1867

Minting material	Weight in grams	Monetary unit	Standard
Gold	3.225	Dos pesos (Quinto de cóndor)	0.900

Description of the seal

Obverse: On the obverse the bust of liberty with an infula on her head that bears the word "Libertad" in relief. The year in which the coin was minted is found beneath the bust. On the circumference the words "ESTADOS UNIDOS DE COLOMBIA" and the nine stars that represent the States of the Union.

Reverse: On the reverse there is the coat of arms of the Republic adorned with the national flags and with the standing condor of the seal. On the circumference, the value, the place in which the coin was minted, the weight, and the standard of the coin are inscribed.

UN PESO
Law of 1867

Minting material	Weight in grams	Monetary unit	Standard
Gold	1.612	Un peso (Décimo de cóndor)	0.900

Description of the seal

Obverse: On the obverse the bust of liberty with an infula on her head that bears the word "Libertad" in relief. The year in which the coin was minted is found beneath the bust. On the circumference the words "ESTADOS UNIDOS DE COLOMBIA" and the nine stars that represent the States of the Union.

Reverse: On the reverse there is the condor with half-spread out wings. On the circumference, the value, the place in which the coin was minted, the weight, and the standard of the coin are inscribed.

VEINTE PESOS
Law of 1873

Minting material	Weight in grams	Monetary unit	Standard
Gold	32.258	Veinte pesos (Doble cóndor)	0.900

Description of the seal

Obverse: On the obverse the bust of liberty with an infula on her head that bears the word "Libertad" in relief. The year in which the coin was minted is found beneath the bust. On the circumference the words "ESTADOS UNIDOS DE COLOMBIA" and the nine stars that represent the States of the Union.

Reverse: On the reverse there is the coat of arms of the Republic adorned with the national flags and with the standing condor of the seal. On the circumference, the value, the place in which the coin was minted, the weight, and the standard of the coin are inscribed.

DIEZ PESOS
Law of 1873

Minting material	Weight in grams	Monetary unit	Standard
Gold	16.129	Diez pesos (Cóndor)	0.900

Description of the seal

Obverse: On the obverse the bust of liberty with an infula on her head that bears the word "Libertad" in relief. The year in which the coin was minted is found beneath the bust. On the circumference the words "ESTADOS UNIDOS DE COLOMBIA" and the nine stars that represent the States of the Union.

Reverse: On the reverse there is the coat of arms of the Republic adorned with the national flags and with the standing condor of the seal. On the circumference, the value, the place in which the coin was minted, the weight, and the standard of the coin are inscribed.

PESO
Law of 1873

Minting material	Weight in grams	Monetary unit	Standard
Gold	1.612	Peso	0.900

Description of the seal

Obverse: On the obverse the bust of liberty with an infula on her head that bears the word "Libertad" in relief. The year in which the coin was minted is found beneath the bust. On the circumference the words "ESTADOS UNIDOS DE COLOMBIA" and the nine stars that represent the States of the Union.

Reverse: On the reverse there is the condor with half-spread out wings. On the circumference, the value, the place in which the coin was minted, the weight, and the standard of the coin are inscribed.

Minting material	Weight in grams	Monetary unit	Standard
Silver	5.00	Dos décimos	0.835

Description of the seal

Obverse: On the obverse the bust of liberty with an infula on her head that bears the word "Libertad" in relief. The year in which the coin was minted is found beneath the bust. On the circumference the words "ESTADOS UNIDOS DE COLOMBIA" and the nine stars that represent the States of the Union.

Reverse: On the reverse there is the coat of arms of the Republic adorned with the national flags and with the standing condor of the seal. On the circumference, the value, the place in which the coin was minted, the weight, and the standard of the coin are inscribed.

DOS DÉCIMOS
Law of 1873

Minting material	Weight in grams	Monetary unit	Standard
Silver	2.500	Décimo	0.835

Description of the seal

Obverse: On the obverse the bust of liberty with an infula on her head that bears the word "Libertad" in relief. The year in which the coin was minted is found beneath the bust. On the circumference the words "ESTADOS UNIDOS DE COLOMBIA" and the nine stars that represent the States of the Union.

Reverse: On the reverse there is the coat of arms of the Republic adorned with the national flags and with the standing condor of the seal. On the circumference, the value, the place in which the coin was minted, the weight, and the standard of the coin are inscribed.

DÉCIMO
Law of 1873

Minting material	Weight in grams	Monetary unit	Standard
Silver	0.625	Cuarto de décimo (Cuartillo)	0.666

Description of the seal

Obverse: On the obverse there is the pomegranate of the coat of arms, with the year of minting on the lower part of the coin.

Reverse: On the reverse there is the value of the coin expressed with the fraction "1/4". On the circumference the place where the coin was minted is given and in the lower part the nine stars of the Union are engraved.

CUARTO DE DÉCIMO
Law of 1873

Minting material	Weight in grams	Monetary unit	Standard
Cupro-nickel		Uno y cuarto centavo (Mitad)	

Description of the seal	
Obverse: On the obverse there is the Phrygian cap, from the central sash of the coat of arms of the Republic, surrounded by the inscription "ESTADOS UNIDOS DE COLOMBIA" and the nine stars that represent the States of the Union.	**Reverse:** On the reverse there is the value of the coin expressed. On the circumference the words: "Un centavo i cuarto" and the year in which the coin was minted are inscribed.

UN CENTAVO Y CUARTO
Law of 1873

Minting material	Weight in grams	Monetary unit	Standard
Silver	12.500	Cincuenta centavos	0.835

Description of the seal	
Obverse: On the obverse there is a bust of a figure symbolizing liberty. She wears a headband bearing the word "Libertad". On the circumference, towards the upper edge the words "REPÚBLICA DE COLOMBIA" are inscribed and near the lower edge the year of minting.	**Reverse:** On the reverse there is the coat of arms of the Republic adorned with the national flags and with the standing condor of the seal. On the circumference, the value, the place in which the coin was minted, the weight, and the standard of the coin are inscribed.

CINCUENTA CENTAVOS
Law of 1894

Minting material	Weight in grams	Monetary unit	Standard
Silver	5.00	Veinte centavos	0.666

Description of the seal	
Obverse: On the obverse there is a bust of a figure symbolizing liberty. She wears a headband bearing the word "Libertad". On the circumference, towards the upper edge the words "REPÚBLICA DE COLOMBIA" are inscribed and near the lower edge the year of minting.	**Reverse:** On the reverse there is the coat of arms of the Republic adorned with the national flags and the standing condor of the seal. On the circumference, the value, the place in which the coin was minted, the weight, and the standard of the coin. *The fabrication of these coins at a standard of 0.666 did not meet the requirements of 0.835 for their precious metal content.*

VEINTE CENTAVOS
Law of 1894

Minting material	Weight in grams	Monetary unit	Standard
Silver	2.50	Diez centavos	0.666

Description of the seal

Obverse: On the obverse there is a bust of a figure symbolizing liberty. She wears a headband bearing the word "LIBERTAD". On the circumference the words "REPÚBLICA DE COLOMBIA" and the minting year.

Reverse: On the reverse there is the coat of arms of the Republic adorned with the national flags and the standing condor of the seal. On the circumference, the value, the place in which the coin was minted, the weight, and the standard of the coin.

The fabrication of these coins at a standard of 0.666 did not meet the requirements of 0.835 for their precious metal content.

DIEZ CENTAVOS
Law of 1894

Minting material	Weight in grams	Monetary unit	Standard
Gold	7.988	Cinco pesos (Libra colombiana)	$0.916_{2/3}$

Description of the seal

Obverse: On the obverse there is a miner, engraved in accordance with a design by Francisco A. Cano. On the circumference the words "REPÚBLICA DE COLOMBIA" and the minting year.

Reverse: On the reverse there is the coat of arms of the Republic adorned with the national flags and with the standing condor of the seal. On the circumference, the value, the weight, and the standard of the coin are inscribed.

CINCO PESOS
Law of 1907

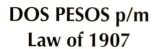

Minting material	Weight in grams	Monetary unit	Standard
Cupro-nickel	3.00	Dos pesos p/m	

Description of the seal

Obverse: On the obverse the principal motif is the head of the figure of the Republic, with the word "Paz" (Peace) engraved on a sash. On the circumference the words "REPÚBLICA DE COLOMBIA" and the minting year.

Reverse: On the reverse there is the value of the coin in numbers in the center of a laurel crown. The initials "p/m" correspond to the abbreviation for "papel moneda", that is, paper money.

DOS PESOS p/m
Law of 1907

Minting material	Weight in grams	Monetary unit	Standard
Cupro-nickel	2.00	Un peso p/m	

Description of the seal

Obverse: On the obverse the principal motif is the head of the figure of the Republic, with the word "Paz" (Peace) engraved on a sash. On the circumference the words "REPÚBLICA DE COLOMBIA" and the minting year.

Reverse: On the reverse there is the value of the coin in numbers in the center of a laurel crown. The initials "p/m" correspond to the abbreviation for "papel moneda", that is, paper money.

UN PESO p/m
Law of 1907

Minting material	Weight in grams	Monetary unit	Standard
Silver	12.500	Cincuenta centavos	0.900

Description of the seal

Obverse: On the obverse the bust of *el Libertador* (the Liberator, Simón Bolívar), facing right. On the circumference the words "REPÚBLICA DE COLOMBIA" and the minting year.

Reverse: On the reverse there is the coat of arms of the Republic adorned with the national flags and with the standing condor of the seal. On the circumference, the value, the weight, and the standard of the coin are inscribed.

CINCUENTA CENTAVOS
Law of 1912

Minting material	Weight in grams	Monetary unit	Standard
Silver	6.250	Veinte centavos	0.900

Description of the seal

Obverse: On the obverse the bust of *el Libertador* (the Liberator, Simón Bolívar), facing right. On the circumference the words "REPÚBLICA DE COLOMBIA" and the minting year.

Reverse: On the reverse there is the coat of arms of the Republic adorned with the national flags and with the standing condor of the seal. On the circumference, the value, the weight, and the standard of the coin are inscribed.

VEINTE CENTAVOS
Law of 1913

Minting material	Weight in grams	Monetary unit	Standard
Silver	1.000	Diez centavos	0.900

Description of the seal

Obverse: On the obverse the bust of *el Libertador* (the Liberator, Simón Bolívar), facing right. On the circumference the words "REPÚBLICA DE COLOMBIA" and the minting year.

Reverse: On the reverse there is the coat of arms of the Republic adorned with the national flags and with the standing condor of the seal. On the circumference, the value, the weight, and the standard of the coin are inscribed.

DIEZ CENTAVOS
Law of 1913

Minting material	Weight in grams	Monetary unit	Standard
Gold	15.9760	Diez pesos (Dos libras colombianas)	0.916 2/3

Description of the seal

Obverse: On the obverse the bust of *el Libertador* (the Liberator, Simón Bolívar), facing right. On the circumference the words "REPÚBLICA DE COLOMBIA" and the minting year.

Reverse: On the reverse there is the coat of arms of the Republic adorned with the national flags and with the standing condor of the seal. On the circumference, the value, the weight, and the standard of the coin are inscribed.

DIEZ PESOS
Law of 1918

Minting material	Weight in grams	Monetary unit	Standard
Gold	7.9880	Cinco pesos (Libra colombiana)	0.916 2/3

Description of the seal

Obverse: On the obverse the bust of *el Libertador* (the Liberator, Simón Bolívar), facing right. On the circumference the words "REPÚBLICA DE COLOMBIA" and the minting year.

Reverse: On the reverse there is the coat of arms of the Republic adorned with the national flags and with the standing condor of the seal. On the circumference, the value, the weight, and the standard of the coin are inscribed.

CINCO PESOS
Law of 1918

Minting material	Weight in grams	Monetary unit	Standard
Silver	12.500	Cincuenta centavos	0.900

Description of the seal

Obverse: On the obverse the bust of *el Libertador* (the Liberator, Simón Bolívar), facing right. On the circumference the words "REPÚBLICA DE COLOMBIA" and the minting year.

Reverse: On the reverse there is the coat of arms of the Republic adorned with the national flags and with the standing condor of the seal. On the circumference, the value, the weight, and the standard of the coin are inscribed.

CINCUENTA CENTAVOS
Law of 1918

Minting material	Weight in grams	Monetary unit	Standard
Gold	3.9940	Dos y medio pesos (1/2 libra colombiana)	0.916 2/3

Description of the seal

Obverse: On the obverse the bust of *el Libertador* (the Liberator, Simón Bolívar), facing right. On the circumference the words "REPÚBLICA DE COLOMBIA" and the minting year.

Reverse: On the reverse there is the coat of arms of the Republic adorned with the national flags and with the standing condor of the seal. On the circumference, the value, the weight, and the standard of the coin are inscribed.

DOS Y MEDIO PESOS
Law of 1919

Minting material	Weight in grams	Monetary unit	Standard
Cupro-nickel	2.00	Un centavo	

Description of the seal

Obverse: On the obverse there is a bust of a figure symbolizing liberty. She wears a headband bearing the word "Libertad". On the circumference the words "REPÚBLICA DE COLOMBIA" and the minting year.

Reverse: On the reverse there is a laurel crown inside of which the value of the coin is stated in Roman numerals and below it the word "centavo".

UN CENTAVO
Law of 1920

Minting material	Weight in grams	Monetary unit	Standard
Cupro-nickel	3.00	Dos centavos	

Description of the seal

Obverse: On the obverse there is a bust of a figure symbolizing liberty. She wears a headband bearing the word "Libertad". On the circumference the words "REPÚBLICA DE COLOMBIA" and the minting year.

Reverse: On the reverse there is a laurel crown inside of which the value of the coin is stated in Roman numerals and below it the word "centavos".

DOS CENTAVOS
Law of 1920

Minting material	Weight in grams	Monetary unit	Standard
Cupro-nickel	4.00	Cinco centavos	

Description of the seal

Obverse: On the obverse there is a bust of a figure symbolizing liberty. She wears a headband bearing the word "Libertad". On the circumference the words "REPÚBLICA DE COLOMBIA" and the minting year.

Reverse: On the reverse there is a laurel crown inside of which the value of the coin is stated in Roman numerals and below it the word "centavos".

CINCO CENTAVOS
Law of 1921

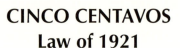

Minting material	Weight in grams	Monetary unit	Standard
Silver	12.50	Cincuenta centavos	0.900

Description of the seal

Obverse: On the obverse the bust of *el Libertador* (the Liberator, Simón Bolívar), facing right. On the circumference the words "REPÚBLICA DE COLOMBIA" and the minting year.

Reverse: On the reverse there is the coat of arms of the Republic adorned with the national flags and with the standing condor of the seal. On the circumference, the value, the weight, and the standard of the coin are inscribed.

CINCUENTA CENTAVOS
Law of 1931

Minting material	Weight in grams	Monetary unit	Standard
Cupro-nickel	4.00	Cinco centavos	

Description of the seal

Obverse: On the obverse there is a bust of a figure symbolizing liberty. She wears a headband bearing the word "Libertad". On the circumference the words "REPÚBLICA DE COLOMBIA" and the minting year.

Reverse: On the reverse there is a laurel crown inside of which the value of the coin is stated in Roman numerals and below it the word "centavos".

CINCO CENTAVOS
Law of 1933

Minting material	Weight in grams	Monetary unit	Standard
Cupro-nickel	3.00	Dos centavos	

Description of the seal

Obverse: On the obverse there is a bust of a figure symbolizing liberty. She wears a headband bearing the word "Libertad". On the circumference the words "REPÚBLICA DE COLOMBIA" and the minting year.

Reverse: On the reverse there is a laurel crown inside of which the value of the coin is stated in Roman numerals and below it the word "centavos".

DOS CENTAVOS
Law of 1933

Minting material	Weight in grams	Monetary unit	Standard
Cupro-nickel	2.0	Un centavo	

Description of the seal

Obverse: On the obverse there is a bust of a figure symbolizing liberty. She wears a headband bearing the word "Libertad". On the circumference the words "REPÚBLICA DE COLOMBIA" and the minting year.

Reverse: On the reverse there is a laurel crown inside of which the value of the coin is stated in Roman numerals and below it the word "centavo".

UN CENTAVO
Law of 1933

Minting material	Weight in grams	Monetary unit	Standard
Copper	2.0	Un centavo	

Description of the seal

Obverse: On the obverse there is the Phrygian cap, surrounded by two branches of laurel. On the circumference the words "REPÚBLICA DE COLOMBIA" and the minting year.

Reverse: On the reverse there is the value of the coin stated in Roman numerals and on either side two branches of a coffee plant. A cornucopia is engraved in the upper part and in the lower part, the word "centavos".

I CENTAVO
Law of 1942

Minting material	Weight in grams	Monetary unit	Standard
Copper	3.0	Cinco centavos	

Description of the seal

Obverse: On the obverse there is the Phrygian cap, surrounded by two branches of laurel. On the circumference the words "REPÚBLICA DE COLOMBIA" and the minting year.

Reverse: On the reverse there is the value of the coin stated in Roman numerals and on either side two branches of a coffee plant. A cornucopia is engraved in the upper part and in the lower part, the word "centavos".

V CENTAVOS
Law of 1943

Minting material	Weight in grams	Monetary unit	Standard
Silver	5.00	Veinte centavos	0.500

Description of the seal

Obverse: On the obverse there is an effigy of General Santander, taken from the sculpture by David. On the circumference the words "REPÚBLICA DE COLOMBIA" and the minting year.

Reverse: On the reverse there is the value of the coin stated in two lines found within a laurel crown. The denomination is written in Arabic numerals on the first line and the second line has the word "centavos".

VEINTE CENTAVOS
Law of 1945

Minting material	Weight in grams	Monetary unit	Standard
Silver	12.50	Cincuenta centavos	0.500

Description of the seal	
Obverse: On the obverse the bust of *el Libertador* (the Liberator, Simón Bolívar), facing letf. On the circumference the words "REPÚBLICA DE COLOMBIA" and the minting year.	**Reverse:** On the reverse there is the value of the coin stated in two lines found within a laurel crown. The denomination is written in Arabic numerals on the first line and the second line has the word "centavos".

CINCUENTA CENTAVOS
Law of 1947

Minting material	Weight in grams	Monetary unit	Standard
Silver	2.50	Diez centavos	0.500

Description of the seal	
Obverse: On the obverse there is an effigy of General Santander, taken from the sculpture by David. On the circumference the words "REPÚBLICA DE COLOMBIA" and the minting year.	**Reverse:** On the reverse there is the value of the coin stated in two lines found within a laurel crown. The denomination is written in Arabic numerals on the first line and the second line has the word "centavos".

DIEZ CENTAVOS
Law of 1949

Minting material	Weight in grams	Monetary unit	Standard
Cupro-nickel	2.50	Diez centavos	

Description of the seal	
Obverse: On the obverse the national coat of arms adorned with the national flags and with the standing condor of the seal. On the circumference the words "REPÚBLICA DE COLOMBIA" and the minting year.	**Reverse:** On the reverse there is the figure of the Cacique (Indigenous chief) Calarcá, circled on both sides by the words "diez centavos".

DIEZ CENTAVOS
Law of 1952

Minting material	Weight in grams	Monetary unit	Standard
Brass	3.0	Dos centavos	

Description of the seal

Obverse: On the obverse there is a bust of a figure symbolizing liberty. She wears a headband bearing the word "Libertad". On the circumference the words "REPÚBLICA DE COLOMBIA" and the year of minting.

Reverse: On the reverse there is a laurel crown inside of which the value of the coin is stated in Roman numerals and below it the word "centavos".

DOS CENTAVOS
Law of 1952

Minting material	Weight in grams	Monetary unit	Standard
Nickel-plated Steel	2.00	Un centavo	

Description of the seal

Obverse: On the obverse there is a bust of a figure symbolizing liberty. She wears a headband bearing the word "Libertad". On the circumference the words "REPÚBLICA DE COLOMBIA" and the year of minting.

Reverse: On the reverse there is a laurel crown inside of which the value of the coin is stated in Roman numerals and below it the word "centavo".

UN CENTAVO
Law of 1952

Minting material	Weight in grams	Monetary unit	Standard
Cupro-nickel	12.50	Cincuenta centavos	

Description of the seal

Obverse: On the obverse the bust of *el Libertador* (the Liberator, Simón Bolívar), facing right. On the circumference the words "REPÚBLICA DE COLOMBIA" and the minting year.

Reverse: On the reverse the coat of arms of the Republic adorned with the national flags and with the standing condor of the seal. On the circumference the words "REPÚBLICA DE COLOMBIA" and the value of the coin.
In 1960 the Banco de la República was authorized to mint coins representing fractions of the peso, in denominations of 1, 2, 5, 10, 20 and 50 centavos, to commemorate the 150th anniversary of Colombian Independence.

CINCUENTA CENTAVOS
Law of 1960

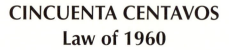

Minting material	Weight in grams	Monetary unit	Standard
Cupro-nickel	5.00	Veinte centavos	

Description of the seal

Obverse: On the obverse the bust of *el Libertador* (the Liberator, Simón Bolívar), facing right. On the circumference the words "REPÚBLICA DE COLOMBIA", the year of the National Independence and the minting year.

Reverse: On the reverse the coat of arms of the Republic adorned with the national flags and with the standing condor of the seal. On the circumference the value of the coin is inscribed.

In 1960 the Banco de la República was authorized to mint coins representing fractions of the peso, in denominations of 1, 2, 5, 10, 20 and 50 centavos, to commemorate the 150th anniversary of Colombian Independence.

VEINTE CENTAVOS
Law of 1960

Minting material	Weight in grams	Monetary unit	Standard
Cupro-nickel	2.50	Diez centavos	

Description of the seal

Obverse: On the obverse the national coat of arms adorned with the national flags and with the standing condor of the seal. On the circumference the words "REPÚBLICA DE COLOMBIA" and the minting year.

Reverse: On the reverse there is the figure of the Cacique (Indigenous chief) Calarcá, circled on both sides by the words "diez centavos".

In 1960 the Banco de la República was authorized to mint coins representing fractions of the peso, in denominations of 1, 2, 5, 10, 20 and 50 centavos, to commemorate the 150th anniversary of Colombian Independence.

DIEZ CENTAVOS
Law of 1960

Minting material	Weight in grams	Monetary unit	Standard
Brass	3.00	Dos centavos	

Description of the seal

Obverse: On the obverse there is a bust of a figure symbolizing liberty. She wears a headband bearing the word "Libertad". On the circumference the words "REPÚBLICA DE COLOMBIA", the year of the National Independence and the year of minting.

Reverse: On the reverse there is a laurel crown inside of which the value of the coin is stated in Roman numerals and below it the word "centavos".

In 1960 the Banco de la República was authorized to mint coins representing fractions of the peso, in denominations of 1, 2, 5, 10, 20 and 50 centavos, to commemorate the 150th anniversary of Colombian Independence.

DOS CENTAVOS
Law of 1960

Minting material	Weight in grams	Monetary unit	Standard
Copper-plated steel	2.00	Un Centavo	

Description of the seal

Obverse: On the obverse there is the Phrygian cap, surrounded by two branches of laurel. On the circumference the words "REPÚBLICA DE COLOMBIA" the year of the National Independence and the year of minting.

Reverse: On the reverse there is the value of the coin stated in Roman numerals and on either side two branches of a coffee plant. A cornucopia is engraved in the upper part and in the lower part, the word "centavo".
In 1960 the Banco de la República was authorized to mint coins representing fractions of the peso, in denominations of 1, 2, 5, 10, 20 and 50 centavos, to commemorate the 150th anniversary of Colombian Independence.

UN CENTAVO
Law of 1960

Minting material	Weight in grams	Monetary unit	Standard
Cupro-nickel	12.5	Cincuenta centavos	

Description of the seal

Obverse: On the obverse the bust of Jorge Eliécer Gaitán. On the circumference the words "JORGE ELIÉCER GAITÁN" and the minting year.

Reverse: On the reverse there is the coat of arms of the Republic adorned with the national flags and with the standing condor of the seal. On the circumference the words "REPÚBLICA DE COLOMBIA" and the value of the coin are inscribed.

CINCUENTA CENTAVOS
Law of 1965

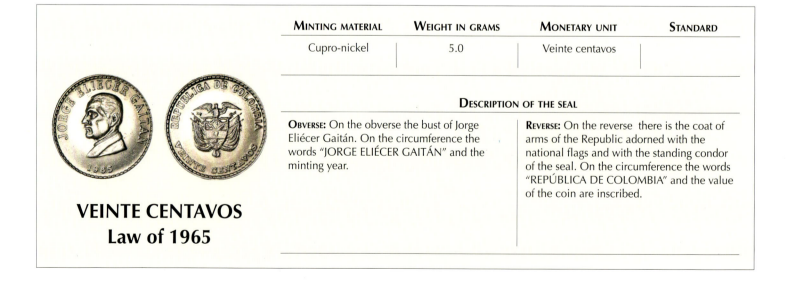

Minting material	Weight in grams	Monetary unit	Standard
Cupro-nickel	5.0	Veinte centavos	

Description of the seal

Obverse: On the obverse the bust of Jorge Eliécer Gaitán. On the circumference the words "JORGE ELIÉCER GAITÁN" and the minting year.

Reverse: On the reverse there is the coat of arms of the Republic adorned with the national flags and with the standing condor of the seal. On the circumference the words "REPÚBLICA DE COLOMBIA" and the value of the coin are inscribed.

VEINTE CENTAVOS
Law of 1965

UN PESO
Law of 1967

Minting material	Weight in grams	Monetary unit	Standard
Cupro-nickel		Un peso (Bolívar de 10 lados)	

Description of the seal

Obverse: On the obverse the bust of *el Libertador* (the Liberator, Simón Bolívar), facing right. On the circumference the words "REPÚBLICA DE COLOMBIA" and the minting year.

Reverse: On the reverse there is the value of the coin stated in two lines found within a laurel crown. The denomination is written in Arabic numerals on the first line and the second line has the word "peso".

CINCUENTA CENTAVOS
Law of 1967

Minting material	Weight in grams	Monetary unit	Standard
Nickel-plated steel	10.00	Cincuenta centavos	

Description of the seal

Obverse: On the obverse there is an effigy of General Santander, taken from the sculpture by David. On the circumference the words "REPÚBLICA DE COLOMBIA" and the minting year.

Reverse: On the reverse there is the value of the coin stated in two lines found within a laurel crown. The denomination is written in Arabic numerals on the first line and the second line has the word "centavos".

VEINTE CENTAVOS
Law of 1967

Minting material	Weight in grams	Monetary unit	Standard
Nickel-plated steel	5.00	Veinte centavos	

Description of the seal

Obverse: On the obverse there is an effigy of General Santander, taken from the sculpture by David. On the circumference the words "REPÚBLICA DE COLOMBIA" and the minting year.

Reverse: On the reverse there is the value of the coin stated in two lines found within a laurel crown. The denomination is written in Arabic numerals on the first line and the second line has the word "centavos".

Minting material	Weight in grams	Monetary unit	Standard
Nickel-plated steel	2.50	Diez centavos	

Description of the seal

Obverse: On the obverse there is an effigy of General Santander, taken from the sculpture by David. On the circumference the words "REPÚBLICA DE COLOMBIA" and the minting year.

Reverse: On the reverse there is the value of the coin stated in two lines found within a laurel crown. The denomination is written in Arabic numerals on the first line and the second line has the word "centavos".

The 1945 dies were used for the minting of these coins.

DIEZ CENTAVOS
Law of 1967

Minting material	Weight in grams	Monetary unit	Standard
Cupro-nickel	10.00	Cinco pesos	

Description of the seal

Obverse: Emblem of four fishes framed within a circle and a square. In the circumference are the words: "XXXIX CONGRESO EUCARÍSTICO INTERNACIONAL" and the minting place

Reverse: On the reverse there is the value of the coin stated in two lines found within a laurel crown. The denomination is written in Arabic numerals on the first line and the second line has the word "pesos". On the circumference the words "REPÚBLICA DE COLOMBIA" and the minting year.

CINCO PESOS
Law of 1968

Minting material	Weight in grams	Monetary unit	Standard
Copper plated steel	4.00	Cinco centavos	

Description of the seal

Obverse: On the obverse there is the Phrygian cap, surrounded by two branches of laurel. On the circumference the words "REPÚBLICA DE COLOMBIA" and the minting year.

Reverse: On the reverse there is the value of the coin stated in Roman numerals and on either side two branches of a coffee plant. A cornucopia is engraved in the upper part and in the lower part, the word "centavos".

CINCO CENTAVOS
Law of 1969

MINTING MATERIAL	WEIGHT IN GRAMS	MONETARY UNIT	STANDARD
Copper plated steel	2.00	Un centavo	

DESCRIPTION OF THE SEAL

OBVERSE: On the obverse there is the Phrygian cap, surrounded by two branches of laurel. On the circumference the words "REPÚBLICA DE COLOMBIA" and the minting year.

REVERSE: On the reverse there is the value of the coin stated in Roman numerals and on either side two branches of a coffee plant. A cornucopia is engraved in the upper part and in the lower part, the word "centavo".

UN CENTAVO
Law of 1969

MINTING MATERIAL	WEIGHT IN GRAMS	MONETARY UNIT	STANDARD
		Cinco pesos	

DESCRIPTION OF THE SEAL

OBVERSE: Emblem of the Pan American Games. In the circumference is the inscription: "VI JUEGOS PANAMERICANOS", and the place where the games were held.

REVERSE: In the center, the value of the coin is given on two lines, with an Olympic torch on either side. The first line gives the denomination in Arabic numerals and the second reads "pesos" On the circumference are the words "REPÚBLICA DE COLOMBIA" and the minting year.

CINCO PESOS
Law of 1971

MINTING MATERIAL	WEIGHT IN GRAMS	MONETARY UNIT	STANDARD
Cupro-nickel	6.8	Un Peso	

DESCRIPTION OF THE SEAL

OBVERSE: On the obverse the bust of *el Libertador* (the Liberator, Simón Bolívar), full-face and in military dress. On the circumference the words "REPÚBLICA DE COLOMBIA" and the minting year.

REVERSE: On the reverse there is the value of the coin in Arabic numerals and below it the word "peso". This inscription is surrounded by two cobs of corn and two arches formed by four concentric lines.

UN PESO
Law of 1974

Minting material	Weight in grams	Monetary unit	Standard
Copper alloy	7.9	Dos pesos	

Description of the seal

Obverse: On the obverse the bust of *el Libertador* (the Liberator, Simón Bolívar), full-face and in military dress. On the circumference the words "REPÚBLICA DE COLOMBIA" and the minting year.

Reverse: On the reverse there is the value of the coin stated in two lines found within a laurel crown. The denomination is written in Arabic numerals on the first line and the second line has the word "pesos".

DOS PESOS
Law of 1977

Minting material	Weight in grams	Monetary unit	Standard
Cupro-nickel	10.0	Diez pesos	

Description of the seal

Obverse: In the center of the obverse there is an equestrian statue of General José María Córdoba. The minting year is given on the left and the word "Córdoba" is engraved below the horse. In the upper part are the words "REPÚBLICA DE COLOMBIA". All of this is framed within an octagon.

Reverse: On the reverse there is the archipelago of San Andrés and Providencia, with the corresponding geographical coordinates around it. In the upper part the inscription "ISLAS DE SAN ANDRÉS Y PROVIDENCIA" and in the lower part "COLOMBIA" is stated. Below the island of Providencia the value of the coin is given in Arabic numerals. All of the above is placed within an octagon.

DIEZ PESOS
Law of 1980

Minting material	Weight in grams	Monetary unit	Standard
Copper alloy	9.0	Cinco pesos	

Description of the seal

Obverse: The obverse shows Policarpa Salavarrieta, martyr of the struggle for independence, seated on a stool, with her hands tied behind her back. On the circumference the words "REPÚBLICA DE COLOMBIA", the minting year, and the name of the heroine engraved between two stars.

Reverse: On the reverse there is the value of the coin written in Arabic numerals on the first line and on the second line the word "pesos". In the background there is an oil refinery.

CINCO PESOS
Law of 1981

VEINTE PESOS
Law of 1983

Minting material	Weight in grams	Monetary unit	Standard
Copper 92%, aluminium 6%, nickel 2%	6.0	Veinte pesos	

Description of the seal

Obverse: On the obverse there is a pre-Columbian "*Poporo*" of the Quimbaya culture, a lime gourd used in *coca* ceremonies. On the right the year in which the coin was minted is given and on the left there is the inscription "POPORO QUIMBAYA". On the circumference the words "REPÚBLICA DE COLOMBIA" and "MUSEO DEL ORO", the Gold Museum where the piece is displayed.

Reverse: On the reverse there is the value of the coin stated in two lines found within a laurel crown. The denomination is written in Arabic numerals on the first line and the second line has the word "pesos".

CINCUENTA PESOS
Law of 1986

Minting material	Weight in grams	Monetary unit	Standard
Copper 65% zinc 20% and nickel 15%	8.4	Cincuenta pesos	

Description of the seal

Obverse: On the obverse the façade of the National Capitol is shown, within a circle, beneath the words "CAPITOLIO NACIONAL - BOGOTÁ" and the nine stars that symbolize the sovereign states that made up the Colombian Federation and were unified by the Constitution of 1886. On the circumference the words "CENTENARIO CONSTITUCIÓN NACIONAL 1886" and in the lower part "1936 REFORMA CONSTITUCIONAL".

Reverse: On the reverse there is the coat of arms of the Republic and the value of the coin written in Arabic numerals on the first line and on the second line the word "pesos". On the circumference the words "REPÚBLICA DE COLOMBIA" and the minting year.

QUINIENTOS PESOS
Law of 1993

Core	Crown	Monetary unit	Weight in grams
Copper 92%, aluminium 6%, nickel 2%	Copper 65%, zinc 20% and nickel 15%	Quinientos pesos	7.4

Description of the seal

Obverse: On the obverse there is a drawing that represents the samán tree of Guacarí. On the circumference the words "REPÚBLICA DE COLOMBIA" and "EL ÁRBOL DE GUACARI".

Reverse: On the reverse there is the value of the coin is stated in Arabic numerals and below this is the word "pesos". The year of minting is seen in the lower part of the external ring or crown.

Minting material	Weight in grams	Monetary unit	Standard
Copper 65%, zinc 20% and nickel 15%	7.08	Doscientos pesos	

Description of the seal

Obverse: On the obverse there is a motif from the pre-Columbian Quimbaya culture. It is made up of the heads of four birds, symmetrically displayed on a circular background and surrounded by a border of 72 small, equidistant dots on the outer edge of the circumference.

Reverse: On the reverse there is the value of the coin in Arabic numerals in the center and below is the word "pesos", all of which is seen against a striated background. On the circumference the words "REPÚBLICA DE COLOMBIA" and the minting year.

DOSCIENTOS PESOS
Law of 1994

Minting material	Weight in grams	Monetary unit	Standard
Copper 92%, aluminium 6%, nickel 2%	5.31	Cien pesos	

Description of the seal

Obverse: On the obverse the national coat of arms adorned with the national flags and with the standing condor of the seal. On the circumference the words "REPÚBLICA DE COLOMBIA" and the minting year.

Reverse: On the reverse there is the value of the coin stated in two lines found within a laurel crown. The denomination is written in Arabic numerals on the first line and the second line has the word "pesos".

CIEN PESOS
Law of 1994

Minting material	Weight in grams	Monetary unit	Standard
Copper 92%, aluminium 6%, nickel 2%	7.3	Mil pesos	

Description of the seal

Obverse: On the obverse, there is the value of the coin stated in Arabic numerals, against a square background made up of thin straight lines and the word "PESOS" below. On the circumference the words "REPÚBLICA DE COLOMBIA" and the minting year. On the outer edge there are perfectly defined and separated dots.

Reverse: On the reverse there is a gold earring of the pre-Columbian Sinú culture, worked in filigree. Three semi-circular segments appear in the design: the middle one is made up of nine double circles framed within the other two, which have a toothed pattern. The other half is completely smooth.

MIL PESOS
Law of 1996

Catalogue of Bills
Issued since 1922

CINCO PESOS

Issuer	Printing firm
Banco de la República	American Bank Note Company Banco de la República (Overlaid seal)

Date of first printing	Edition
Law of: 1915 **Law of:** 1934 Overlaid seal	

Description

Obverse: LA REPÚBLICA DE COLOMBIA, CINCO PESOS ORO. José María Córdoba on the left, condor on the right, three signatures.
Reverse: Coat of arms of Colombia.
In 1931 the Banco de la República put a new seal on these bills for a provisional issue of the silver certificate, a black seal on the reverse that reads: "Certificado de plata cambiable a su presentación en el Banco de la República por igual valor en monedas legales de plata." (Silver Certificates Exchangeable on Presentation at the Banco de la República).
Imprint: "AMERICAN BANK NOTE COMPANY".
Signatories: Miembros junta de conversion (Members of the Conversion Board).

DOS Y MEDIO PESOS

Issuer	Printing firm
Banco de la República	American Bank Note Company Banco de la República (Overlaid seal)

Date of first printing	Edition
Law of: 1919 **Law of:** 1923 Overlaid seal	

Description

Obverse: CASA DE MONEDA DE MEDELLÍN, 2 1/2 PESOS. Seated woman with mirror, in center.
Reverse: Coat of arms of Colombia.
Overlaid seal "Banco de la República - Billete provisional".
Provisional bank notes issued in 1923, with overlaid seal of the Banco de la República printed on Gold Certificates from the Mint of Medellín.
Imprint: "AMERICAN BANK NOTE COMPANY".

UN PESO

Issuer	Printing firm
Banco de la República	American Bank Note Company

Date of first printing	Edition
Law of: 1923	15,000,000

Description

Obverse: EL BANCO DE LA REPÚBLICA, UN PESO ORO.
Francisco José de Caldas, in the center.
Signature of the Governor and the Secretary.
Reverse: Emblem of the Banco de la República.
Signature of the Cashier.
Imprint: "AMERICAN BANK NOTE COMPANY", on the obverse and the reverse.
Signatories: José Joaquín Pérez - Governor
Gustavo Michelsen - Secretary
Gonzalo Posada - Cashier

DOS PESOS

Issuer	Printing firm
Banco de la República	American Bank Note Company

Date of first printing	Edition
Law of: 1923	2,500,000

Description

Obverse: EL BANCO DE LA REPÚBLICA, DOS PESOS ORO.
Camilo Torres, in the center.
Signatures of the Gerente and the Secretary.
Reverse: Emblem of the Banco de la República.
Imprint: "AMERICAN BANK NOTE COMPANY", on the obverse and the reverse.
Signatories: José Joaquín Pérez - Governor
Gustavo Michelsen - Secretary
Gonzalo Posada - Cashier

CINCO PESOS

Issuer	Printing firm
Banco de la República	American Bank Note Company

Date of first printing	Edition
Law of: 1923	2,400,000

Description

Obverse: EL BANCO DE LA REPÚBLICA, CINCO PESOS ORO.
José María Córdoba, on the left.
Signatures of the Governor and the Secretary.
Reverse: Emblem of the Banco de la República.
Signature of the Cashier.
Imprint: "AMERICAN BANK NOTE COMPANY", on the obverse and the reverse.
Signatories: José Joaquín Pérez - Governor
Gustavo Michelsen - Secretary
Gonzalo Posada - Cashier

DIEZ PESOS

Issuer	Printing firm
Banco de la República	American Bank Note Company

Date of first printing	Edition
Law of: 1923	800,000

Description

Obverse: EL BANCO DE LA REPÚBLICA, DIEZ PESOS ORO.
Antonio Nariño, on the right.
Signatures of the Governor and the Secretary.
Reverse: Emblem of the Banco de la República.
Signature of the Cashier.
Imprint: "AMERICAN BANK NOTE COMPANY", on the obverse and the reverse.
Signatories: José Joaquín Pérez - Governor
Gustavo Michelsen - Secretary
Gonzalo Posada - Cashier

CINCUENTA PESOS

Issuer	Printing firm
Banco de la República	American Bank Note Company

Date of first printing	Edition
Law of: 1923	80,000

Description

Obverse: EL BANCO DE LA REPÚBLICA, CINCUENTA PESOS ORO.
Antonio José de Sucre, on the left.
Signatures of the Governor and the Secretary.
Reverse: Emblem of the Banco de la República.
Signature of the Cashier.
Imprint: "AMERICAN BANK NOTE COMPANY", on the obverse and the reverse.
Signatories: José Joaquín Pérez - Governor
Gustavo Michelsen - Secretary
Gonzalo Posada - Cashier

CIEN PESOS

Issuer	Printing firm
Banco de la República	American Bank Note Company

Date of first printing	Edition
Law of: 1923	30,000

Description

Obverse: EL BANCO DE LA REPÚBLICA, CIEN PESOS ORO.
Francisco de Paula Santander, in the center.
Signatures of the Governor and the Secretary.
Reverse: Emblem of the Banco de la República.
Signature of the Cashier.
Imprint: "AMERICAN BANK NOTE COMPANY", on the obverse and the reverse.
Signatories: José Joaquín Pérez - Governor
Gustavo Michelsen - Secretary
Gonzalo Posada - Cashier

QUINIENTOS PESOS

(Reverse not available)

Issuer	Printing firm
Banco de la República	American Bank Note Company

Date of first printing	Edition
Law of: 1923	6,000

Description

Obverse: EL BANCO DE LA REPÚBLICA, QUINIENTOS PESOS ORO.
Simón Bolívar, on the right.
Signatures of the Governor and the Secretary.
Imprint: "AMERICAN BANK NOTE COMPANY".
Signatories: José Joaquín Pérez - Governor
Gustavo Michelsen - Secretary
Gonzalo Posada - Cashier

UN PESO

Issuer	Printing firm
Banco de la República	American Bank Note Company

Date of first printing	Edition
Law of: 1926	8,000,000

Description

Obverse: EL BANCO DE LA REPÚBLICA, UN PESO ORO.
Simón Bolívar, in the center.
Signatures of the Governor and the Secretary.
Reverse: Emblem of the Banco de la República.
Signature of the Cashier.
Imprint: "AMERICAN BANK NOTE COMPANY", on the obverse and the reverse.
Signatories: Félix Salazar - Governor
Mariano Ospina Vásquez - Secretary
Gonzalo Posada - Cashier

DOS PESOS

Issuer	Printing firm
Banco de la República	American Bank Note Company

Date of first printing	Edition
Law of: 1926	2,000,000
Law of: 1942 - 1955	5,000,000

Description

Obverse: EL BANCO DE LA REPÚBLICA, DOS PESOS ORO.
Camilo Torres, in the center.
Signatures of the Governor and the Secretary.
Reverse: Emblem of the Banco de la República.
Imprint: "AMERICAN BANK NOTE COMPANY", on the obverse and the reverse.
Signatories: Félix Salazar, Julio Caro, Luis Ángel Arango - Governor
Mariano Ospina Rodríguez, Luis Ángel Arango, Ignacio Copete, Jaime Londoño, Eduardo Aria Robledo - Secretary
Gonzalo Posada - Cashier

CINCO PESOS

Issuer	Printing firm
Banco de la República	American Bank Note Company

Date of first printing	Edition
Law of: 1926 and 1928	2,000,000

Description

Obverse: EL BANCO DE LA REPÚBLICA, CINCO PESOS ORO.
José María Córdoba, on the left.
Signatures of the Governor and the Secretary.
Reverse: Emblem of the Banco de la República.
Imprint: "AMERICAN BANK NOTE COMPANY", on the obverse and the reverse.
Signatories: Félix Salazar, Julio Caro - Governor
Mariano Ospina Vásquez - Secretary
Gonzalo Posada - Cashier

DIEZ PESOS

Issuer	Printing firm
Banco de la República	American Bank Note Company

Date of first printing	Edition
Law of: 1926 and 1928	800,000
Law of: 1941 - 1963	2,000,000

Description

Obverse: EL BANCO DE LA REPÚBLICA, DIEZ PESOS ORO.
Antonio Nariño, on the right.
Signatures of the Governor and the Secretary.
Reverse: Emblem of the Banco de la República.
Imprint: "AMERICAN BANK NOTE COMPANY", on the obverse and the reverse.
Signatories: Félix Salazar, Julio Caro, Luis Ángel Arango, Eduardo Arias Robledo - Governor
Mariano Ospina Vásquez, Luis Ángel Arango, Ignacio Copete Lizarralde - Secretary
Gonzalo Posada, Jaime Londoño, Germán Botero de los Ríos - Cashier

CINCUENTA PESOS

Issuer	Printing firm
Banco de la República	American Bank Note Company

Date of first printing	Edition
Law of: 1926 and 1928	40,000
Law of: 1958 - 1967	10,000,000

Description

Obverse: EL BANCO DE LA REPÚBLICA, CINCUENTA PESOS ORO.
Antonio José de Sucre, on the left.
Signatures of the Governor and the Secretary.
Reverse: Emblem of the Banco de la República.
Signature of the Cashier.
Imprint: "AMERICAN BANK NOTE COMPANY", on the obverse and the reverse.
Signatories: Félix Salazar, Ignacio Copete L., Jorge Cortés Boshell, Eduardo Arias Robledo - Governor
Mariano Ospina Vásquez, Jorge Cortés Boshell, Germán Botero de los Ríos - Secretary

DIEZ PESOS

Issuer	Printing firm
Banco de la República	Thomas de la Rue & Co. Ltd.

Date of first printing	Edition
Law of: 1927	1,000,000

Description

Obverse: EL BANCO DE LA REPÚBLICA, DIEZ PESOS ORO. Antonio Nariño, on the left; Mercury and scene of boat on river. Signatures of the Governor and the Secretary.
Reverse: Building of the Banco de la Repoblación, Medellín. Signature of the Cashier.
Imprint: "THOMAS DE LA RUE & COY LTD. LONDRES, INGLATERRA", on the obverse and the reverse.
Signatories: Julio Caro - Governor
Mariano Ospina Vásquez - Secretary
Gonzalo Posada - Cashier

CINCO PESOS

Issuer	Printing firm
Banco de la República	Thomas de la Rue & Co. Ltd.

Date of first printing	Edition
Law of: 1927	2,000,000

Description

Obverse: EL BANCO DE LA REPÚBLICA, CINCO PESOS ORO. José María Córdoba and seated allegorical woman, on the left; Simón Bolívar in watermark, on the right.
Signatures of the Governor and the Secretary.
Reverse: First building of the Banco de la República in Bogotá. Signature of the Cashier.
Imprint: "THOMAS DE LA RUE & COY. LTD. LONDRES, INGLATERRA", on the obverse and the reverse.
Signatories: Julio Caro - Governor
Mariano Ospina Vásquez - Secretary
Gonzalo Posada - Cashier.

VEINTE PESOS

Issuer	Printing firm
Banco de la República	Thomas de la Rue & Co. Ltd.

Date of first printing	Edition
Law of: 1927	500,000

Description

Obverse: EL BANCO DE LA REPÚBLICA, VEINTE PESOS ORO.
Francisco José de Caldas, on the left; Simón Bolívar in watermark, on the right.
Signatures of the Governor and the Secretary.
Reverse: Building of the Banco de la República, Barranquilla.
Signature of the Cashier.
Imprint: "THOMAS DE LA RUE & COY LTD. LONDRES, INGLATERRA", on the obverse and the reverse.
Signatories: Julio Caro - Governor
Mariano Ospina Vásquez - Secretary
Gonzalo Posada - Cashier

CIEN PESOS

Issuer	Printing firm
Banco de la República	American Bank Note Company

Date of first printing	Edition
Law of: 1928 - 1957	100,000

Description

Obverse: EL BANCO DE LA REPÚBLICA, CIEN PESOS ORO.
Francisco de Paula Santander, in the center.
Signatures of the Governor and the Secretary.
Reverse: Emblem of the Banco de la República.
Signature of the Cashier.
Imprint: "AMERICAN BANK NOTE COMPANY", on the obverse and the reverse.
Signatories: Julio Caro, Luis Ángel Arango, Ignacio Copete Lizarralde - Governor
Mariano Ospina Vásquez, Luis Ángel Arango, Ignacio Copete Lizarralde, Jaime Londoño, Eduardo Arias Robledo - Secretary
Gonzalo Posada - Cashier (until 1928)

UN PESO

Issuer	Printing firm
Banco de la República	American Bank Note Company

Date of first printing	Edition
Law of: 1929	22,000,000

Description

Obverse: EL BANCO DE LA REPÚBLICA, UN PESO ORO.
Francisco de Paula Santander, on the left; effigy of Simón Bolívar, on the right.
Signatures of the Governor and the Secretary.
Reverse: Emblem of the Banco de la República.
Imprint: "AMERICAN BANK NOTE COMPANY", on the obverse and the reverse.
Signatories: Julio Caro - Governor
Mariano Ospina Vásquez - Secretary

UN PESO PLATA

Issuer	Printing firm
Banco de la República	American Bank Note Company

Date of first printing	Edition
Law of: 1932	9,000,000

Description

Obverse: EL BANCO DE LA REPÚBLICA, CERTIFICADO DE PLATA.
Effigy of Francisco de Paula Santander (David), in the center.
On both sides of the effigy the inscription "1 PESO PLATA".
Signatures of the Governor and the Secretary.
Reverse: Emblem of the Banco de la República.
Imprint: "AMERICAN BANK NOTE COMPANY", on the obverse and the reverse.
Signatories: Julio Caro - Governor
Mariano Ospina Vásquez - Secretary

CINCO PESOS PLATA

Issuer	Printing firm
Banco de la República	American Bank Note Company

Date of first printing	Edition
Law of: 1932	1,400,000

Description

Obverse: EL BANCO DE LA REPÚBLICA, CINCO PESOS SILVER.
Antonio Nariño, in the center.
Signatures of the Governor and the Secretary.
Reverse: Emblem of the Banco de la República.
Imprint: "AMERICAN BANK NOTE COMPANY", on the obverse and the reverse.
Signatories: Julio Caro - Governor
Mariano Ospina Vásquez - Secretary

MEDIO PESO

Issuer	Printing firm
Banco de la República	American Bank Note Company

Date of first printing	Edition
Law of: 1935	4,000,000

Description

Obverse: EL BANCO DE LA REPÚBLICA, MEDIO PESO ORO.
Busto de Francisco José de Caldas, on the left; effigy of Simón Bolívar, on the right.
Reverse: Emblem of the Banco de la República.
Imprint: "AMERICAN BANK NOTE COMPANY", on the obverse and the reverse.
Signatories: Julio Caro - Governor
Mariano Ospina Vásquez - Secretary

UN PESO

Issuer	Printing firm
Banco de la República	American Bank Note Company

Date of first printing	Edition
Law of: 1938	3,000,000

Description

Obverse: EL BANCO DE LA REPÚBLICA, UN PESO ORO.
Gonzalo Jiménez de Quesada (founder of Bogotá) in the center of a medallion flanked by two angels.
Signatures of the Governor and the Secretary.
Reverse: Portrayal of the founding of Bogotá.
Imprint: "AMERICAN BANK NOTE COMPANY", on the obverse and the reverse.
Commemorative issue for the IV centennial of the foundation of Bogotá in 1538.
Signatories: Julio Caro - Governor
Mariano Ospina Vásquez - Secretary

CINCO PESOS

Issuer	Printing firm
Tesorería República de Colombia	American Bank Note Company

Date of first printing	Edition
Law of: 1938	2,000,000

Description

Obverse: LA REPÚBLICA DE COLOMBIA, CINCO PESOS ORO.
José María Córdoba, in the center.
Reverse: Coat of arms of Colombia.
Imprint: "AMERICAN BANK NOTE COMPANY", on the obverse and the reverse.
Signatories: Gonzalo Restrepo J. - Minister of Finance and Public Credit
Carlos Lleras Restrepo - Controller General
Andrés Rocha - General Treasurer

DIEZ PESOS

Issuer	Printing firm
Banco de la República	American Bank Note Company

Date of first printing	Edition
Law of: 1938	586,142

Description

Obverse: LA REPÚBLICA DE COLOMBIA, DIEZ PESOS ORO. Effigy of Francisco de Paula Santander (David), on the left; effigy of Simón Bolívar, on the right.
Reverse: Coat of arms of Colombia.
Imprint: "AMERICAN BANK NOTE COMPANY", on the obverse and the reverse.
Signatories: Gonzalo Restrepo - Minister of Finance and Public Credit
Carlos Lleras Restrepo - Controller General
Andrés Rocha - General Treasurer

UN PESO PLATA

Issuer	Printing firm
Banco de la República	American Bank Note Company

Date of first printing	Edition
Law of: 1941	4,000,000

Description

Obverse: EL BANCO DE LA REPÚBLICA, UN PESO PLATA. Effigy of Francisco de Paula Santander (David), on the left. Signatures of the Governor and the Secretary.
Reverse: Emblem of the Banco de la República.
Imprint: "AMERICAN BANK NOTE COMPANY", on the obverse and the reverse.
Signatories: Julio Caro - Governor
Mariano Ospina Vásquez - Secretary

CINCO PESOS PLATA

Issuer	Printing firm
Banco de la República	American Bank Note Company

Date of first printing	Edition
Law of: 1941	2,000,000

Description

Obverse: EL BANCO DE LA REPÚBLICA, CINCO PESOS PLATA. Antonio Nariño on the left.
Signatures of the Governor and the Secretary.
Reverse: Emblem of the Banco de la República.
Imprint: "AMERICAN BANK NOTE COMPANY", on the obverse and the reverse.
Signatories: Julio Caro - Governor
Mariano Ospina Vásquez - Secretary

MEDIO PESO PARTIDO

Issuer	Printing firm
Banco de la República	American Bank Note Company

Date of first printing	Edition
Law of: 1942	1,000,000 of 1942 250,000 of 1943

Description

Obverse: Overlaid seal with the inscription "Banco de la República, provisional, MEDIO PESO".
Reverse: Overlaid seal: MEDIO PESO.
Half of the bank note of 1 PESO of 1942 or 1943, with overlaid seal on both faces.
Imprint: In some bills there is the imprint: "LITOGRAFÍA COLOMBIANA S.A. - BOGOTÁ".

QUINIENTOS PESOS

Issuer	Printing firm
Banco de la República	American Bank Note Company

Date of first printing	Edition
Law of: 1942 - 1964	20,000

Description

Obverse: EL BANCO DE LA REPÚBLICA, QUINIENTOS PESOS ORO.
Effigy of Simón Bolívar, on the right.
Signatures of the Governor and the Secretary.
Reverse: Emblem of the Banco de la República
Imprint: "AMERICAN BANK NOTE COMPANY".
Signatories: Julio Caro, Luis Ángel Arango, Eduardo Arias R. - Governor
Luis Ángel Arango, Ignacio Copete L., Jaime Londoño, Eduardo Arias R. - Secretary
Germán Botero de los Ríos - Cashier

VEINTE PESOS

Issuer	Printing firm
Banco de la República	American Bank Note Company

Date of first printing	Edition
Law of: 1943 - 1963	500,000

Description

Obverse: EL BANCO DE LA REPÚBLICA, VEINTE PESOS ORO.
Francisco José de Caldas, on the left; effigy of Simón Bolívar, on the right.
Signatures of the Governor and the Secretary.
Reverse: Emblem of the Banco de la República.
Pie de impre1nta: "AMERICAN BANK NOTE COMPANY", on the obverse and the reverse.
Signatories: Julio Caro, Luis Ángel Arango, Eduardo Arias Robledo - Governor
Luis Ángel Arango, Ignacio Copete, Jaime Londoño, Germán Botero de los Ríos - Secretary

MEDIO PESO

Issuer	Printing firm
Tesorería República de Colombia	American Bank Note Company

Date of first printing	Edition
Law of: 1948	10,000,000

Description

Obverse: REPÚBLICA DE COLOMBIA, MEDIO PESO ORO.
Antonio Nariño, in the center.
Reverse: Coat of arms of Colombia.
These notes were popularly known as the "Lleritas".
Imprint: "AMERICAN BANK NOTE COMPANY", on the obverse and the reverse.
Signatories: José María Bernal - Minister of Finance and Public Credit
Antonio Ordóñez Ceballos - Controller General
Andrés Rocha - General Treasurer

UN PESO

Issuer	Printing firm
Banco de la República	Waterlow and Sons Ltd. Londres

Date of first printing	Edition
Law of: 1953	100,000,000

Description

Obverse: EL BANCO DE LA REPÚBLICA, UN PESO ORO.
Statue of Simón Bolívar on the left, Bridge of Boyacá in the center and portrait of Francisco de Paula Santander on the right.
Signatures of the Governor and the Secretary.
Reverse: Emblem of the Banco de la República.
Imprint: "WATERLOW AND SON LIMITED, LONDRES", on the obverse and the reverse. All of the bills have special characteristics of printing control in the lower left hand corner of the obverse and reverse
Signatories: Luis Ángel Arango - Governor
Eduardo Arias Robledo - Secretary

CINCO PESOS

Issuer	Printing firm
Banco de la República	Thomas de la Rue & Co. Ltd.

Date of first printing	Edition
Law of: 1953	50,000,000
Law of: 1960	30,000,000

Description

Obverse: EL BANCO DE LA REPÚBLICA, CINCO PESOS ORO. José María Córdoba and seated allegorical woman, on the left. Signatures of the Governor and the Secretary.
Reverse: Building of the Banco de la República in Bogotá.
Imprint: "THOMAS DE LA RUE & COY LTD., LONDRES, INGLATERRA".
Signatories: Luis Ángel Arango, Jorge Cortés Boshell - Governor
Eduardo Arias Robledo, Germán Botero de los Ríos - Secretary

DIEZ PESOS

Issuer	Printing firm
Banco de la República	Thomas de la Rue & Co. Ltd.

Date of first printing	Edition
Law of: 1953 - 1961	25,000,000

Description

Obverse: EL BANCO DE LA REPÚBLICA, DIEZ PESOS ORO. Antonio Nariño, on the left; Mercury and scene of boat on river. Signatures of the Governor and the Secretary.
Reverse: Building of the Banco de la República in Cali.
Imprint: "THOMAS DE LA RUE & COY LTD. LONDRES, INGLATERRA".
Signatories: Luis Ángel Arango, Ignacio Copete L., Eduardo Arias Robledo - Governor
Eduardo Arias Robledo, Jorge Cortés Boshell, Germán Botero de los Ríos - Secretary

VEINTE PESOS

Issuer	Printing firm
Banco de la República	Thomas de la Rue & Co. Ltd.

Date of first printing	Edition
Law of: 1953 - 1965	25,000,000

Description

Obverse: EL BANCO DE LA REPÚBLICA, VEINTE PESOS ORO. Francisco José de Caldas, on the left; emblem of the Banco de la República, on the right.
Signatures of the Governor and the Secretary.
Reverse: Building of the Banco de la República in Barranquilla.
Imprint: "THOMAS DE LA RUE & COY LTD. LONDRES, INGLATERRA".
Signatories: Luis Ángel Arango, Ignacio Copete, Eduardo Arias Robledo - Governor
Eduardo Arias Robledo, Jorge Cotés Boshell, Germán Botero de los Ríos - Secretary

CIEN PESOS

Issuer	Printing firm
Banco de la República	American Bank Note Company

Date of first printing	Edition
Law of: 1958 - 1967	10,000,000

Description

Obverse: EL BANCO DE LA REPÚBLICA, CIEN PESOS ORO. Francisco de Paula Santander, on the right.
Signatures of the Governor and the Secretary.
Reverse: Emblem of the Banco de la República.
Imprint: "AMERICAN BANK NOTE COMPANY", on the obverse and the reverse.
Signatories: Ignacio Copete L., Eduardo Arias R. - Governor
Jorge Cortés Boshell, Germám Botero de los Ríos - Secretary

UN PESO

Issuer	Printing firm
Banco de la República	Imprenta de Billetes del Banco de la República

Date of first printing	Edition
Law of: 1959	100,000,000

Description

Obverse: EL BANCO DE LA REPÚBLICA, UN PESO ORO.
Effigy of Simón Bolívar, on the left; portrait of Francisco de Paula Santander, on the right.
Signatures of the Governor and the Secretary.
Reverse: Condor and view of the Tequendama falls.
Imprint: Without imprint.
First issue of this denomination from the presses of the Banco de la República.
Signatories: Ignacio Copete Lizarralde - Governor
Jorge Cortés Boshell - Secretary

CINCO PESOS

Issuer	Printing firm
Banco de la República	Imprenta de Billetes del Banco de la República

Date of first printing	Edition
Law of: 1961	4,000,000

Description

Obverse: EL BANCO DE LA REPÚBLICA, CINCO PESOS ORO.
José María Córdoba, on the right; condor, on the left.
Signatures of the Governor and the Secretary.
Reverse: Walls of Cartagena.
Imprint: Without imprint.
Signatories: Eduardo Arias Robledo, Germán Botero de los Ríos, Rafael Gama Quijano - Governor
Germán Botero de los Ríos, Antonio José Gutiérrez, Francisco J. Ortega - Secretary

DIEZ PESOS

Issuer	Printing firm
Banco de la República	Imprenta de Billetes del Banco de la República

Date of first printing	Edition
Law of: 1963 - 1980	15,000,000

Description

Obverse: EL BANCO DE LA REPÚBLICA, DIEZ PESOS ORO. Antonio Nariño, on the left; condor, on the right. Signatures of the Governor and the Secretary.
Reverse: San Agustín Archaeological Park
Imprint: Without imprint.
First issue of this denomination from the presses of the Banco de la República.
Signatories: Eduardo Arias Robledo, Germán Botero de los Ríos, Rafael Gama Quijano - Governor
Germán Botero de los Ríos, Antonio J. Gutiérrez, Francisco J. Ortega - Secretary

VEINTE PESOS

Issuer	Printing firm
Banco de la República	Imprenta de Billetes del Banco de la República

Date of first printing	Edition
Law of: 1966 - 1983	50,000,000

Description

Obverse: EL BANCO DE LA REPÚBLICA, VEINTE PESOS ORO. Francisco José de Caldas with celestial sphere, on the right. Signatures of the Governor and the Secretary.
Reverse: Pieces from the Gold Museum of Bogotá.
Imprint: Without imprint.
First issue of this denomination from the presses of the Banco de la República.
Signatories: Eduardo Arias Robledo, Germán Botero de los Ríos, Rafael Gama Quijano, Hugo Palacio Mejía - Governor
Germán Botero de los Ríos, Antonio José Gutiérrez, Francisco J. Ortega - Secretary

CIEN PESOS

Issuer	Printing firm
Banco de la República	Thomas de la Rue & Co. Ltd.

Date of first printing	Edition
Law of: 1968 - 1971	10,000,000

Description

Obverse: EL BANCO DE LA REPÚBLICA, CIEN PESOS ORO. Francisco de Paula Santander, on the right; Simón Bolívar in watermark, on the left.
Signatures of the Governor and the Secretary.
Reverse: Building of National Parliament.
Imprint: "THOMAS DE LA RUE & COMPANY LIMITED".
Signatories: Eduardo Arias R., Germán Botero de los Ríos - Governor
Germán Botero de los Ríos, Antonio J. Gutiérrez - Secretary

QUINIENTOS PESOS

Issuer	Printing firm
Banco de la República	American Bank Note Company

Date of first printing	Edition
Law of: 1968 y 1971	10,000,000

Description

Obverse: EL BANCO DE LA REPÚBLICA, QUINIENTOS PESOS ORO. Simón Bolívar, on the right; effigy of the Liberty in watermark, on the left.
Signatures of the Governor and the Secretary.
Reverse: Cathedral of Salt in Zipaquirá.
Imprint: "AMERICAN BANK NOTE COMPANY", on the obverse and the reverse.
After a robbery, the color of this bill was changed to red.
Signatories: Eduardo Arias Robledo, Germán Botero de los Ríos - Governor
Germán Botero de los Ríos, Antonio José Gutiérrez - Secretary

CINCUENTA PESOS

Issuer	Printing firm
Banco de la República	Thomas de la Rue & Co. Ltd.

Date of first printing	Edition
Law of: 1969	20,000,000

Description

Obverse: EL BANCO DE LA REPÚBLICA, CINCUENTA PESOS ORO. Camilo Torres, on the right; in watermark, on the left. Signatures of the Governor and the Secretary.
Reverse: Colombian orchids.
Imprint: "THOMAS DE LA RUE & COMPANY LIMITED", on the obverse and the reverse.
Signatories: Germán Botero de los Ríos - Governor
Antonio José Gutiérrez - Secretary

DOS PESOS

Issuer	Printing firm
Banco de la República	Imprenta de Billetes del Banco de la República

Date of first printing	Edition
Law of: 1972 - 1977	100,000,000 first edition

Description

Obverse: EL BANCO DE LA REPÚBLICA, DOS PESOS ORO. Policarpa Salavarrieta, on the left. Signatures of the Governor and the Secretary.
Reverse: Pre-Columbian gold figurine of raft, from Gold Museum of Bogotá.
Imprint: Without imprint
Signatories: Germán Botero de los Ríos - Governor
Antonio José Gutiérrez - Secretary

CIEN PESOS

Issuer	Printing firm
Banco de la República	Thomas de la Rue & Co. Ltd.

Date of first printing	Edition
Law of: 1973 - 1980	

Description

Obverse: EL BANCO DE LA REPÚBLICA, CIEN PESOS ORO. Francisco de Paula Santander, on the right; effigy of the Liberty in watermark, on the left.
Signatures of the Governor and the Secretary.
Reverse: Building of the National Parliament.
Imprint: "THOMAS DE LA RUE & COMPANY LIMITED".
1973-74 dark blue
1977-80 violet
Signatories: Germán Botero de los Ríos, Rafael Gama Quijano - Governor
Antonio José Gutiérrez, Francisco J. Ortega - Secretary

QUINIENTOS PESOS

Issuer	Printing firm
Banco de la República	American Bank Note Company

Date of first printing	Edition
Law of: 1973	10,000,000

Description

Obverse: EL BANCO DE LA REPÚBLICA, QUINIENTOS PESOS ORO. Simón Bolívar, on the right; in watermark, on the left.
Signatures of the Governor and the Secretary.
Reverse: Cathedral of Salt in Zipaquirá.
Imprint: "AMERICAN BANK NOTE COMPANY", on the obverse and the reverse.
Signatories: Germán Botero de los Ríos - Governor
Antonio José Gutiérrez - Secretary

DOSCIENTOS PESOS

Issuer	Printing firm
Banco de la República	Thomas de la Rue & Co. Ltd. 1974-80 Imprenta de Billetes del Banco de la República 1980-82

Date of first printing	Edition
Law of: 1974 - 1982	

Description

Obverse: EL BANCO DE LA REPÚBLICA, DOSCIENTOS PESOS ORO. Simón Bolívar y Cathedral of Bogotá, on the right; Simón Bolívar in watermark, on the left.
Signatures of the Governor and the Secretary.
Reverse: Coffee harvester.
Imprint: "THOMAS DE LA RUE & COMPANY LIMITED".
First issue of this denomination from the presses of the Banco de la República.
Signatories: Germán Botero de los Ríos, Rafael Gama Quijano - Governor
Antonio José Gutiérrez, Francisco J. Ortega - Secretary

QUINIENTOS PESOS

Issuer	Printing firm
Banco de la República	American Bank Note Company

Date of first printing	Edition
Law of: 1977 and 1979	

Description

Obverse: EL BANCO DE LA REPÚBLICA, QUINIENTOS PESOS ORO. Francisco de Paula Santander, on the left; in watermark, on the right.
Signatures of the Governor and the Secretary.
Reverse: Cathedral of Salt in Zipaquirá.
Imprint: "AMERICAN BANK NOTE COMPANY".
Signatories: Germán Botero de los Ríos, Rafael Gama Quijano - Governor
Antonio José Gutiérrez, Francisco J. Ortega - Secretary

MIL PESOS

Issuer	Printing firm
Banco de la República	American Bank Note Company

Date of first printing	Edition
Law of: 1979	

Description

Obverse: EL BANCO DE LA REPÚBLICA, MIL PESOS ORO.
José Antonio Galán, on the right; in watermark, on the left.
Signatures of the Governor and the Secretary.
Reverse: Nariño Presidential Palace.
Imprint: "AMERICAN BANK NOTE COMPANY", on the obverse and the reverse.
First issue of this denomination from the presses of the Banco de la República.
Signatories: Rafael Gama Quijano - Governor
Francisco J. Ortega - Secretary

QUINIENTOS PESOS

Issuer	Printing firm
Banco de la República	Thomas de la Rue & Co. Ltd. 1981-86 Imprenta de Billetes del Banco de la República 1986-93

Date of first printing	Edition
Law of: 1981	

Description

Obverse: EL BANCO DE LA REPÚBLICA, QUINIENTOS PESOS ORO.
Francisco de Paula Santander, on the left; in watermark, on the right.
Signatures of the Governor and the Legal Deputy Governor.
Reverse: Casa de la Moneda (Mint) in Bogotá.
Imprint: "IMPRENTA DE BILLETES - BOGOTÁ".
Signatories: Francisco J. Ortega, Rafael Gama Quijano, Hugo Palacio M. - Governor
Francisco J. Ortega 1981,
Roberto Salazar M.- Legal Deputy Governor

Issuer	Printing firm
Banco de la República	Thomas de la Rue & Co. Ltd. 1982-87 Imprenta de Billetes del Banco de la República 1987-1995

Date of first printing	Edition
Law of: 1982 - 1995	

MIL PESOS

Description

Obverse: EL BANCO DE LA REPÚBLICA, MIL PESOS ORO. Simón Bolívar, on the left; in watermark, on the right. Signatures of the Governor and the Secretary.
Reverse: Monument of the battle of the Pantano de Vargas.
Imprint: "THOMAS DE LA RUE & CO. LTD."
Signatories: Rafael Gama Quijano, Hugo Palacio M., Francisco J. Ortega, Miguel Urrutia- Governor
Francisco J. Ortega - Secretary
Roberto Salazar - Legal Deputy Governor 1984-87
Luis Carlos León Cuervo - Secretary
Fernando Copete - Executive Governor, from 1990

Issuer	Printing firm
Banco de la República	Imprenta de Billetes del Banco de la República

Date of first printing	Edition
Law of: 1983 - 1991	

CIEN PESOS

Description

Obverse: EL BANCO DE LA REPÚBLICA, CIEN PESOS ORO. Antonio Nariño, on the left; in watermark, on the right. Signatures of the Governor and the Secretary.
Reverse: Villa de Leiva, Antonio Nariño press.
Imprint: "IMPRENTA DE BILLETES - BOGOTÁ".
Signatories: Hugo Palacio Mejía, Francisco J. Ortega - Governor
Francisco J. Ortega - Secretary (1983) Roberto Salazar
1984-89 Legal Deputy Governor
1990 Secretary

DOSCIENTOS PESOS

Issuer	Printing firm
Banco de la República	Thomas de la Rue & Co. Ltd. April 1983 Imprenta de Billetes del Banco de la República April 1983
Date of first printing	**Edition**
Law of: 1983 - 1991	

Description

Obverse: EL BANCO DE LA REPÚBLICA, DOSCIENTOS PESOS ORO. José Celestino Mutis and Astronomical Observatory, on the left. José Celestino Mutis in watermark, on the right. Signatures of the Governor and the Secretary.
Reverse: Colegio del Rosario.
Imprint: "IMPRENTA DE BILLETES DE SANTA FE DE BOGOTÁ".
Signatories: Hugo Palacio Mejía, Francisco J. Ortega - Governor
Francisco J. Ortega - Secretary (1983) Roberto Salazar
Abogado subgerente 1984 Roberto Salazar
Secretary 1991 Luis Carlos León Cuervo

DOS MIL PESOS

Issuer	Printing firm
Banco de la República	Thomas de la Rue & Co. Ltd. 1983-86 Imprenta de Billetes del Banco de la República 1986-98
Date of first printing	**Edition**
Law of: 1983 - 1998	

Description

Obverse: EL BANCO DE LA REPÚBLICA, DOS MIL PESOS ORO. Simón Bolívar, on the left; in watermark, on the right. Signatures of the Governor and the Secretary.
Reverse: Scene of the passing of the páramo de Pisba, after F.A. Cano.
Imprint: "THOMAS DE LA RUE & CO. LTD."
Signatories: Hugo Palacio Mejía, Francisco J. Ortega, Miguel Urrutia - Governor
Francisco J. Ortega, Luis Carlos León - Secretary
Roberto Salazar M. - Legal Deputy Governor
Fernando Copete - Executive Governor

CINCO MIL PESOS

Issuer	Printing firm
Banco de la República	Bundesdruckerei (Germany) 1986 Instituto Poligrafico e Zecca dello Stato (Italy) 1987- 88 Imprenta de Billetes del Banco de la República 1990

Date of first printing	Edition
Law of: 1986 - 1995	

Description

Obverse: EL BANCO DE LA REPÚBLICA, CINCO MIL PESOS. Rafael Núñez, on the left; in watermark, on the right. Signatures of the Governor and the Legal Deputy Governor
Reverse: Monument to Miguel Antonio Caro.
Imprint: BUNDESDRUCKEREI, FEDERAL GERMANY
Signatories: Francisco J. Ortega, Miguel Urrutia - Governor
Roberto Salazar M. - Legal Deputy Governor
Luis Carlos León Cuervo - Secretary
Fernando Copete - Executive Governor

DIEZ MIL PESOS

Issuer	Printing firm
Banco de la República	Imprenta de Billetes del Banco de la República

Date of first printing	Edition
Law of: 1992 - 1994	

Description

Obverse: EL BANCO DE LA REPÚBLICA, DIEZ MIL PESOS ORO. Embera indigenous woman, on the right; in watermark, on the left. Signatures of the Governor and the Secretary.
Reverse: Colombian birds, globe and caravel.
Imprint: "IMPRENTA DE BILLETES – SANTA FE DE BOGOTÁ".
Signatories: Francisco J. Ortega, Miguel Urrutia - Governor
Luis Carlos León Cuervo, Fernando Copete - Secretary

As from 1993 the legend stating the amount of gold pesos that the Banco de la República would pay to the bearer was eliminated. This had lost its meaning with the abandonment of convertibility in the 1930´s.

CINCO MIL PESOS

Issuer	Printing firm
Banco de la República	Imprenta de Billetes del Banco de la República

Date of first printing	Edition
Law of: 1995 -	

Description

Obverse: EL BANCO DE LA REPÚBLICA, CINCO MIL PESOS.
José Asunción Silva (Colombian poet), on the right; in watermark, in the center.
Signatures of the Governors General and Executive.
Reverse: Landscape evocative of the best known "Nocturne" of Silva.
Imprint: "IMPRENTA DE BILLETES – SANTA FE DE BOGOTÁ".
Signatories: Miguel Urrutia - Governor General
Fernando Copete - Executive Governor

DIEZ MIL PESOS

Issuer	Printing firm
Banco de la República	Imprenta de Billetes del Banco de la República

Date of first printing	Edition
Law of: 1995 -	

Description

Obverse: EL BANCO DE LA REPÚBLICA, DIEZ MIL PESOS.
Policarpa Salavarrieta, on the right; in watermark, on the left.
Signatures of the Governors General and Executive.
Reverse: View of the town of Guaduas at the beginning of the nineteenth century.
Imprint: "IMPRENTA DE BILLETES – SANTA FE DE BOGOTÁ".
Signatories: Miguel Urrutia - Governor General
Fernando Copete - Executive Governor

DOS MIL PESOS

Issuer	Printing firm
Banco de la República	Imprenta de Billetes del Banco de la República

Date of first printing	Edition
Law of: 1996 -	

Description

Obverse: EL BANCO DE LA REPÚBLICA, DOS MIL PESOS. Francisco de Paula Santander, on the left, after an engraving done in Paris on the basis of a sketch by José María Espinosa. In background a view of a marsh in los llanos orientales (eastern plains); in watermark, on the right.
Signatures of the Governors General and Executive.
Reverse: Façade of the Casa de la Moneda in Santa Fe de Bogotá.
Imprint: "IMPRENTA DE BILLETES – SANTA FE DE BOGOTÁ".
Signatories: Miguel Urrutia - Governor General
Fernando Copete - Executive Governor

VEINTE MIL PESOS

Issuer	Printing firm
Banco de la República	Imprenta de Billetes del Banco de la República

Date of first printing	Edition
Law of: 1996 -	

Description

Obverse: EL BANCO DE LA REPÚBLICA, VEINTE MIL PESOS. Julio Garavito A. (Colombian astronomer), on the right; in watermark, on the lef. The moon, in the center.
Signatures of the Governors General and Executive.
Reverse: The earth and in the background geometrical figures and the Astronomical Observatory of Bogotá.
Imprint: "IMPRENTA DE BILLETES – SANTA FE DE BOGOTÁ".
Signatories: Miguel Urrutia - Governor General
Fernando Copete - Executive Governor

CINCUENTA MIL PESOS

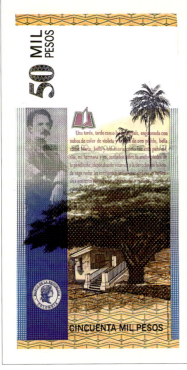

ISSUER	PRINTING FIRM
Banco de la República	Imprenta de Billetes del Banco de la República

DATE OF FIRST PRINTING	EDITION
Law of: 2000 -	

DESCRIPTION

OBVERSE: BANCO DE LA REPÚBLICA, 50 MIL PESOS.
Jorge Isaac (Colombian writer) in the lower part (in vertical sense), figure of María, the heroine of his novel.
Signatures of the Governors General and Executive
REVERSE: Landscape of the Valley of Cauca and the house of the hacienda El Paraíso (setting of his novel)
IMPRINT: "IMPRENTA DE BILLETES – SANTA FE DE BOGOTÁ".
SIGNATORIES: Miguel Urrutia - Governor General
Fernando Copete - Executive Governor

ONOMASTIC INDEX

A

Abadía Méndez, Miguel, 76, 97, 128, 129
Agudelo Villa, Hernando, 163, 275
Arango, Alejandro, 65, 66
Alter, Gerald, 158
Álvarez Restrepo, Antonio, 163
American Bank Note company, 65, 92, 117
Andrade, Eugenio, 99, 100
Arango, Luis Ángel, 154, 155
Arango, Marcelino, 76
Archila, Aristóbulo, 104
Arias Robledo, Eduardo, 168
Arias, Leopoldo, 65
Avella Gómez, Mauricio, 28, 65, 133, 167

B

Banco Americano, 48
Banco Cafetero, 21, 159
Banco Central, 86, 88, 89, 90, 91, 94, 95, 97, 111, 112
Banco Central Hipotecario (BCH), 19, 24, 140, 141, 159, 173
Banco Colombiano, 49, 99
Banco de Antioquia, 50
Banco de Barranquilla, 50
Banco de Bogotá, 39, 47, 50, 51, 54, 6, 76, 91, 110, 111, 112, 181
Banco de Bolívar, 50, 57
Banco de Boyacá, 48
Banco de Cartagena, 54
Banco de Colombia, 48, 50, 62, 111, 112
Banco de Cundinamarca, 50
Banco de Importadores y Exportadores, 148
Banco de la Nueva Granada, 45
Banco de la República, 28, 95, 97, 99, 101, 102, 103, 104, 105, 106, 107, 108, 109, 110, 111, 112, 113, 115, 116, 117, 118, 119, 120, 121, 123, 125, 126, 128, 129, 130, 133, 134, 135, 136, 137, 138, 139, 140, 141, 143, 144, 145, 148, 149, 150, 153, 155, 156, 157, 158, 159, 160, 164, 165, 167, 168, 172, 173, 175, 176, 177, 178, 179, 180, 183, 184, 187, 188, 189, 190
Banco de Márquez, 51, 56
Banco de Medellín, 54
Banco de Pamplona, 54
Banco de Riohacha, 50
Banco de Santander, 54
Banco de Sopetrán, 54
Banco del Cauca, 50, 56.
Banco del Estado Soberano de Bolívar, 59
Banco del Estado Soberano de Cauca, 59
Banco del Norte, 56
Banco del Progreso de Medellín, 50
Banco Ganadero, 21, 159
Banco Internacional, 57, 157
Banco López, 109, 110, 111
Banco Mercantil, 50, 55
Banco Nacional, 13, 28, 86, 59, 62, 63, 64, 65, 66, 67, 68, 69, 71, 74, 75, 76, 77, 78, 79, 90
Banco Popular, 21, 159
Banco Popular de Bogotá, 54
Banco Popular de Soto, 57
Banco Santander, 50
Banco Tequendama, 49
Banco Unión, 57
BANCOLDEX, 21
Bank bond, 102
Bank of America, 181
Bank of England, 15, 95
Bank Superintendency, 107, 149, 175, 179
Banking Association, 175
Barco, Virgilio, 180
Bejarano, Jesús Antonio, 85, 275
Bergquist, Charles, 71, 73, 90
Bernal, Eusebio, 47, 50
Betancur, Belisario, 179
Bic, 181
Billetes Nacionales, National Bank Notes, 93, 117
Bonos del Tesoro, Treasury Bonds, 95, 99, 106, 112, 116
Borda, José, 65, 66, 68
Botero de los Ríos, Germán, 168
Bustamante, Darío, 36, 275

C

Caballero Argáez, Carlos, 184, 187
Caballero, Lucas, 96, 97
Caja Agraria, 19, 173
Caja de Crédito Agrario, 139, 141, 159
Calderón, Carlos, 96, 97
Camacho Carrizosa, José, 68, 86, 96, 97, 275
Camacho, Nemesio, 8
Camacho Roldán, Salvador, 62, 68
Cano, Francisco Antonio, 93
Caraqueña, 31
Caro, Miguel Antonio, 68, 71, 73, 74, 75
Caro, Julio, 82, 108, 125, 129, 130, 134, 140, 155
Casa de Moneda of Medellín, 94, 107, 111
Casabianca, Manuel, 109, 155
Cédulas Bancarias, 94, 116
Cédulas de Tesorería, 94, 104, 105, 106, 109, 112
Cédulas Hipotecarias, 95, 106, 107, 141
Cerruti, Ernesto, 82
Certificado de Depósito, 148
Certificado de Oro, 111, 112
Certificado de Plata, 106, 116
Chambers of Commerce, 136, 137, 156
Chinas, 31.
Cipriano de Mosquera, Tomás, 33, 39, 45
Clavijo, Sergio, 184
Cocobola, 64

Coffee-Growers Federation, 137, 156, 159, 165, 176
Concha, José Vicente, 94, 96
Cóndor, 35, 89, 93
Conversion Fund, 92
Copete Lizarralde, Ignacio, 168
Coriolano Amador, Carlos, 49
Coronado, Carlos Eduardo, 77
Corporación Colombiana de Crédito, 141
Cortés Boshell, Jorge, 168
Credencial, 181
Credibanco-Visa, 13, 15, 24, 28, 181
Cuartillo de plata, 36
Cuartillo de real, 33
Cuartillos, 31, 33
Cuarto de cóndor, 93
Cuarto de décimo, 64
Cuéllar, María Mercedes, 184
Currie, Lauchlin, 13, 145, 157, 158, 167, 174, 175, 183

D

De Brigard, Juan, 59, 65, 76, 77
De Herrera, Simón, 51
De Márquez, José Ignacio, 44
De Pombo, Lino, 35, 37
Décimo de Real, 35
Décimos, 64
Del Castillo, José María, 35
Diners, 181
Doble cóndor, 89, 93
Doblón, 33

E

El Correo Nacional, 71, 75
El Espectador, 179
El Telegrama, 71, 75
El Tiempo, 101, 112
El Zancudo, 65, 71, 75

Escudo, 33, 35
Esguerra, Nicolás, 51, 54
Espinosa Valderrama, Abdón, 169
Espinosa, José María, 31

F

Fairchild, Frederick Rogers, 101, 102, 104
Farrington, Robert M., 99
Financiera Eléctrica Nacional (FEN), 21, 185
First World War, 17, 96
Flórez, Luis Bernardo, 184, 189
Fondo de Capitalización Empresarial (FCE), 172
Fondo de Contratistas de Obras Públicas (FCOP), 172
Fondo de Inversión Privada (FIP), 172
Fondo de Promoción de Exportadores (PROEXPO), 172
Fondo Financiero Agrícola, 172
Fondo Financiero Agropecuario (FFAP), 172, 185
Fondo Financiero Agropecuario (FINAGRO), 21, 185, 188
Fondo Financiero de Desarrollo Urbano (FFDU), 172
Fondo Financiero Eléctrico, 185
Fondo Financiero Industrial (FFI), 172

G

Gaitán, Jorge Eliécer, 147, 150, 157
Gama, Rafael, 168, 171
Garcés, Modesto, 68, 96
García, Antonio, 157
García, Francisco, 65, 66
García Paredes, Roberto, 155
Gaviria, César, 183, 184, 192
Gómez, Eugenio, 99, 100

Gómez, Laureano, 155, 160
González, Florentino, 36, 45
Granadino de oro, 33
Granadino de plata, 33, 35
Great Depression, 17, 125
Greham, Thomas, 36
Grove, David, 158, 159, 167
Gutiérrez de Alba, José María, 37
Gutiérrez de Piñeres, Germán, 39, 44

H

Hernández Gamarra, Antonio, 13, 184, 186, 189
Hernández Rodríguez, Guillermo, 157
Herrera Umaña, Roberto, 105
Herrera, Simón, 65, 66, 76
Holguín, Carlos, 65, 71, 74, 75
Holguín, Jorge, 65, 68, 69, 99
Hommes, Rudolf, 183, 184

I

Ibáñez, Jorge Enrique, 28
India, 31
Instituto Colombiano de Comercio Exterior (INCOMEX), 167
Instituto de Crédito Territorial, 159
Instituto de Fomento Industrial (IFI), 21, 140, 159
International Monetary Fund, 17, 179, 188

J

Jaramillo, Esteban, 90, 95, 97, 101, 103, 105, 118, 129, 133, 134, 137
Jaramillo Ocampo, Hernán, 154
Jaramillo, Pedro, 88
Jefferson, Howard M., 101, 104
Junguito, Roberto, 179, 184, 189
Junta de Amortización, 86, 89

Junta de Conversión, Conversion Board, 91, 92, 93, 96, 106, 118
Junta de Emisión, Emission Board, 85
Junta Depositaria, Depository Board, 85
Junta Militar de Gobierno Military Junta, 161, 163
Junta Monetaria Monetary Board, 167, 168, 169, 183

K

Kalmanovitz, Salomón, 184, 186
Kemmerer, Edwin W., 101, 102, 103, 104, 108, 109, 110, 111, 128, 130, 153
Keynes, 17
Koppel, Bendix, 47
Koppel, Salomón, 47, 82
Koppel, Sam B., 109

L

Lemos, Antonio José, 157
Lemos, Carlos, 184
León Valencia, Guillermo, 164, 165,167
Liévano Aguirre, Indalecio, 69,71
Lleras, Alberto, 153, 157, 163
Lleras Restrepo, Carlos, 118, 144, 169
Lloreda, Rodrigo, 184
López Martínez, Alejandro, 28
López Michelsen, Alfonso, 117
López Pumarejo, Alfonso, 122, 143, 144, 147
López, José Hilario, 40, 45
López, Pedro A., 110
Luquiens, Frederick, 101, 102, 104

M

Macuquina, 31, 33
Malo O'Leary, Arturo, 65, 74, 77, 78
Marroquín, José Manuel, 81, 82, 83
Martínez Silva, Carlos, 71, 73, 74, 75, 76

Martínez, Néstor Humberto, 186
Mastercard, 181
Media onza, 33
Medina, Bernardino, 65
Medio cóndor, 89, 93
Medio décimo, 64
Medio décimo de real, 35
Medio peso, 33
Medio real, 33
Medios cuartillos, 31
Meisel Roca, Adolfo, 28
Mejía, Manuel, 155
Melo, Jorge Orlando, 59
Mendoza Neira, Plinio, 157
Michelsen, Gustavo, 111, 115
Monsalve, Diego, 110, 125, 130
Montenegro, Santiago, 125, 136, 278
Morillo, Pablo, 31
Mosquera, Manuel María, 40, 43
Murillo Toro, Manuel, 40, 47

N

Nariño, Antonio, 31
National Coffee Fund, 147, 165
National Defense Bond, 137, 147
National Planning Department, 167, 183
Núñez, Rafael, 59, 62, 64, 65, 69, 71, 73, 74

O

O'Leary, Carlos, 47
Ocampo, José Antonio, 28, 125, 136, 184
Olaya Herrera, Enrique, 101, 126, 128, 130
Onza, 33, 35
Ortega, Francisco, 168, 184
Osorio, Nicolás, 65, 74, 77, 78
Ospina Pérez, Mariano, 149
Ospina Vázquez, Mariano, 108

Ospina, Pedro Nel, 100, 101, 104, 109, 110, 113, 115
Ossa Escobar, Carlos, 184
Osuna, Hector, 154, 174, 179

P

Palacio Rudas, Alfonso, 167, 183
Palacio Mejía, Hugo, 168
Palau, Emigdio, 51, 54
Pardo, Juan María, 59, 66
Parra, Aquileo, 40, 51, 55
Pastrana, Andrés, 184
Pastrana Borrero, Misael, 164, 174
Paul, Felipe, 59, 65
Pérez, José Joaquín, 108, 111,115
Perry, Guillermo, 184
Peseta, 31, 33, 89
Peso colombiano de oro, 33
Peso colombiano de plata, 33
Peso fuerte, 31
Plata, José María, 36
Posada, Gabriel, 109

Q

Quijano Wallis, José María, 51, 54
Quintero, Miguel, 65

R

Real, 33
Real de plata, 33
Recamán, Jaime Mz., 158
Regeneration, 17, 50, 59, 62, 67, 69, 71
Restrepo Ochoa, Bernardo, 155
Restrepo, Carlos E., 99
Restrepo, Juan Camilo, 184
Restrepo, Vicente, 76
Reyes, Rafael, 86, 88, 89, 91
Robinson, Guillermo, 35

Robinson, Joan, 13
Rojas Pinilla, Gustavo, 160, 161, 163
Roldán, Antonio, 65
Román, Soledad, 64
Roosevelt, 24, 148
Russell Lill, Tomas, 101

S

Salazar, Félix, 109, 118, 120, 108, 110
Samper Pizano, Ernesto, 184, 188, 190
Samper, Miguel, 47, 62, 68, 81
Sánchez Torres, Fabio, 28
Sanclemente, Manuel, 81, 82
Santos, Eduardo, 144
Santos, Juan Manuel, 184, 192
Sanz de Santa María, Carlos, 167
Schloss, Carlos, 47
Second World War, 133, 143, 146, 148, 149, 159
Sierra, Juan María, 88, 91
Sociedad Botero, Arango e Hijos, 50
Sociedad de Agricultores, Farmers Society, 136, 137
Sociedad Minera del Zancudo, 49
Soto, Focion, 81
Special Exchange Account, 144
Suárez, Marco Fidel, 94, 95, 96, 99, 101

T

Tanco, Mariano, 50
Tenjo, Fernando, 184
Torres, Carlos Arturo, 89
Torres García, Guillermo, 28, 51, 77, 90

U

Ulloa, Benito, 82
Urdinola, Antonio, 184
Uribe, José Vicente, 65, 66
Uribe Uribe, Rafael, 83, 94, 96, 97
Urrutia, Miguel, 168, 184, 189, 171,
Urueta, Carlos Adolfo, 109, 110

V

Valenzuela, Carlos, 108
Valenzuela, Tobías, 92
Vargas, Francisco de P., 157
Vélez, Marceliano, 71, 74
Villa, Vicente, 101
Villamizar Gallardo, José María, 51, 54
Villar, Leonardo, 184, 186, 189
Villaveces, Carlos, 65, 153, 154, 155, 157
Visa Colombia, 13
Visa International, 181

W

War of the thousand days, 15, 81, 84, 90, 96, 117, 158
War with Peru, 133, 139, 143, 144
Wiesner, Eduardo, 169, 279
World Bank, 19, 179

Z

Zea, Francisco Antonio, 33

BIBLIOGRAPHY

Abadía Méndez, Miguel. (1884) *Informe del Ministro del Tesoro al Congreso Nacional (Report of the Treasury Minister to the National Congress)*. Imprenta de Vapor de Zalamea Hermanos.

Andrade, José Arturo. (1927) *El Banco de la República. Nociones Sobre su Organización y Funcionamiento (The Banco de la República. Ideas on its Organization and Functioning)*. Editorial Minerva. Bogotá.

____ . (1929) *El Banco de la República. Glosas y Comentarios (The Banco de la República. Notes and Commentaries)*. Editorial Minerva. Bogotá.

Agudelo Villa, Hernando. (1967) *Cuatro Etapas de la Inflación en Colombia (Four Stages of Inflation in Colombia)*. Ediciones Tercer Mundo. Bogotá.

Arango, Luis Angel. (1948) *XXV Informe Anual del Gerente a la Junta Directiva, período de julio 1 de 1947 a junio 30 de 1948 (XXV Annual Report of the Governor to the Board of Directors, period: June 1, 1947 to June 30, 1948")*. Imprenta del Banco de la República. Bogotá.

Avella Gómez, Mauricio. (1987) *Pensamiento y Política Monetaria en Colombia 1886-1945 (Monetary Thought and Policy in Colombia, 1886-1945)*. Contraloría General de la República.

____ . (2000) *Hacienda Pública, Moneda y Café. El papel protagónico de Alfonso Palacio Rudas (Public Finance, Money and Coffee. The leading role of Alfonso Palacio Rudas)*. Común Presencia Editores. Bogotá.

Banco de la República. (1990) *El Banco de la República. Antecedentes, Evolución y Estructura (The Banco de la República. Background, Evolution and Structure)*. Departamento Editorial de Banco de la República.

____ . (1994) *Kemmerer y el Banco de la República. Diarios y Documentos (Kemmerer and the Banco de la República. Diaries and Documents)*. Banco de la República. Bogotá.

____ . (1998) *Principales Indicadores Económicos 1923-1997 (Main Economic Indicators 1923-1997)*. Banco de la República. Bogotá.

Barro, Robert J. (1973) "El Dinero y la Base Monetaria en Colombia 1967-1972" ("Money and the Monetary Base in Colombia 1967-1972".) *Revista de Planeación y Desarrollo*. April-June.

Bejarano, Jesús Antonio. (1987) "El Despegue Cafetero: 1900-1928" ("The Takeoff of Coffee: 1900-1928".) In Ocampo, Editor. 1987.

Berquist, Charles. (1973) *Coffee and Conflict in Colombia, 1886-1904: Origins and Outcome of the War of the Thousand Days*. Ph.D. Dissertation. Stanford University.

Botero de los Ríos, Germán. (1963) "Breve Exégesis de las Funciones Monetarias del Banco de la República" ("Brief Explanation of the Monetary Functions of the Banco de la República".) *Revista del Banco de la República*. August.

____ . (1976) *Informe Anual del Gerente a la Junta Directiva (Annual Report of the Governor to the Board of Directors)*. Imprenta del Banco de la República. Bogotá.

Bustamante R., Darío. (1974) "Efectos Económicos del Papel Moneda durante la Regeneración" ("Economic Effects of Paper Money during the Regeneration".) *Cuadernos Colombianos*. No. 4.

Caballero Argaez, Carlos. Editor (1979). *El sector financiero en los años ochenta (The financial sector in the nineteen-eighties)*. Asocación Bancaria de Colombia.

____ . (1987) 50 *Años de Economía: De la Crisis del Treinta a la del Ochenta (50 years of Economy: From the Crisis of Nineteen-Thirty to the Crisis of Nineteen-Eighty)*. Asociación Bancaria de Colombia.

Caballero Escovar, Enrique. (1986) *Historia Económica de Colombia (Economic History of Colombia)*. Editorial Oveja Negra. Bogotá.

Camacho Carrizosa, José. (1903) *Estudios Económicos (Economic Studies)*. Imprenta La Crónica. Bogotá.

Caro, Miguel Antonio. (1956) *Escritos sobre Cuestiones Económicas (Writings on Economic Questions)*. Imprenta del Banco de la República. Bogotá.

Caro, Julio. (1931). *Octavo Informe Anual Presentado por el Gerente a la Junta Directiva, período de julio 1 de 1930 a junio 30 de 1931 (Eighth Annual Report Presented by the Governor to the Board of Directors, period: July 1, 1930 to June 30, 1931)*. Editorial Minerva, Bogotá.

____. (1932). *Noveno Informe Anual Presentado por el Gerente a la Junta Directiva, período de julio 1 de 1931 a junio 30 de 1932 (Ninth Annual Report Presented by the Governor to the Board of Directors, period: July 1, 1931 to June 30, 1932)*. Editorial Minerva, Bogotá.

____. (1933). *Décimo Informe Anual Presentado por el Gerente a la Junta Directiva, período de julio 1 de 1932 a junio 30 de 1933 (Tenth Annual Report Presented by the Governor to the Board of Directors, period: July 1, 1932 to June 30, 1933)*. Editorial Minerva, Bogotá.

CURRIE, LAUCHLIN. (1951) *Bases de un Programa de Fomento para Colombia (Bases of a Program of Development for Colombia)*. Chapters XIV and XXVII. Facsimile of the second edition. Editorial Presencia. Bogotá.

____. (1952) *Reorganización de la Rama Ejecutiva del Gobierno de Colombia (Reorganization of the Executive Branch of the Government of Colombia)*. Chapter XVII. Imprenta Nacional. Bogotá.

____. (1973) *La Política Monetaria y el Nivel de Precios (Monetary Policy and the Level of Prices)*: Revista de Planeación y Desarrollo. April-June.

____. (1984) *Evaluación de la Asesoría Económica a los Países en Desarrollo. El caso colombiano (Evaluation of Economic Consultancy for the Developing Countries. The Colombian case)*. Fondo Editorial CEREC. Bogotá.

____. (1987). *Moneda en Colombia: Comportamiento y Control (The Supply and Control of Money in Colombia)*. Fondo Cultural Cafetero. Bogotá.

DEPARTAMENTO NACIONAL DE PLANEACIÓN. (National Planning Department, 1998) *Estadísticas Históricas de Colombia (Historical Statistics of Colombia)*. Volume 1. Tercer Mundo Editores. Bogotá.

DRAKE, PAUL W. (1983) "Primera Misión Kemmerer, Prosperidad al Debe 1923-28" ("The First Kemmerer Mission, Debt Prosperity 1923-28".) *Revista Economía Colombiana*. October.

ECHAVARRÍA. JUAN JOSÉ. (1999) *Crisis e Industrialización. Las lecciones de los Treinta (Crisis and Industrialization. The lessons of the Thirties)*. Tercer Mundo Editores. Bogotá.

ECHEVERRY G., JUAN CARLOS. (1998) "Summary of the Minutes of the Monetary Board 1971-1988". *Borradores Semanales de Economía*, No. 88. Banco de la República.

ESPINOSA VALDERRAMA, AUGUSTO. (1986) *Escritos Políticos y Económicos (Political and Economic Writings)*. Volume I. Contraloría General de la República. Bogotá.

FAJARDO M., CARLOS JAIME AND RODRÍGUEZ ARDILA, NÉSTOR. (1980) "Tres Décadas del Sistema Financiero Colombiano: 1950-1979" ("Three Decades of the Colombian Financial System: 1950-1979".) In: Mauricio Cabrera Galvis, Editor. *Sistema Financiero y Política Antiinflacionaria 1974-1980 (The Financial System and Anti-inflationary Policy 1974-1980)*. Asociación Bancaria de Colombia.

FLOREZ ENCISO, LUIS BERNARDO. (2001) "Colombia Tras Diez Años de Reformas Políticas y Económicas". Photocopy.

FRANCO HOLGUÍN, JORGE. (1960) *Evolución de las Instituciones Financieras en Colombia (Evolution of Financial Institutions in Colombia)*. Fondo de Cultura Económica. Mexico.

GARCÍA, ANTONIO. (1949) *Problemas de la Nación Colombiana (Problems of the Colombian Nation)*. Nuevo Mundo. Bogotá.

GÓMEZ O., HERNANDO; FRANCISCO J. ORTEGA AND PATRICIA SANCLEMENTE. Editors. (1976) *Lecturas sobre Moneda y Banca en Colombia (Readings on Money and Banking in Colombia)*. Fedesarrollo-Editorial Stella. Bogotá.

GROVE, DAVID L. (1988). "Deficiencias en la Estructura de la Banca Central Colombiana" ("Deficiencies in the Structure of the Colombian Central Bank".) *Banca y Finanzas*. March-April.

____. (1988b) "Memorandum sobre Reorganización del Banco de la República" ("Memorandum on the Reorganization of the Banco de la República".) *Banca y Finanzas*. No. 2. March-April.

GRUPO DE ESTUDIOS DEL CRECIMIENTO ECONÓMICO COLOMBIANO - GRECO - (Study Group of Colombian Economic Growth, 1999). *El Desempeño Macroeconómico Colombiano - Series Estadísticas, 1905-1997 (Colombian Macroeconomic Performance - Statistical Series, 1905-1997)*. Second version. Borradores de Economía. No. 121. May.

HERNÁNDEZ GAMARRA, ANTONIO AND JOSÉ TOLOSA. (2001) "La Política Monetaria en Colombia en la Segunda Mitad de los Años Noventa" ("Monetary Policy in Colombia in the Second Half of the Nineties".) *Revista del Banco de la República*. February.

HERNÁNDEZ GAMARRA, ANTONIO AND IGNACIO LOZANO E. (2001) "El Estado de las Finanzas Públicas en Colombia a Fines del Siglo XX" ("The State of Public Finances in Colombia at the end of the 20th Century".) In: Gabriel Misas Arango, Editor. *Desarrollo Económico y Social en Colombia. Siglo XX (Social and Economic Development in Colombia. 20th Century)*. Editorial Unibiblos. Bogotá.

HERNÁNDEZ GAMARRA, ANTONIO. (1973). "Política de Redescuento 1950-1970" ("Rediscount Policy 1950-1970".) *Revista de Planeación y Desarrollo*. April-June.

____. (1991) "La transparente claridad del Emisor" ("The transparency of the Central Bank".) *Revista Economía Colombiana*. September-October.

____. (2000) "Emisiones Clandestinas" ("Hidden Emissions".) *Revista del Banco de la República*. August.

____. (2001) "La Banca Central en Colombia" ("The Central Bank in Colombia".) *Revista Credencial Historia*. March.

HERNÁNDEZ, CARLOS. (2000). *Catálogo de Billetes de Colombia (Catalogue of Colombian Bank Notes)*. Casa Editorial El Búho.

HOLGUÍN, CARLOS (1894) *Aclaraciones al Congreso Nacional (Clarifications to the National Congress)*. Imprenta de Antonio María Silvestre. Bogotá.

HOLGUÍN, JORGE. (1892) *La Bestia Negra (The Black Beast)*. Imprenta de la Nación. Bogotá.

"Informe de la Comisión Investigadora de la Cámara de Representantes presentado a la Plenaria de la Corporación el 14 Noviembre de 1894", en las obras Obras completas de Carlos Martínez Silva, *Las Emisiones Clandestinas del Bank Nacional y otros Escritos*. ("Report of the Investigating Commission of the House of Representatives, presented to the full session of the House on November 14, 1894, as transcribed in the complete works of Dr. Carlos Martínez Silva: *The Hidden Emissions of the Banco Nacional and other writings*".) Volume IX. Imprenta Nacional. 1938.

JARAMILLO OCAMPO, HERNÁN. (1949) "Exposición de Motivos al Proyecto de Ley Sobre Orientación del Crédito Bancario" ("Statement of Reasons for the proposed Law On the Orientation of Banking Credit".) *Revista del Banco de la República*. December.

Junta Directiva del Banco de la República (Board of Directors of the Banco de la República). (1999). "Informe Adicional al Congreso de la República" ("Supplementary Report to the Congress of the Republic".) *Revista del Banco de la República*. October.

KALMANOVITZ K., Salomón and Mauricio Avella G. (1998) "Barreras del Desarrollo Financiero: Las Instituciones Monetarias Colombianas en la Década de 1950" ("Barriers to Financial Development: Colombian Monetary Institutions in the decade of the 1950´s".) *Borradores de Economía*. No. 104. Banco de la República.

KEMMERER, EDWIN W. (1923) *Exposición de Motivos Referente al Proyecto de Ley Orgánica del Banco de la República (Statement of Reasons for the proposed Organic Law for the Banco de la República)*. Imprenta Nacional. Bogotá.

LIÉVANO AGUIRRE, INDALECIO. (1985) *Rafael Núñez*. El Áncora Editores.

LÓPEZ PUMAREJO, ALFONSO. "El Principio del Fin" ("The Beginning of the End".) In: *Aproximación a Alfonso López, Testimonio para una Biografía (An Approach to Alfonso López, Testimony for a Biography)*. Aníbal Noguera Mendoza, Editor (1986). Volume 1. Banco de la República.

LÓPEZ C., HUGO. (1975) "La Inflación en Colombia en la Década de los Veintes" ("Inflation in Colombia in the decade of the Twenties".) *Cuadernos Colombianos*. No. 5.

LOW MURTRA, ENRIQUE. (1986) "Historia Monetaria de Colombia: 1886 - 1986" ("Monetary History of Colombia: 1886 - 1986".) In: Oscar Rodríguez Salazar, compiler. *Estado y Economía en la Constitución de 1886 (State and Economy in the Constitution of 1886)*. Contraloría General de la República. Bogotá.

LLERAS DE LA FUENTE, CARLOS. (1995) "El Régimen de Banca Central en la Constitución de 1991: La Búsqueda del Consenso"

("The Regime for a Central Bank in the Constitution of 1991: The Search for Consensus".) In: Steiner, compiler, 1995.

LLOREDA CAICEDO, RODRIGO. (1995) "La Banca Central en la Constituyente: Una Visión de Conjunto" ("The Central Bank in the Constituent Assembly: A Joint Vision".) In: Steiner, compiler, 1995.

MARTÍNEZ SILVA, CARLOS. (1884) *Discurso en la sesión del 12 de noviembre, sobre emisiones clandestinas del Banco Nacional (Speech in the session of November 12, on the hidden emissions of the Banco Nacional)*. Imprenta de El Correo Nacional.

MC GREEVEY, WILLIAM PAUL. (1975) *Historia Económica de Colombia 1845 - 1930 (Economic History of Colombia 1845 - 1930)*. Ediciones Tercer Mundo.Bogotá.

MEISEL ROCA, ADOLFO. (1988) "La Historia Monetaria de Mauricio Avella: Hamlet con tres Príncipes" ("The Monetary History of Mauricio Avella: Hamlet with three Princes".) *Ensayos sobre Política Económica*. June.

____. (1998) "La Banca Central en Colombia: de la Autonomía Privada a la Autonomía Pública, 1923 - 1997" ("The Central Bank in Colombia: from Private Autonomy to Public Autonomy, 1923 - 1997".) *Coyuntura Económica*. March.

____. (2001) "Orígenes de la Banca Comercial en Colombia. La Banca Libre, 1870 - 1886" ("Origins of Commercial Banking in Colombia. The Free Banks, 1870 - 1886".) *Revista Credencial Historia*. March.

MELO, JORGE ORLANDO. (1987) "Las Vicisitudes del Modelo Liberal 1850 - 1899" ("The Vicissitudes of the Liberal Model 1850 - 1899".) In: Ocampo, 1987.

MENESES OLIVAR, ALVARO. (1971) *El Manejo de la Política Monetaria en Colombia (The Management of Monetary Policy in Colombia)*. Superintendencia Bancaria. Bogotá.

MENDOZA NEIRA, PLINIO. (et. alia). (1947) "Proyecto de Ley, por la cual se dictan algunas disposiciones sobre el Banco de la República y se organiza la Corporación Colombiana de Crédito, Fomento y Ahorro" ("Proposed Law, by which some provisions are dictated for the Banco de la República and the Colombian Corporation of Credit, Development and Saving is organized".) *Anales del Congreso*, September 3.

MISCELLANEOUS AUTHORS. (1931) *Leyes Financieras presentadas al gobierno de Colombia por las misiones de expertos americanos en los años de 1923 y 1930 y exposición de motivos de estas (Financial Laws presented to the government of Colombia by the missions of American experts in 1923 and 1930 and a statement of the reasons for them)*. Editorial Cromos. Bogotá. 1931.

OCAMPO, JOSÉ ANTONIO AND SANTIAGO MONTENEGRO. (1982) "La Crisis Mundial de los Años Treinta en Colombia" ("The World Crisis of the Nineteen-Thirties in Colombia".) *Revista Desarrollo y Sociedad*. January, 1982.

____. Editor. (1987). *Historia Económica de Colombia (Economic History of Colombia)*. Siglo Veintiuno Editores. Bogotá.

OTERO MUÑOZ, GUSTAVO. (1948) *El Banco de la República 1923 - 1948*. Imprenta del Banco de la República.

PALACIO, JULIO H. (1992) *La Historia de mi Vida. Crónicas Inéditas (The Story of my Life. Unpublished Chronicles)*. Edición Uninorte.

PALACIO RUDAS, ALFONSO. (1995) "Los Instrumentos que Maneja el Banco de la República como Autoridad Monetaria, Cambiaria y Crediticia" ("The Powers of the Banco de la República as a Monetary, Exchange and Credit Authority".) In Steiner, 1995.

POSADA, CARLOS ESTEBAN. (1976) "La Crisis del Capitalismo Mundial y la Deflación en Colombia" ("The Crisis of World Capitalism and Deflation in Colombia".) *Cuadernos Colombianos*. Numbers 10 and 11.

RECAMAN MZ, JAIME. (1980) *Historia Jurídica del Banco de la República (Legal History of the Banco de la República)*. Banco de la República. Bogotá.

RESTREPO, JUAN CAMILO. (1991) "La Política Monetaria de la Regeneración" ("The Monetary Policy of the Regeneration".) *Boletín Cultural y Bibliográfico*. Biblioteca Luis Ángel Arango. No. 26.

RODRÍGUEZ, OSCAR. (1973) *Efectos de la Gran Depresión sobre la Industria Colombiana (Effects of the Great Depression on Colombian Industry)*. Edición Tigre de Papel. Medellín.

ROSAS, LUIS EDUARDO. (1973) "La Política Monetaria" ("Monetary Policy".)

Revista de Planeación y Desarrollo. April-June.

Romero, Carmen Astrid. (1991) "La Regeneración y el Banco Nacional" ("The Regeneration and the Banco Nacional".) *Boletín Cultural y Bibliográfico.* Biblioteca Luis Ángel Arango. No. 26.

Romero Baquero, Carmen Astrid. (1987) *Historia Monetaria en Colombia 1880 - 1905 (Monetary History of Colombia 1880 - 1905).* Degree thesis, faculty of economics. Universidad Nacional, Bogotá.

Salazar, Felix. (1924) *Primer Informe Anual Presentado por el Gerente a la Junta Directiva (First Annual Report Presented by the Governor to the Board of Directors).* Editorial Minerva. Bogotá.

Sandilands, Roger J. *(1990) Vida y Política Económica de Lauchlin Currie (The Life and Economy Policy of Lauchlin Currie).* Legis Editores. Bogotá.

Sánchez Torres, Fabio. Editor. (1994) *Ensayos de Historia Monetaria y Bancaria de Colombia (Essays on the Monetary and Banking History of Colombia).* Tercer Mundo Editores. Bogotá.

Sanz de Santamaría, Carlos. (1965) *Una Época Difícil (A Difficult Epoch).* Tercer Mundo Editores. Bogotá.

Samper, Miguel. (1977) *Escritos Políticos-Económicos de Miguel Samper (Political-Economic Writings of Miguel Samper).* Volume III, publicaciones del Banco de la República. Bogotá.

Steiner, Roberto. Compiler (1995) *La Autonomía del Banco de la República (The Autonomy of the Banco de la República).* Fedesarrollo Tercer Mundo Editores. Bogotá.

Torres García, Guillermo. (1980) *Historia de la Moneda en Colombia (History of Money in Colombia).* Fondo Rotatorio de Publicaciones FAES. Medellín.

Triffin, Robert. (1944) "La Moneda y las Instituciones Bancarias en Colombia" ("Money and Banking Institutions in Colombia".) Supplement to number 202, *Revista del Banco de la República,* August, 1944. Imprenta del Banco de la República. Bogotá.

Uribe Escobar, José Darío. (1997) "Notas sobre la Política Cambiaria en Colombia" ("Notes on Exchange Policy in Colombia".) In: *Política Cambiaria en los Países Miembros del FLAR (Exchange Policy in the Member Countries of the Latin American Reserve Fund).* Fondo Latinoamericano de Reserva. Cali.

Urrutia, Miguel and Mario Arrubla. (1970) *Compendio de Estadísticas Históricas de Colombia (Compendium of Historical Statistics on Colombia).* Universidad Nacional. Bogotá.

Urrutia, Miguel. (2000) "La Estrategia de la Política Monetaria" ("The Strategy of Monetary Policy".) *Revista del Banco de la República.* October.

Velásquez Cock, Alvaro. (1979) "Las Corporaciones Financieras. Evolución, Problemas Actuales y Perspectivas" ("The Financial Corporations: Their Evolution, Current Problems and Prospects".) In: Caballero, 1979.

Vélez García, Jorge. Editor. (1963) *Devaluación 1962. Historia Documentada de un Proceso Económico (The 1962 Devaluation: Documented History of an Economic Process).* Ediciones Tercer Mundo. Bogotá.

Villate Bonilla, Eduardo. (1979). "Las Corporaciones de Ahorro y Vivienda. Importancia en la Financiación de la Construcción. Perspectivas Futuras de Operación" ("The Savings and Housing Loans Corporations. Their Importance in the Financing of Construction. Future Prospects for their Operations".) In: Caballero, 1979.

Villaveces R., Carlos. (1949) "Política Anticíclica" ("Anti-cylical Policy".) *Revista del Banco de la República.* Vol 22. No. 266. December.

Vistas Fiscales y Alegatos del Procurador General de la Nación en el Proceso por Delitos Cometidos en el Banco Nacional (Prosecution Hearings and Allegations of the Attorney-General of the Nation in the Trial for Crimes Committed in the Banco Nacional). (1895). Imprenta de Vapor de Zalamea Hermanos. Bogotá.

Wiesner Durán, Eduardo. (1978) "Devaluación y Mecanismo de Ajuste en Colombia" ("Devaluation and the Adjustment Mechanism in Colombia".) In: Eduardo Wiesner Durán, Editor, *Política Económica Externa de Colombia 1978 (External Economic Policy of Colombia, 1978).* Asociación Bancaria de Colombia. Bogotá.